More Than Victims of Horace

Public Schools 1914 –1918

Wolverhampton Military Studies No.41

Timothy Halstead

To my Mother

Helion & Company Limited
Unit 8 Amherst Business Centre
Budbrooke Road
Warwick
CV34 5WE
England
Tel. 01926 499 619
Email: info@helion.co.uk
Website: www.helion.co.uk
Twitter: @helionbooks
Visit our blog at blog.helion.co.uk

Published by Helion & Company 2023
Designed and typeset by Mach 3 Solutions (www.mach3solutions.co.uk)
Cover designed by Paul Hewitt, Battlefield Design (www.battlefield-design.co.uk)

Text © Timothy Halstead 2023
Images © as individually credited
Cover: Oundle Munitions Workers, summer 1915. (Oundle School)

Every reasonable effort has been made to trace copyright holders and to obtain their permission for the use of copyright material. The author and publisher apologize for any errors or omissions in this work and would be grateful if notified of any corrections that should be incorporated in future reprints or editions of this book.

ISBN 9-7-81913336-21-9

British Library Cataloguing-in-Publication Data.
A catalogue record for this book is available from the British Library.

All rights reserved. No part of this publication may be reproduced, stored in a retrieval system, or transmitted, in any form, or by any means, electronic, mechanical, photocopying, recording or otherwise, without the express written consent of Helion & Company Limited.

For details of other military history titles published by Helion & Company Limited contact the above address or visit our website: http://www.helion.co.uk.

We always welcome receipt of book proposals from prospective authors.

Contents

List of Illustrations	iv
List of Abbreviations	v
Series Editor's Preface	vii
Acknowledgements	ix
Introduction	x
1 Victims of Horace?	25
2 Public Schools in the Victorian Age	44
3 A Lack of Common Purpose: The Army and the Public Schools, 1901–1914	59
4 Building from Scratch: Public Schools and the New Army, 1914–1915	83
5 Drawing on Their Own Resources: Public School OTCs, 1914-1915	103
6 Setting and Raising the Standard: The OTC 1916-1919	125
7 Status, Class, Curriculum and Connections: Public Schoolboys and Military Service	146
8 Home Front	167
Conclusion	187
Bibliography	193
Index	211

List of Illustrations

Oakham OTC at Rugely Camp in August 1914, so rapid was army mobilisation that the school's cadets were left to cook for themselves. (Oakham School) 79

St Albans School, site of the school library in the 1914 which was requisitioned by the army as a military prison. (James Halstead) 79

Oundle Munitions Workers, summer 1915. Apart from munitions production being part of regular school life, school holidays were also devoted to production. (Oundle School) 80

Sherborne OTC Band 1915. Many public schools had corps bands. (Sherborne School) 80

Uppingham OTC Camp c.1916. The obvious exhaustion of the boys demonstrates the demanding nature of their training. (Uppingham School) 81

Inns of Court OTC Training Trenches. Some 13,000 yards of excavated works was where Eton, Harrow, Westminster, Berkhamsted and Merchant Taylors OTC contingents took part in military exercises. (James Halstead) 81

Edmund Blunden with fellow Christ's Hospital Old Boys. The photograph depicts the famous 'Feast of Five' at St Omer in 1917. Blunden (front right) is in the company of four Old Blues all serving with the Royal Sussex Regiment. Two were killed within a few months and a third committed suicide in 1924. (Christ's Hospital) 82

'Mill Hill School War Memorial. School memorials were both sacred and secular. Not only did the school erect this arch but it also erected a science block in memory of old boys who lost their lives during the conflict. (Open source) 82

List of Abbreviations

BEF	British Expeditionary Force
CIGS	Chief of the Imperial General Staff
CO	Commanding Officer
ESA	Epsom School Archives
HMC	Headmasters' Conference
IWM	Imperial War Museum
LHCMA	Liddell Hart Centre for Military Archives
MC	Military Cross
MHM	Mill Hill Magazine
OTC	Officer Training Corps
OU	Old Uppinghamiam
POW	Prisoner of War
RAF	Royal Airforce
RAMC	Royal Army Medical Corps
RAOC	Royal Army Ordnance Corps
RASC	Royal Army Service Corps
RFC	Royal Flying Corps
RGA	Royal Garrison Artillery
RMA	Royal Military Academy
RMC	Royal Military College
RNAS	Royal Naval Air Service
RMLI	Royal Marine Light Infantry
RND	Royal Naval Division
RNVR	Royal Naval Volunteer Reserve
SA	Somme Association
SASA	St Albans School Archives
SGSM	St Georges School Magazine
SR	Special Reserve
SSA	Sherborne School Archives
TF	Territorial Force
TNA	National Archives
USA	Uppingham School Archives
USC	United Services College

USM	Uppingham School Magazine
UVF	Ulster Volunteer Force
VAD	Volunteer Aid Detachment
VC	Victoria Cross
WO	War Office

The Wolverhampton Military Studies Series
Series Editor's Preface

As series editor, it is my great pleasure to introduce the *Wolverhampton Military Studies Series* to you. Our intention is that in this series of books you will find military history that is new and innovative, and academically rigorous with a strong basis in fact and in analytical research, but also is the kind of military history that is for all readers, whatever their particular interests, or their level of interest in the subject. To paraphrase an old aphorism: a military history book is not less important just because it is popular, and it is not more scholarly just because it is dull. With every one of our publications we want to bring you the kind of military history that you will want to read simply because it is a good and well-written book, as well as bringing new light, new perspectives, and new factual evidence to its subject.

In devising the *Wolverhampton Military Studies Series*, we gave much thought to the series title: this is a *military* series. We take the view that history is everything except the things that have not happened yet, and even then a good book about the military aspects of the future would find its way into this series. We are not bound to any particular time period or cut-off date. Writing military history often divides quite sharply into eras, from the modern through the early modern to the mediaeval and ancient; and into regions or continents, with a division between western military history and the military history of other countries and cultures being particularly marked. Inevitably, we have had to start somewhere, and the first books of the series deal with British military topics and events of the twentieth century and later nineteenth century. But this series is open to any book that challenges received and accepted ideas about any aspect of military history, and does so in a way that encourages its readers to enjoy the discovery.

In the same way, this series is not limited to being about wars, or about grand strategy, or wider defence matters, or the sociology of armed forces as institutions, or civilian society and culture at war. None of these are specifically excluded, and in some cases they play an important part in the books that comprise our series. But there are already many books in existence, some of them of the highest scholarly standards, which cater to these particular approaches. The main theme of the *Wolverhampton Military Studies Series* is the military aspects of wars, the preparation for wars or their prevention, and their aftermath. This includes some books whose main theme is the technical details of how armed forces have worked, some books on wars and battles, and some books that re-examine the evidence about the existing stories, to show in a different light what everyone thought they already knew and understood.

As series editor, together with my fellow editorial board members, and our publisher Duncan Rogers of Helion, I have found that we have known immediately and almost by instinct the kind of books that fit within this series. They are very much the kind of well-written and challenging books that my students at the University of Wolverhampton would want to read. They are books which enhance knowledge and offer new perspectives. Also, they are books for anyone with an interest in military history and events, from expert scholars to occasional readers. One of the great benefits of the study of military history is that it includes a large and often committed section of the wider population, who want to read the best military history that they can find; our aim for this series is to provide it.

Stephen Badsey
University of Wolverhampton

Acknowledgements

This volume would not have been possible without the assistance of many. If there is anyone I have missed, please accept my apologies for the unintentional oversight.

Brian Curragh and John Spencer have been rocks as I wrote the manuscript. They have given up their valuable to read my first draft and point out with honesty and kindness where improvements could be made.

Schools and their archivists have been of great help in letting me look at their papers and patiently answering my questions. Their insights and answers have been of great help. My thanks are due to Simon Batten (Bloxham), Nicholas Hooper (Bradford Grammar School), James Harrison (Brighton College), the staff of Cheltenham College Archives, Bill Richards (Christ's Hospital), Paul Jordan (Eastbourne College), Rebecca Jallot Elizabeth Manterfield and Alan Scadding (Epsom), Jane Everard (Haileybury Society), Lesley Edwards (Lancing), Gráinne Lenehan (Marlborough), Peter Elliot (Mill Hill), George Hay (The National Archives), Charlotte (Oakham), Elspeth Langsdale (Oundle), Katy de la Rivière (Sedbergh), Rachel Hassall and Patrick Ferguson (Sherborne), Robin Brooke-Smith (Shrewsbury), David Knight (Stonyhurst), David Walsh (Tonbridge), Jerry Rudman (Uppingham) and Suzanne Foster (Winchester). William Richardson of the Headmasters' and Headmistresses' Conference gave me access to a range of papers which provided important oversight of the approach of public schools both before and during the Great War.

Hunting down information can be a long and tortuous exercise. Books cannot be written in isolation and I am most grateful to those who have patiently acted as a sounding board and offered helpful suggestions. Dr Jim Beech, John Bibby, Dr Timothy Bowman, Rhodri Davies, Professor Richard Grayson, Ella Halstead, Mark Leslie, Nigel Richardson, Andrew Rice, Trevor Robinson, Malcolm Tozer, David Underdown, Anne Wares (St Albans & Hertfordshire Architectural & Archaeological Society) and the Late Lieutenant-Colonel Bob Wyatt all offered much appreciated assistance and support. My son, James, has acted as an immediately available in-house sounding board. In addition, he has tramped round trenches and other sites with me and acted as a far superior photographer of these visits. Charles Fair's work on Officer Cadet Battalions has meant we have had many shared areas of interest. His generous sharing of his own research has led me down some highly productive areas for further investigation and led me towards insights I might never have picked up on. It is my hope that the information I have been able to share with him will be of equal use. Above all, my wife, Ann, has been a source of unstinting support and interest even when I have at times become overenthusiastic. All errors are solely my responsibility.

Introduction

To children ardent for some desperate glory,
The old Lie: Dulce et decorum est
Pro patria mori.[1]

'It is sweet and right to die for one's country,' the old lie, as Wilfred Owen saw it, has become for many the definitive statement about Britain's involvement in the Great War. This is especially so in the case of public schoolboys where it is claimed their education was largely based on the classics including the study of Horace from whose *Odes* Owen, who was not educated at public school, took this line. The public schools and the Great War have been spoken and written about extensively but much of this discussion concentrates on the ideological aspects of their involvement.[2] The public's understanding of public schools during the war continues to be dominated by perceptions presented through art and literature (such as Owen's biting criticism of Horace) and the occasional polemic. When one starts to explore public schools and the Great War, it is surprising, considering the volume and ferocity of opinion on the subject how little thorough scholarly research has been done on it. In addition, much of the work has concentrated on those who died in the war and relatively little on those who survived. Averages are a crude measure but typically 20 percent of the old boys who served were killed and 80 percent survived yet many accounts of public school involvement talk mainly about those who died. By looking at those who survived a greater understanding will be gained of the contribution of public schools to the Great War. Public schools were not homogenous bodies. The background of the of the schools varied and the approach to its curriculum by each school differed in its emphasis. Public schools involvement is far more nuanced than has been previously recognised in terms of both their individual and collective contributions to the national war effort between 1914 and 1918.The traditional narrative has been one of boys who had been indoctrinated by the exploits of the military heroes in the classics going to war as the junior officers of the army. This book will argue that the involvement of the schools needs to be seen within a broader context.

---

1   Wilfred Owen, 'Dulce et Decorum est' in Brian Gardener (ed) *Up the Line to Death: The War Poets 1914-1918* (London: Methuen, 1956), passim.
2   The definition of a public school is discussed in the 'Structure' section of this chapter below.

Public Schools in History, Literature and Memoir

There are a variety of secondary sources which discuss public school involvement during and before the Great War. These sources can be broken down into eight major areas of literature which contribute to this study: general history, memoirs, fiction, examinations of public attitudes to the war in general, studies of public schools, histories of education and studies of army recruitment and training before and during the war. This section discusses the historiography relating to public schools and identifies the gaps and shortcomings which have led to this study.

General histories have examined the role of public schools in the Great War as part of a more common discussion about the war and the decline of the British Empire. Corelli Barnett in *The Collapse of British Power* identified the shortcomings of the public school system as one of the reasons for that decline. In this less than flattering assessment of public schools he claimed that only Nazis and Communists were subject to a more intense instillation of values.[3] Christian morality was to be more important than scientific knowledge.[4] Education in the public schools, he claimed, had a romantic bias which was religious and intellectual.[5] It was these values that made public school boys so willing to volunteer to serve in the Great War. In the latter half of the 20th Century, when Europe had suffered from the consequences of the spread of Nazism and Communism, memories of this were still fresh in the 1970s and it is not surprising that there was cynicism about anything which smacked of ideology. The 1960s and 1970s also saw the rise of social and economic liberalism and the end of deference to one's supposed betters. The combination of an approach which was influenced by the events in Europe during the 20th Century and the emergence of a less deferential approach within society has meant other aspects of public school involvement in the war have had less attention than they deserve.

This approach which is critical of the public schools is reflected in the literary accounts published after the war by disillusioned public schoolboys.[6] For the most part, however, these works were published at a time when some authors, although not all, started to take a more jaundiced attitude to the war. They continue to be influential because of their literary merit but they should not be seen primarily as works of history. These writers set out to state a personal point of view of how they perceived the war based on their own experience. This experience was based on their personal circumstances and lacked the advantage of being able to consider all the factors involved. The role of the historian, on the other hand, is to examine the available evidence and

---

3   Corelli Barnett, *The Collapse of British Power* (Gloucester: Alan Sutton, 1984), passim. pp. 24-25. See also Martin J Weiner, *English Culture and the Decline of the Industrial Spirit 1850-1980* (London: Penguin, 1987), passim.
4   Barnett, *The Collapse of British Power*, p. 25.
5   Ibid., pp. 27-28.
6   See, for example Edmund Blunden, *Undertones of War* (London: Penguin, 2010), passim. and Robert Graves, *Good-bye to All That* (London: Jonathan Cape, 1929), passim.

place it within the wider context of the war. This is not to diminish the contribution of these literary figures: Their contribution is significant and it is important to understand what they wrote and why as well as how others have chosen to interpret it over the years. By understanding this we gain a better insight into public schools and their old boys during the war. Other public school old boys, such as Guy Chapman, produced less jaundiced memoirs which can be used to help build a wider picture of their involvement in the war but, again, they only form a small part of the story of the involvement of the schools and their old boys.[7]

The same problems of placing too much emphasis on the personal account occurs with fiction based on public schools. Public school fiction is not a homogeneous genre. Within it there are a variety of approaches, not all of them tie in with the traditional narrative about public school ethos. The most often cited books were published in a period between 1857 and 1917; over this length of time it was inevitable that attitudes would change and the genre would evolve. An examination of *Tom Brown's Schooldays*, *The Complete Stalky & Co.*, *Mike A Public School Story* and *The Loom of Youth* reveals a variety of approaches from a semi-autobiography to gently poking fun at public schools.[8] It is also a mistake to assume that the writers were always faithfully recording their own experience and that their work reflected the experience of their contemporaries.[9] This is not to diminish the use of fiction as a source of evidence, Gary Sheffield has described war fiction as a useful source. The same may be said of public school fiction but its use must be within the wider context of other evidence.[10]

One significant problem with studies of, and accounts about, individual public schools and the Great War is that they have centred on the schools themselves with research focussed on how they fitted in with the wider effort. It is important to consider the extent to which public school attitudes accorded with the rest of the population. Studies such as those by Alexander Watson have made a connection between civilian and army life.[11] Other writers such as Adrian Gregory have focussed on the role and attitudes of the home front.[12] The latter's book concentrates on how the civilian population supported the war and places into context the public schools' contributions to supporting the war effort beyond their involvement in the armed forces. The

---

7   Guy Chapman, *A Passionate Prodigality: Fragments of an Autobiography* (London: Buchan & Enright, 1985), passim.
8   Thomas Hughes, *Tom Brown's Schooldays* (London: Virtue & Company, 1857), passim; Rudyard Kipling, *The Complete Stalky & Co.*, (Oxford: Oxford University Press, 1999), passim; P G Wodehouse, *Mike A Public School Story* (Rockville Maryland, 2008), passim and Alec Waugh, *The Loom of Youth* (London: Methuen, 1984), passim.
9   See Chapter 1 for a fuller discussion of this topic.
10 Gary Sheffield, 'Officer-man Relations: Morale and Discipline in the British Army, 1902–22' (PhD thesis, London, 1994), p. xiii.
11 Alexander Watson, *Enduring the Great War Combat: Morale and Collapse in the German and British Armies* (Cambridge: Cambridge University Press, 2009), passim.
12 Adrian Gregory, *The Last Great War British Society and the First World War* (Cambridge: Cambridge University Press, 2008), passim.

cultural aspects of the war have been covered in detail by Jay Winter whose work provides a deeper level of analysis of British attitudes to the war.[13] It is also valuable in understanding how attitudes towards the conflict developed after the war and how perceptions about public schools changed. Winter provided an analysis which considered how cultural perceptions of the war developed. This is important as there are a number of writers who have attempted to analyse this including Martin Stephens and Dan Todman.[14] Stephens's approach to addressing the myths of the war is helpful in understanding how public schools and their old boys saw the war. Todman argued that many of our perceptions of the war have been affected by developments in our general attitude towards war. He illustrated this by demonstrating how the views of veterans in the 1960s would have been influenced by changing attitudes.[15] This analysis is helpful in understanding the views of all those involved with public schools during the war. Catriona Pennell addressed attitudes in Britain and Ireland before the outbreak of the war arguing that there was not the level of enthusiasm for war that some have argued existed at this time.[16] She demonstrated that even amongst those who sent their sons to public schools there were severe reservations about the prospect of war. Former public schoolboys were often placed in positions of leadership but this does not mean they necessarily held significantly different views about the war to other sections of the population. The danger with taking an ideological approach is that it leads to an assumption which places an over-emphasis on exceptionalism within the public schools.

This is not to say that there were not unique factors in the contribution of the schools to the war effort. Discussion about public schools and the Great Wars has formed part of wider works. The debate about their involvement has revolved around the schools' ethos and it has been argued that it was these values and qualities, regardless of academic ability, which made a commission in the First World War the expected rank of public school old boys.[17] As Sheffield observed: 'It was widely believed that there was a direct connection between the ethos of public schools … and the ability to lead men in battle.'[18] These discussions ignore the military training public schoolboys had through the OTC and their predecessor cadet corps. However, it is mistaken to assume that all public schools made a similar contribution to the military effort and the army in particular. Simon Robbins discussed the varying contributions of schools

---

13   For example, see Jay Winter, *Sites of Memory Sites of Mourning* (Cambridge: Cambridge University Press, 1996), passim.
14   See Martin Stephen, *The Price of Pity Poetry, History and Myth in the Great War* (London: Leo Cooper, 1996), passim. and Dan Todman, *The Great War Myth and Memory* (London: Hambledon and London, 2005), passim.
15   Todman *The Great War Myth and Memory*, p. 204.
16   Catriona Pennell, *A Kingdom United: Popular Responses to the Outbreak of the First World War in Britain and Ireland* (Oxford: Oxford University Press, 2014), passim.
17   Barnett, *The Collapse of British Power*, p. 227.
18   Sheffield, *Officer-man Relations*, pp. 119-120.

in his examination of British leadership on the Western Front.[19] He demonstrates through statistical analysis that there were 10 public schools (five of whom formed part of the original group of nine public schools) that dominated the leadership on the Western Front. [20] There is no reason to assume that this was not the case in other theatres of war. The contribution of public schools outside this top 10 is more one of their old boys leading a citizen army as junior officers. Writers such as Jon Lewis-Stempel and Moore-Bick offer relevant analysis to the public schools although their work focusses on the infantry officer.[21] Neither of these works consider the characteristics of public schools in 1914 as a contributing factor.

The development of the public school in the Victorian and Edwardian periods has been covered more extensively than their involvement in the war. Peter Parker is one of the few authors to cover the subject in depth.[22] His analysis fails to cover the broader issues which affected the public schools up to and including the war and mainly focusses on the experience of the public school boy, as well as being literary in its approach. The weakness of his work can be found in his assertion that the memoirs of the public school boys represented a superior form of evidence to all other sources. Scholarly works include that of John de Honey who provides a scholarly and valuable analysis of the development of the Victorian public school serves as a useful background for the development of understanding public school ethos.[23] It does not, however, cover the period immediately leading up to the war. Other writers such as Brian Gardener and Jonathon Galthorne-Hardy have covered this period but have taken a less scholarly approach than Honey.[24] There are a number of works which examine the development of the cult of games by writers such as J A Mangan and

---

19 Simon Robbins, *British Generalship in the First World War*, 1914-1918 unpublished PhD thesis, (London 2001).
20 The 10 schools were: Charterhouse, Cheltenham, Clifton, Eton, Haileybury, Harrow, Marlborough, Rugby, Wellington College and Winchester.
21 John Lewis-Stempel, *Six Weeks: The Short and Gallant Life of the British Officer in the First World War* (London: Orion, 2011), passim and Christopher Moore-Bick, *Playing the Game: The British Junior Infantry Officer on the Western Front 1914-1918* (Solihull: Helion, 2011), passim. Lewis- Stempel's prologue offers an account of the death of Second Lieutenant Lewes on the Somme. He states that Lewes went to Uppingham but his name appears neither on the school's list of OU's who died or the CWGC list of dead. There is no trace of this individual on the school roll. This demonstrates the importance of establishing the veracity of all information which appears about public school participation in the war.
22 Peter Parker, *The Old Lie* (London: Hambledon Continuum, 1987), passim.
23 J R de. S Honey, *Tom Brown's Universe: The Development of the Victorian Public School* (London: Millington, 1977), passim.
24 Brian Gardner, *The Public Schools* (London: Hamish Hamilton, 1973), passim. and Jonathan Galthorne-Hardy, *The Public School Phenomenon* (London: Hodder and Stoughton, 1977), passim.

Malcom Tozer.²⁵ For a more general analysis of the mobilisation of youth, writers such as John Springhall address this topic although information on public schools is limited.²⁶ The literature in this area concentrates on the development of the public school ethos in the years before the war and there is no broad ranging scholarly overview of public schools in 1914.

In contrast a great deal has been written about the public schools between 1914 and 1918. Anthony Seldon and David Walsh's *Public Schools and The Great War: The Generation Lost* argued that the public schools' involvement should not be treated with disdain and that the qualities of a public school education were important to victory.²⁷ The book is an important contribution but does not discuss the public schools' activities as institutions during the Great War and their relationship with government. This gap includes the role of public schools in preparing its boys to serve as officers. The participation of public schools in the war also needs to be understood in terms of the pre-war Liberal government's army reforms initiated by Lord Haldane, its development of the Officer Training Corps (OTC) as well as the army's connection with public schools. For Haldane's reforms, E M Spiers provides a useful account of the factors which drove the reforms and the role of the public schools in them.²⁸ Ian Worthington discussed the development of the relationship between the army and the public schools but this only covers the period from 1849 to 1908 when the OTC came into existence.²⁹ Most recently, the publication of *The Edwardian Army* by Timothy Bowman and Mark Connelly and *From Boer War to Great War* by Spencer Jones has increased understanding of the development of the British Army between 1902 and 1914.³⁰ Despite this, relatively little has been written about the development of the OTC during this period. To date, very limited work has been done to examine the evidence available at a national level and at individual schools to gain a better understanding.³¹

---

25 J A Mangan, *Athleticism in the Victorian and Edwardian Public Schools* (Cambridge: Cambridge University Press, 1981) and Malcolm Tozer, *The Ideal of Manliness The Legacy of Thring's Uppingham* (Truro: Sunnyrest Books, 2015), passim.
26 Springhall, J., *Youth, Empire and Society: British Youth Movements, 1883-1940* (London: Croom Helm, 1977), passim.
27 Anthony Seldon and David Walsh, *Public Schools and The Great War The Generation Lost* (Barnsley: Pen and Sword Military, 2013), passim.
28 E M Spiers, *Haldane: An Army Reformer* (Edinburgh: Edinburgh University Press, 1980), passim.
29 Ian Worthington, 'Antecedent Education and Officer Recruitment: An Analysis of the Public School-Army Nexus, 1849-1908' (PhD thesis, Lancaster 1982).
30 Timothy Bowman and Mark Connelly, *The Edwardian Army: Recruiting, Training, and Deploying the British Army, 1902-1914*, (Oxford: Oxford University Press, 2012) and Spencer Jones, *From Boer War to Great War: Tactical Reform of the British Army 1902-1914* (Oklahoma: University of Oklahoma Press 2012), passim.
31 For example, Bowman and Connelly in their analysis draw on papers in the University of London Special Collections.

In contrast to the limited general work on public schools there have been many accounts focussing on the individual schools and their involvement in the war. In the main, these accounts have concentrated on the old boys who lost their lives in the war. This is problematic; by concentrating on those who died it omits the contribution of those who survived. This approach also requires judgements about who to include. Eton lost 1,200 old boys in the war and Alexandra Churchill's account of the school in this period is only able to discuss 120 (10 per cent) of them.[32] Of the accounts on those who died one of the more useful is Sue Smart's *When Heroes Die* about Gresham and the Great War.[33] Although it has no bibliography or footnotes it draws on the school archives to provide a useful account of life on the front line. The centenary of the end of the war led to a fresh batch of books about individual schools. Colin Pendrill's *And We Were Young Oundle and The Great War* provides accounts of all the old boys who died but in addition discusses life at the school during the war.[34] This is a useful contribution as little to date has been written about public schools and the home front outside of Seldon and Walsh's balanced approach and Parker's more limited commentary. In general, books about individual schools can be parochial in their nature and do not consider how they fit into the wider context. This writer's *A School in Arms: Uppingham and the Great War* is a case study of the school and the war and attempts to explain how it fitted into the wider war effort.[35] It discusses both those who survived as well as those who died and examines areas such as the skills Old Uppinghamians contributed as well as its involvement on the home front. Its limitations are that while it considers the wider war effort this is inevitably from the point of view of Uppingham. Even if the differences were subtle, each school had a different approach; a case study by its nature even when employed to test current theories cannot reflect these differences. Considering a wider group of schools will greatly enhance an understanding of public schools in the Great War.

The studies of public schools in the Great War have in many cases focussed on their ethos and ignored other aspects of their involvement. Therefore, this book will address the contributions of public schools to the Great War and examine the limitations of the 'ideology' model in understanding their contributions. Public schools did not sit in isolation from the rest of society in the years leading up to and during the Great War. Their role also needs to be better understood in terms of their relationship with the government and army, the training of its pupils to be officers and the nature of public schools in 1914.

---

32 Alexandra Churchill, *Blood and Thunder: The Boys of Eton College and the First World War* (Stroud: The History Press, 2014), passim.
33 Sue Smart, *When Heroes Die: A Forgotten Archive Reveals the Last Days of the School Friends Who Died for Britain* (Derby: Breedon Books, 2001), passim.
34 Colin Pendrill, *And We Were Young: Oundle School and the Great War* (Solihull: Helion 2017), passim.
35 Timothy Halstead, *A School in Arms: Uppingham and the Great War* (Solihull: Helion, 2017), passim.

Structure

To understand the role of public schools, therefore, it is necessary to consider several different themes so that a broader understanding can be gained. Developing this understanding requires that an approach which is not strictly chronological approach is taken. In explaining why the alumni of public schools are 'More than Victims of Horace' it is necessary to examine public schools, their ethos and values before and during the war. Chapter 1 examines the literature (both as fiction and history) and theories that have appeared on this subject. It will discuss the strengths and weaknesses of such work and assist in providing a greater understanding about how the ideas around the 'ideology' of public schools developed.

Chapter 2 considers the development of the schools from the Public Schools Act in 1868 until the end of Queen Victoria's reign in 1901. The legislation set the direction for the development of the public school movement and formed part of the wider educational reform initiated by Gladstone's Liberal Government which also included the Endowed Schools Act 1869 and the Elementary Education Act 1870. This chapter demonstrates that despite assertions to the contrary the public school movement was not monolithic in its nature. Schools within the movement differentiated themselves by addressing different educational requirements. Only a few of these schools were substantial sources of junior officers for the army. The Boer War (1899-1902) demonstrated that this arrangement was far from satisfactory and there were severe differences between the army and the schools over the education potential cadets should receive.

Chapter 3 examines the evolution of public schools from 1901 to 1914. The government took an increasingly interventionist approach to education and a series of important legislative acts followed in the years up to 1914 including the major reforms of the Education Act 1902. The government's relationship with the public schools changed as it sought to increase its control of them in the years leading up to the war. This educational reform was partly designed to address the technological, educational changes and developments in the professions which took place within society before 1914.It influenced the development of education at public schools before 1914 but also created tensions between them and the government which need to be considered. Education was not the only area where significant reforms took place in the years leading up to 1914. The army's failures during the Boer War and the increasing concern about the threat of Germany to the British Empire led to significant military reforms. The difficult relationship between the army and schools continued in the 1900s. The priorities of the schools clashed with those of the army. There was far from a cosy relationship between the two bodies and the schools placed their own needs ahead of the country's military requirements. The debate about the role of the schools in supporting the army led, in 1908, to the formation of the OTC. Only after 1911 was there a thawing in the relationship.

When the war broke out in August 1914 Britain rapidly expanded its army as Kitchener created his 'New Armies'. These new armies required junior officers which the small pre-war professional army could not supply. A key source was the public schools with OTC units; a belief within the army that the social qualities of their old boys made them an obvious and instant source for junior officers. Britain's army was unprepared for a large scale European war and it was only with the appointment of Lord Kitchener as Secretary of State for War in August 1914 that steps were taken to remedy this. However, the new armies did not have the luxury of time of a carefully managed development towards becoming an effective fighting force. The urgency of the situation, especially with an overstretched War Office, made improvisation necessary to achieve this.

Chapters 5 and 6 consider the active role of public schools, during the war, of preparing their boys to be junior officers. To date, the day to day involvement of public schools in military training has not been examined. Instead, the perceived militarism of the schools has been given the most attention by writers including Barnett, Parker and Tozer. Chapter 5 looks at how the public schools were left to fend for themselves during 1914 and 1915 in providing officer training by a disorganised War Office. Chapter 6 shows that from 1916 the War Office had recovered sufficiently to be able to take a firmer control of the way it managed its junior officer corps and trained its men. As a result, it started to become more prescriptive about the way this should be done and in the role of the public schools in this. Both chapters examine the public schools' commitment to providing boys with the technical skills to become officers. This did not mean that there were no disagreements between the army and public schools and this is also examined in these chapters.

Chapter 7 examines how the individual public schools contributed different skills to the army and the extent to which this was influenced by their individual curricula. As discussed, earlier in this introduction, much of the histography about junior officers has centred on those who served in the infantry. Not only did the army grow in size during the war but also in terms of its complexity. The size of the organisation and the increasing use of technology meant that a wider range of skills was required to ensure its efficient operation. It also considers the extent to which public schools contributed to the army both in terms of senior and junior officers and demonstrating that it was not the traditional army schools which provided a higher proportion of old boys to the ranks of the senior officers.

Chapter 8 examines the efforts of public schools on the Home Front discussing how they supported food production alongside other schools as part of a national effort. The start of 1916 saw a significant development in the British war effort. During 1914-15 the army relied on volunteers as recruits. This did not prove sufficient for recruiting enough men for the army and also meant that skilled workers often needed for the home front volunteered to serve in the army thus impeding the efforts of vital industries such as munitions. A response was needed and from the start of 1916 conscription was introduced giving the government far more power to direct resources as it saw fit.[36] Despite this the country increasingly suffered from a manpower shortage. There

---

36 See R J Q Adams and Philip P Poirier, *The Conscription Controversy in Great Britain 1900-1918* (Basingstoke: MacMillan, 1987), passim and Keith Grieves, *The Politics of Manpower, 1914-1918* (Manchester: Manchester University Press, 1988), passim.

were conflicting demands from different sectors including farming where workers in the early stages of the war had tended to stay at home to support the war effort through agricultural production. As these problems became increasingly severe public schools became involved in food production. With an approach increasingly based on 'National Efficiency', the Ministry of National Service was created in March 1917 to direct the use of manpower and the schools found themselves increasingly required to support agriculture.[37] Some schools made other significant contributions to the war effort and the extent and its connection with the educational ethos of individual schools is considered. Finally, the chapter briefly touches on commemoration at public schools and the sacred as well as the secular elements to it. As with the rest of British society, the war had a considerable effect on the public schools. The establishment of memorials to those who had died was undertaken by all the public schools. The debate about the most appropriate memorials was at times extremely strong within the schools and amongst their old boys. Different approaches to memorials were taken ranging from the religious to the utilitarian. This is considered and compared against the concepts of gentlemanliness and chivalry which some writers have argued were prevalent at public schools before and during the war.

Sources

The question of what precisely a public school is continues to promote a great deal of academic debate.[38] It can descend into semantics and there are a number of valid approaches, but for the purposes of this book a public school will be one that had representation on the Headmaster's Conference (HMC) in 1914. Membership of the HMC was considerably smaller in 1914 than it is today, and many of the schools which are members today but were not in 1914, had pupils from substantially different backgrounds to those they draw on today. However, even among the public schools of 1914 the background of the pupils of different schools varied and each school had its own emphasis within its curriculum; Oundle was known for its emphasis on science and engineering and Uppingham for the quality of its music. In addition, there was a social hierarchy of schools headed by Eton and Harrow.

The contribution of the public school movement needs to be understood within the context of these variations. In researching this book, it has been necessary to ensure a representative sample of schools is examined. To achieve this, John Honey's approach has been employed, which developed a five grade scale for ranking public schools, split into I to IV with a fifth category (henceforth NC) formed by those schools which were not graded by him. The methodology for this grading system was to use a number of

---

37 See G R Searle, *The Quest for National Efficiency: A Study in British Politics and Political Thought, 1899-1914* (Oxford: Blackwell, 1971), passim.
38 For a fuller discussion, see J R de S Honey, *Tom Brown's Universe* (London 1977), pp. 238-295.

different criteria to establish the status of individual schools. These included which other schools any individual school played at games, the number of scholarships a school's pupils won to Oxford and Cambridge and how successful a school's pupils were in passing army and Civil Service entrance exams.[39] To ensure that the research for the book investigated was representative of public schools in 1914, a sample of schools across all categories was selected for detailed research. The sample consists of 11 schools, Christ's Hospital (NC) Epsom (III), Lancing (II), Mill Hill (NC), Oundle (IV), Sherborne (I), Shrewsbury (III), Stonyhurst (NC), Tonbridge (I), Uppingham (I) and Winchester (I). An overview of these schools, their history and background appear in Chapter 2, but they represent schools who varied because of their curriculum, social background and religious faith. The analysis of this core group of schools has been supplemented by drawing on material relating to a wider group of schools which have shed more light on issues which all public schools faced before and after the war.

In addition to the secondary literature discussed above a variety of research sources have been employed both from the 11 schools identified above and from other schools. These include records held by The National Archives (TNA), the Headmasters' Conference (HMC), school magazines, the reports of headmasters to governing bodies, governing body minutes, rolls of service, school rolls, unpublished diaries and memoirs and other working papers such as those relating to the OTC and previous research projects.[40]

The National Archives has a variety of relevant material. This includes instructions, minutes and memorandum from the War Office, Ministry of National Service and Board of Education as well as officer files. The War Office (WO) files are especially useful for providing a high-level view of the development of officer training by the army and the development and evolution of the relationship with the public schools. It has not been possible to identify files which provide information about the rationale behind the army's thinking about its relationship with the Junior OTC and public schools. To a certain extent, it has been possible to fill these gaps through other sources such as the HMC archives. The WO officer files are variable in their quality as a result of weeding over the years. Some files have been the subject of especially ferocious weeding and are of limited use. Others which have been treated more mercifully, provide useful background on the reasons for the recruitment of junior officers. This has been especially useful when examining a selection of files for old boys from the core sample of schools. The files relating to the Ministry of National Service and the Board of Education are especially valuable in understanding the government's approach to all schools in the country. They are also useful in placing the contribution of public schools to food production in a wider context.

---

39 Honey, *Tom Brown's Universe*, p. 264.
40 For example, Oundle School Archives holds the research papers Richard John Palmer, 'The Life of F W Sanderson (1857-1922) with special reference to his work and influence at Oundle School (1892-1922)' (PhD thesis, Hull 1981).

In understanding public school involvement, the HMC archives are extremely useful. They contain the minutes of the annual meeting of the HMC's members as well as committee reports. The HMC comprised of public school headmasters who met to discuss matters of mutual interest; they did not represent their governing bodies but themselves as the individuals who were in charge of the schools. The minutes reflect the issues they were dealing with in the running of their schools. Those covered include the relationship with the government and army, the OTC, supporting the war effort, curriculum and public examinations. The minutes have been examined for the period 1900 and 1919. It has been possible to gain an understanding of the main issues which were of concern to them in this period. These views were not necessarily those of their governors with whom the relationship could be tense. To examine the position of the governing bodies the reports of headmasters to them and their own minutes are available for a number of the schools but not all. Despite this it is possible to gain an understanding of the views of the governors and the areas of tension. Furthermore, in making a comparison it is possible to gain an understanding of the common concerns for all schools; especially, when compared against HMC records. Several school magazines have been consulted; many schools have made these available online. They often address the issues faced by all public schools, such as OTC work during the war. Combining this commentary helps to provide a better understanding of the activities of other schools. For example, one magazine may state that an army instruction has been received to carry out certain activities, whereas another magazine will report the activity without reference to the instruction. School magazines are important as a chronicle of the life of the community they were published for. By their nature they were introspective and, if they were to succeed, had to publish what was of interest to their readers; sport was a strong interest to many and therefore was prominent. As such they were not censored but they could not publish material which would upset their readers or sponsors at school. The magazines provide useful biographical material about staff, pupils and old boys which is helpful in understanding public school life.[41] They are also of use as in validating general attitudes and values which studies of public schools have ascribed to them.

Apart from school magazines there are other sources which provide information about the participation of public schools in the Great War. Extremely useful primary sources are the rolls of service which were published by individual schools during and after the war. These documents recorded the known military careers of their old boys and were dependent on the school's ability to gather the relevant information. The compilers of these documents used sources such as announcements of commissions in *The Times* for news of old boys. It was more difficult to track old boys serving in the ranks and this was not helped by the alumni of public schools displaying varying levels of diligence in reporting back to their schools on their exploits. Uppingham's

---

41 J A Mangan, *Athleticism in the Victorian and Edwardian Public Schools* (Cambridge: Cambridge University Press, 1981). pp. 243-245.

roll of service recorded 2,198 as having served, subsequent research raised this total to 2,343 and the master responsible for tracking the activity of old boys claimed to have a list of 2,500 although it can no longer be located.[42] Christ's Hospital's roll lists just over 2000, although those responsible for its compilation believed that around 3000 served.[43] This can be attributed to the difficulties in gathering information at the time and, possibly, the fact of the School's move from London to Horsham in 1902. Many of those in service would have left School before the move and may have felt less of a connection to the school in its new location in the country. Lancing's roll of service is only complete to July 1918.[44] Promotions and officer commissions could be missed. Ralph Vaughan Williams was appointed a Second Lieutenant in the Royal Garrison Artillery (RGA) on Christmas Eve 1917 having served as private in the Royal Army Medical Corps (RAMC).[45] The Charterhouse roll of service does not record his promotion.[46] Other rolls of service suffered from similar deficiencies. Despite this the rolls of service provide a statistically significant sample which provide a wealth of biographical information. From this statistical analysis can be carried out to investigate topics including which areas of the forces old boys served in and the proportion of ranks held. This is also useful in making comparisons between different schools to identify factors which led to this. School rolls produced by most but not all schools can also be employed to supplement this analysis. They provide basic autobiographical information which assists further analysis for example in establishing the location of the National Archives (Kew) officer files.

Summary

The focus of the general work on public schools to date has been on their ethos and ideology. Much of this appeared when the experience of Europe pointed towards the undesirable effects that an ideological approach had had upon the continent. It is not surprising that in the 1960s and 1970's when deference to perceived social betters had been eroded that public school ideology should be critically examined in the light of this experience. Much of the literature about individual public schools and the Great War also concentrates on those who died. It is right that this personal tragedy should be examined but it must also be remembered that in the region of 80 percent

---

42 Halstead, *A School in Arms*, pp. xiii-xiv.
43 *Christ's Hospital Roll of Honour and Service Names of Governors, Members of Staff, and Old Blues serving in His Majesty's and Allied Forces in the World War 1914-1918* (Privately published,1920), passim.
44 *Lancing College Roll of Service Ninth Issue, July 1918* (Privately published, 1918), passim.
45 TNA WO/ 374/75055: Second Lieutenant Ralph Vaughan Williams.
46 Final *A List of Caruthusians who served in His Majesty's Forces and the Allied Armies August, 1914- November 1918 and in the Subsequent Russian Campaigns* (Privately published: 1919), p. 27.

of public school boys survived the war and their contribution deserves detailed study. Alongside this public school involvement manifested itself in several ways including the training of its pupils for military service and food production. Existing literature has overlooked much of this and these areas need to be considered to give a broader understanding of public schools, one which goes beyond the matters of ethos and ideology. Before considering the wider aspects of public school involvement it is necessary to examine the ethos of public schools.

1

Victims of Horace?

Public school ethos, alongside patriotism, public enthusiasm and a deep concern about the German threat, has formed a central part of the explanation for the involvement of public school old boys in the Great War. Before examining the involvement of public schools in wider terms it is necessary to examine this and associated literature to place it in context. An examination of Uppingham School and public ethos reveals more nuanced circumstances than the historiography sometimes allows.[1] This literature needs to be examined to consider these variations and how they apply across all the public schools in the years before the war. A more detailed examination of public schools and the boys who attended them will be examined in Chapter Two. This chapter examines the educational approach of the schools and the cult of games which developed there in the later years of Queen Victoria's reign and reached its peak in the years leading up to 1914. In support of theories about the ethos of public schools, fiction about them, together with the works of the war poets and the memoirs of the 'disillusioned' public school boys have often been cited. Memoirs, poetry and fiction should not be dismissed because they inevitably reflect the bias of the authors and poets; instead, they need to be considered in the context in which they were written and their value as evidence to the general debate. Discussion of this forms the second and third parts of this chapter.

Public School Ethos, Education and the Cult of Games

Wellington famously credited victory at Waterloo as having been won on the playing fields of Eton. The statement is apocryphal but echoes the argument that the playing of games by public school boys imbued them with the leadership qualities which made them effective junior officers during the Great War.[2] Even if true the statement ignores

---

1 Halstead, *A School in Arms*.
2 Oxford Academic, *Misquotation: 'The Battle of Waterloo was won on the playing fields of Eton'* <https://oupacademic.tumblr.com/post/57740288322/misquotation-the-battle-of-waterloo-was-won-on> (8 August 2022).

the substantial changes which took place in the 19th Century. The public school playing fields of 1815 and 1914 were not readily comparable. In 1815 there were no organised games and at Eton one of the main activities of boys outside the classroom was fighting.[3] In the years before 1914 boys were diverted from this by organised games such as rugby and cricket. From the school playing fields in the years leading up to 1914 it is argued that the old boys developed qualities to equip them to be junior officers. The playing of games at public schools was important but equally important was the way they were played; the playing of games was to reflect the chivalric way life which was to be lived. By 1914 this way was termed 'gentlemanliness' which 'stressed honour, bravery, loyalty, courtesy, generosity, mercy and self-sacrifice'.[4] From this flowed a sense of responsibility towards team members and in the Great War manifested itself in a sense of paternalism towards their men and their welfare. The public school education, it is argued, producing these gentlemen consisted of a series of influences which, in addition to games, were scholastic, ethical, religious and military.[5]

Correlli Barnett, a trenchant critic of public schools, attributed to Thomas Arnold, Headmaster of Rugby, the primary responsibility for giving English education its 'concern with moral conduct and its distinctive mark of romanticism'.[6] It was an approach shared by Edward Thring, Headmaster of Uppingham School, who believed 'that the highest education must work in the region of the highest life'.[7] Christian morality was to be more important than scientific knowledge.[8] However, from 1890 to 1914 this Christian romanticism became fused with a patriotic romanticism. The English principles of truth, liberty, equality and religion must be taken to the rest of the world. The public school response to the foreign threat became idealised and the school playing field was seen as a preparation for the battles the Empire would be involved in. Education in the public schools had a romantic bias which was religious and intellectual.[9] However, as an analysis of a sample of senior late Victorian army officers demonstrates, at the end of the 19th century, officers were drawn from a restricted group.[10] The sample consists of 316 officers out of which the schools of 82 of them are known. Of that 82, 43 percent went to Eton and the rest are spread out over several schools. Of prominent figures in the Roberts and Wolseley rings, Roberts was educated at Eton, family financial circumstances meant Wolseley was educated in Dublin and Evelyn Wood went to Marlborough, which he disliked intensely.[11]

---

3   Sir Llewellyn Woodward, *The Age of Reform 1815-1870, Second Edition* (Oxford: Oxford University Press, 1962) p. 485.
4   Sheffield, *Officer-man Relations*, p. 129.
5   John Keegan, *The Face of Battle* (Paperback edition, London: Pimlico, London, 1991), p. 273.
6   Barnett, *The Collapse of British Power*, pp. 24-25.
7   Ibid., p. 29.
8   Ibid., p. 25.
9   Ibid., pp. 27-28.
10 I am grateful to Brian Curragh for sharing his research on this topic.
11 Steven Manning, *Evelyn Wood VC: Pillar of Empire* (Barnsley: Pen and Sword, 2007), pp. 6-7.

It's difficult to see public school ethos playing a key part of the army's defence of the Empire at the end of the 19th century. Until the Great War there was no widespread deployment of public schoolboys in the junior officer corps. The roots of their education can be attributed to Arnold who was appointed to Rugby in 1828, 84 years before the outbreak of the Great War. His appointment was the key event in the transformation of public schools from anarchic institutions to ones whose aim was to produce Christian gentlemen.[12] Its importance needs to be understood because it is from this that the idea of public school, ethos developed. The Eton of 1815 (and other public schools) were run on the basis that boys were allowed to make their own rules and impose their own punishments. Boys and masters were in a state of constant conflict where boys demanded more privileges and less tyranny from the masters. David Newsome described this as 'mob rule' which impeded good learning and any prospect of a climate where the right moral culture prevailed.[13] The only way for masters to keep control was by expulsion and mass flogging. This lawlessness continued into the middle of the nineteenth century. The last public school rebellion took place at Marlborough in 1851, long after Arnold's arrival at Rugby.[14] His approach was not only to provide boys with an education but offer them a set of values. It was not only the curriculum he was concerned with but also the way the school was run. There were five key features of this: firstly, he obtained from the governing body the right to have independence in the day to day business of the school and the imposition of discipline. Secondly, he improved the status of masters by awarding them higher salaries and involving them in the management of the school. His third innovation was to introduce the house system where assistant masters exercised supervisory and pastoral care over boarders. His fourth change complemented the introduction of the house system by developing the prefect system. A select group of boys were appointed not to enforce the system but to support Arnold in developing the right moral culture. This select group was not to be dictators but leaders with a great deal of independence in how each house was run. Finally, in support of his quest for higher moral standards, he had no hesitation in removing unsuitable boys.[15] Although Arnold secured the power to run the school as he thought best, he shared these responsibilities with the masters and prefects. His explanation of sharing with prefects the task of achieving higher moral standards was to compare their role with that of the army or navy officer where the lack of moral courage would be considered to be cowardice.[16] The boys in his care were to be trained to be leaders both in the way the school operated and what they were taught.

On the face of it Arnold made few changes to the curriculum. Classics continued to be at its heart but the purposes for which they were taught changed radically in that

---

12   J A Mangan, *Athleticism*, pp. 14-15.
13   David Newsome, *Godliness & Good Learning* (London: Cassell, 1961), pp. 38-39.
14   Honey, *Tom Brown's Universe*, p. 6.
15   Ibid., pp. 7-11.
16   Newsome, *Godliness & Good Learning*, pp. 41-42.

they were now to be used to teach moral values.[17] In Arnold's curriculum 16 of the 20 periods in each week were devoted to the classics, scripture and history with the remaining four periods divided equally between mathematics and modern languages. That classics was at the heart of his syllabus is demonstrated by the emphasis of the work in history and scripture. History mainly involved reading the works of classical authors such as Herodotus and Thucydides while scripture partly involved the study of the New Testament in Greek.[18] There was a shift in the curriculum from Latin to Greek with Arnold using a combination of classics and history to explain political and social problems.[19] In hindsight, Arnold may be criticised for excluding sciences from the timetable; he believed that there was not time to accommodate them in the timetable and that in any event they were unsuitable subjects. His main concern was with the education of the mind.[20] That his ideas were influential can be seen in a number of different ways. The Public School Commissioners (led by Lord Clarendon) in their report of 1864 identified Arnold's approach as good practice and recommended it form the basis for the curricula of other more conservative schools such as Eton. Benson at Wellington College and Prince Lee at King Edward's Birmingham drew upon Arnold's ideas as they developed their own curricula.[21] Benson's first post as a teacher was at Rugby in 1852 having attended King Edward's under Prince Lee so it is little surprise that the ideas of Arnold should have so heavily influenced him. Arnold's ideas became widespread; 23 of his assistant teachers became headmasters at other public schools between 1842 and 1899 and his ideas were taken up by the Christian Socialists.[22]

At the heart of Arnold's classical teaching lay Plato's *Republic* whose aim 'to produce ideal citizens to play their part in the ideal community.' Citizens were to serve the community by putting the needs of others ahead of their own. For Plato perfect happiness came from the proper use of abilities and gifts. The proper application of these would lead to a soul aspiring to the three qualities of truth, courage and self-control. These were the qualities which were at the centre of the concept of manliness. For Plato education was achieved through 'music' (music, literature and visual arts) and 'gymnastic' (to achieve a simple life and diet as well as maintaining good health.[23] Arnold appears to have had no interest in games as an activity to promote the 'gymnastic'. The myth that he introduced games to the curriculum is the result of Pierre de Coubertin (founder of the modern Olympic

---

17 Honey, *Tom Brown's Universe*, p. 10.
18 Newsome, *Godliness & Good Learning*, p. 64.
19 Malcolm Tozer, '"To the Glory that was Greece": Classical Images in Public School Athleticism' in Tom Winnifrith and Cyril Barratt (eds.) *Leisure in Art and Literature* (London: Macmillan, 1992), p. 109.
20 Newsome, *Godliness & Good Learning*, p. 68.
21 Ibid., p. 66.
22 Tozer, '"To the Glory that was Greece"', p. 112.
23 Ibid., pp. 111-112.

Games) incorrectly taking *Tom Brown's Schooldays* to be representative of Arnold's educational approach.[24] The development of games at Rugby was more a consequence of his decision to ban hunting and poaching and close down the boys' pack of hounds than an active decision to promote games; instead the boys' found other activities to fill their spare time such as the already popular cricket and Rugby's version of football.[25] Other headmasters introduced games and athletics to the public schools with the earliest innovations in this area having more to do with keeping boys out of trouble. When Charles Vaughan, a former pupil of Arnold, was appointed Headmaster of Harrow in 1844 the number of pupils was in decline and problems of ill-discipline needed to be addressed. His solution was to adopt Arnold's educational approach and introduce the playing of games to fill much of the boys' spare time. Vaughan had no interest in sports apart from its use to burn off the surplus energy of boys. George Cotton, who had taught at Rugby under Arnold, was appointed to be Master of Marlborough College in 1852. Like Vaughan he was faced with a situation where for the pupils lawlessness was a way of life. Although he would propound the value of games Cotton's main motivation for introducing them was to bring an out of control school back to order. The introduction of games was only one part of his reforms which also addressed the school's poor facilities. The importance of Cotton and Vaughan, Mangan argued, is because once their approach had been shown to work others created an ideology to justify it.[26]

Ideology is a strong word, and in light of the two world wars of the 20th century one with negative connotations. It is often understood to be a set of political beliefs such as Communism or Nazism. The British have tended to recoil from this idea and the adverse commentary on the cult of games and public schools can be seen in this light. Edward Thring appointed as Headmaster of Uppingham in 1853 ranks alongside Arnold as the other great innovator in the Victorian public school movement. His vision was to provide every boy with an education which was relevant to his needs.[27] To this end, he insisted on taking boys of all abilities. The curriculum he developed for their education expanded on that of Arnold. He developed a wider curriculum where moral training was linked to the teaching of the classics.[28] Gymnastics and physical education were introduced to not only provide a fit body and a range of physical skills but also train a boy in truth, courage and self-control from which would come a spirit of selflessness and service.[29] It was an approach which lasted for only a short time. The Public Schools Commission had been established following complaints that while the intellectual education of the schools was

---

24 Mangan, *Athleticism*, pp. 16-17.
25 Tozer, *The Ideal of Manliness*, p. 206.
26 Mangan, *Athleticism*, pp. 22-28.
27 Ibid., p. 45.
28 Tozer, "'To the Glory that was Greece'", pp. 123-124.
29 Tozer, *The Ideal of Manliness*, p. 114.

adequate there was a complete lack of moral training. The Commission drew the wrong conclusions from the work of Cotton, Thring, Vaughan and others. Instead of seeing the playing of games, which a useful tool for maintaining discipline it recommended that games, and not gymnastics, should provide moral training. By setting out a template for the running of public schools the Commission made it inevitable that in a time when the system was rapidly expanding all schools would play games. Given this endorsement and as schools sought to make themselves attractive to parents there was an expansion in matches between schools and within schools, the awarding of colours, the provision of professional coaches and improved facilities.[30] Playing games became an end in themselves rather than the moral training the Commission had identified. From this followed the rise in importance of the games player whom it is argued became deified. Harrow and other schools started to select prefects from games players rather than scholars. Team games it was argued promoted the idea of thinking of others by working together and provided training in leadership.[31] To achieve this *Esprit de Corps* it was important to select the right games to play. Gymnastics and other sports such as tennis were too individual; the preferred sporting activities were cricket, rowing and football (with rugby being the dominant code).[32] The leadership skills they produced, it is argued by Barnett and others, made the products of public schools ideal candidates to run the British Empire which expanded rapidly between 1850 and 1899. During the period before 1914, the country perceived itself to be at different times at risk from threats from France and Germany. The first public school corps was formed at Rossall in 1860, closely followed by Eton but only initiated at many other public schools from 1880, when it was believed there was a serious threat from France. In what some have described as an increasing climate of imperialism the public schools believed they should be playing their part in defending the Empire. The linking of the playing of games and its *Esprit de Corps* with the skills needed to fight in battle it has been argued led to a spirit of militarism within the public schools.[33] This, it is claimed, was reflected in the way the classics were taught. The emphasis changed from the teaching of Plato to one where Homer was the centre of study. No longer was the emphasis on the Platonic concept of service but on the Homeric emphasis on honour and war for its moral worth. Death in war in the Homeric version was seen as swift, sweet and painless.[34] From this, it is argued, stemmed the patriotic romanticism of public school boys. Public school boys had been indoctrinated by the classics taught to them and provided on the school playing fields with the basic skills to fight and lead men in battle.

---

30   Ibid., pp. 208-211.
31   Ibid., pp. 245-246.
32   Tozer, '"To the Glory that was Greece"', p. 118.
33   Tozer, *The Ideal of Manliness*', p. 294.
34   Tozer, '"To the Glory that was Greece"', p. 124.

However, there is no indication of teaching emphasis in terms of the way classics taught in these records to suggest a Homeric tone had taken hold in the way classics were taught. Examining records from Winchester and Epsom College all the elements of Arnold's curriculum are included. In the Sixth Form at Winchester the Classical Divisions' reading included Thucydides, Cicero and Euripides as part of wide-ranging reading.[35] At Epsom the Sixth Form reading included Cicero, Homer, Plato and Thucydides. On the classical side the Middle IV studied Julius Caesar's *Gallic War* (*De Bello Gallico*) which was a justification and celebration of Caesar through an account of his military success. This was written in Latin the average schoolboy would have found easier to understand and promoted the idea of the military hero leading to the boys developing a romantic idealism about their role in the Empire.[36] A contrary view of the influence of classics on the average boy argues that in the 19th century classroom most of those in receipt of a classical education believed it was irrelevant. The more it was forced on the boys the more they resisted and resented it. Edward Lyttleton, who was Headmaster of Haileybury and Eton, remarked that teaching was centred on abstract language work which had the effect of making games an attractive alternative to most boys.[37] By the start of the 20th Century there is little evidence that the classics were taught for moral education and more that they were taught in a way which concentrated on the technical aspects and included a heavy reliance on memory work.[38] Attempts at reform were made but in general met with resistance from many Headmasters. At the 1902 meeting of the HMC a motion to reduce the importance of Latin and Greek as entrance requirements to Oxford and Cambridge was watered down.[39] The problems with the teaching of the classics continued and in January 1912 *The Times* reported on a scathing assessment of the teaching of classics which had recently been published in *The Times Educational Supplement*.[40] Written anonymously by 'A Public School Master' who complained that huge endowments skewed teaching towards the classics with the result that the average schoolboy received an unsuitable education. He estimated that only 20 percent of boys got what they required from an education, with the remaining 80 percent ill-equipped to go forward in the world.

The fudge at the 1902 HMC meeting concealed differences about how the classics were taught. Reverend Albert David, who had previously been Headmaster of Clifton and was the newly appointed Headmaster of Rugby in 1909, believed in the importance of a classical education was best but that there should be less grammar and more

---

35 Winchester College Archives's (hereinafter WCA), Winchester College Calendar July 1907, p. 97.
36 Epson College Archives (Hereafter ECA), Epsom College Midsummer 1914, pp. 34-35.
37 Mangan, *Athleticism*, pp. 111-112.
38 Honey, *Tom Brown's Universe*, pp. 127-128.
39 The Headmasters' Conference, Report of the Thirtieth Meeting of the Headmasters' Conference December 1902, pp. 42-57
40 *The Times*, 3 January 1912, p. 2.

literature.⁴¹ W. H. D. Rouse, Headmaster of the Perse School, reformed his school's teaching of the classics and introduced the direct method of teaching Greek and Latin.⁴² In his view boys were introduced to the classics too early and too much time was spent teaching in a way which was 'dull and stupid' using unsuitable text books.⁴³ An assistant master at Uppingham, E. Hockliffe (an Old Etonian), where the amount of compulsory classics had been significantly reduced, compared the way the classics were taught to 'scholastic medievalism' and better ways of teaching them needed to be found.⁴⁴ Another classicist, Nowell Smith, Headmaster of Sherborne, blamed Oxford and Cambridge for insisting on them as a condition of entry. To him, testing the proficiency of boys in Latin and Greek was not the right way to assess their suitability for many of the subjects boys would study at the two universities.⁴⁵ His views in this area were shared by his predecessor as Headmaster, F. B. Westcott, also a classicist. Keen to promote the growth of the Moderns at Sherborne, he believed their growth was being impeded by the 'ancient universities' insisting on boys having some Greek.⁴⁶ Smith removed Greek from class teaching and arranged for it to be taught in sets below the Sixth Form allowing 'Modern' boys to learn German and extra French in the freed time. In addition, he introduced a course of elementary chemistry and physics for all boys once they reached the middle part of the school.⁴⁷ He noted that fewer boys were studying the classics, despite the requirements of Oxbridge, and argued 'a more nutritious intellectual diet can be provided than the bare elements of Greek Grammar.' He still believed that the ancient civilisations provided valuable lessons but he was doing this by introducing the teaching of history of the Greeks and Romans while maintaining the teaching of modern history.⁴⁸ To his mind, the average boy was likely to get far more from a broad study of the classics than an overemphasis on the 'niceties of Greek and Latin idiom.'⁴⁹ The concerns of Rouse and Smith were not the only the challenge the classics faced. Lyttleton complained that parents warned their sons that the hard work required to study the classics would make them unpopular with their fellow students. This, he believed, led to games playing too important a part in life at school for many boys, who saw them as a pleasant alternative to Latin and Greek.⁵⁰ In many ways Lyttleton was being unfair, the type of education parents expected did not require the classics. By the early 20th century, it was no longer necessary to take a paper in Latin as part of the Army Entrance Exam. Many parents sought an education

41 Sherborne School Archives (hereafter SSA), Diaries of H R King, 5 November 1909.
42 Hugh Pattenden, 'Old Perseans and the Great War: A Study in the Alumni of a Minor Public School', *History of Education*, 47: 5 (April 2018), p. 630.
43 *The Times,* 4 January 1912, p. 8.
44 Ibid., 9 January 1912, p. 4.
45 *The Times,* 15 January 1912, p. 6.
46 SSA, Headmaster's Report to the Governors for 1907, p. 6.
47 SSA, Headmaster's Report to the Governors for 1909, pp. 7-8.
48 SSA, Headmaster's Report to the Governors for 1910, pp. 10-11.
49 SSA, Headmaster's Report to the Governors for 1911, p. 11.
50 Mangan, *Athleticism*, p. 133.

which would prepare their sons to go into the family business, where the study of the Moderns was more relevant. The connection between games and the classics in the training of boys to be leaders was tenuous. They were often in conflict with each other; many games players had no aptitude for the classics. The demands of games also stood in the way of OTC training. Alan Haig Brown, the officer commanding the Lancing College OTC, complained that those in charge of the Corps had 'been watched with a jealous eye to see that they did not encroach an inch upon the claims of work or the necessities of games.'[51] At many schools the OTC was not compulsory before 1914 (Winchester and Uppingham are examples of this approach) and many of the top athletes (the games bloods) preferred to practice instead of spending some time each week on parade with the OTC.

The playing of games, a classical education and training with the OTC did not work together to produce a group of leaders in the way that some writers have argued. The Army did see some benefits in the playing of games. Boys learned on the playing field to take rapid decisions, take risks and disregard their personal safety. An interest in games was not a monopoly of public school boys and the working classes too had a strong interest in watching and playing sport, the foundation of the Football League in 1888 was one part of this. It was a shared interest which helped to put the public school boy in a good position to win the respect of his men.[52] It was taken advantage of by using it to package training as a form of sporting activity.[53] The playing of games it is claimed developed a sense a sense of responsibility towards fellow team members and in the war which would manifest itself in a sense of paternalism towards the men and their welfare.[54] There is no doubt that these qualities were important for a junior officer but they were never sufficient during the Great War. The failings of the British Army during the Boer War led to its reform into a professional fighting force on a limited budget which restricted its size to 200,000. When the Great War broke out, in August 1914, and it was decided to rapidly expand it there was a need to quickly recruit junior officers to lead it. The public schoolboy was an obvious source for these officers as the army was forced to improvise to meet this requirement. It was an good short-term solution but before the war there had been significant concern within the army about the ability of the public schools to provide cadets with the type of education required.

The attitude of the army demonstrates there are limitations to the idea the public school playing field was preparation for the battlefield. Likewise, the idea that the schools promoted militarism should be treated with some scepticism. There is no doubt that from 1900 to 1914 tensions between Germany and Britain increased considerably. German ambitions caused a great deal of concern and the expansion of its navy was seen

---

51   Captain Alan R Haig-Brown, *The OTC and the Great War* (London: Country Life, 1915) p. 62.
52   Sheffield, *Officer-man Relations*, pp. 122-123.
53   Ibid., p. 127.
54   Ibid., p. 129.

as a serious threat to the Empire. British prosperity was built on trade with its Empire and the rest of the world. British prosperity rested on its status as a leading exporter of manufactured goods while Germany produced for consumption within the country.[55] For Britain there was a clear interest in international trade and any threat to this was bound to be a factor in increasing British concern about Germany. Although many of the British newspapers in this period were campaigning for more action to meet the threat this should not be confused with an overwhelming lust for war. Within business there was serious concern about the effects of war.[56] This included the businessmen who sent their sons to public school, such as Leopold de Rothschild, the banker whose sons were at Harrow, who in July 1914 was actively involved in steps to stop Britain entering the war. At home many boys were the subject to the influence of those who recognised the disadvantages of war. At school, militarism was not as prevalent as has been suggested. A study of debates at Greshams and Harrow has demonstrated that the empire was accepted as a way of life (mundane imperialism) but were not incapable of criticising imperial propaganda.[57] Studies of other schools reveals similar attitudes. At Uppingham a motion supporting conscription was easily defeated.[58] Mill Hill Debating Society passed a motion in support of conscientious objection.[59] While such views were unusual it demonstrates there was no unquestioning militarism.

Once war broke out public schools did not always present their fallen old boys as military heroes. Charles Sorley, the poet, was educated at Marlborough a school which was known for its strong army connections. His obituary in the *Malburian* in November 1915 did not celebrate his military prowess but rather his poetry and his love of it, together with ideals and his plans to give his life to working with the less fortunate.[60] He had gone to war out of a sense of duty and not because he had an enthusiasm for war.[61] This was not just the view of poets; Arthur Lee, a 37 year old solicitor and Old Uppinghamian, expressed similar sentiments saying that it while he had severe reservations neither he nor his wife any doubts he should serve. His approach was not jingoistic nor militaristic and he disliked the war because of the damage it would do to his career, the loss of income and the problems this would create for the education of his children.[62] Edmund Blunden (Christ's Hospital), took *De Bello Gallico* with him to the front after he had joined up in 1915; his subsequent poetry and memoirs do not suggest a public schoolboy imbued with romantic ideal-

---

55 David Edgerton, *The Rise and Fall of the British Nation: A Twentieth-Century History* (London: Allen Lane, 2018), p. 132.
56 Pennell, *A Kingdom United*, pp. 25-26.
57 Edward Whiffin, 'Public Schools, Politics and Associational Culture in England, 1899-1939,' PhD thesis, (University College London Institute of Education 2021).
58 *Uppingham School Magazine*, November 1914, pp. 257-261.
59 *The Mill Hill Magazine*, No. 269, Vol. XL., No. 4. December.,1912, pp. 150-151.
60 *The Malburian*, Vol L, No. 755, 24 November 1915, pp. 173-176.
61 Pennell, *A Kingdom United*, pp. 159-160.
62 Imperial War Museum, (hereafter IWM) 66/121/, Colonel A N Lee Papers.

ism.⁶³ Old boys, whatever their age, were not guaranteed to unquestioningly adopt the militaristic views it is claimed they were imbued with. Public schools did not produce men possessed of nothing but a romantic idealism. Public school ethos, public opinion, parental influence or educational background were not guarantees that an old boy would hold a particular set of views. Apart from Sorley, Marlborough produced a number of old boys with varying attitudes to the war. Henry Wilson became CIGS in 1918, the poet Siegfried Sassoon who served made a highly publicised protest to the War Office about the way the war was being conducted, and the mountaineer Geoffrey Winthrop Young became a conscientious objector. The Shove brothers, both educated at Uppingham, had entirely different views of the war. Ralph became a barrister and later a County Court Judge and served in the war. After graduating Gerald was a Cambridge academic, a member of the Apostles and during the war was a conscientious objector.⁶⁴ Clement Atlee's brother, Tom, had objections to war so strong that he refused to serve in any capacity and went to prison rather than compromise on them.⁶⁵ Both brothers were educated at Haileybury (another school popular with the army whose *alumni* included Edmund Allenby) and by 1914 were socialists, but Clement's views differed significantly from those of his brother. For him socialism and patriotism went hand in hand.⁶⁶ A classical education and a love of Horace had not left him with a romantic view of war.⁶⁷ Donald Hankey, educated at Rugby, devoted his life to working with the less privileged.⁶⁸ In 1914 he enlisted as a private to continue this work and only later was he persuaded to accept a commission, and was killed on the Somme in October 1916. As 'A Student in Arms' writing for the *Spectator* he set out to explain the moral dilemmas of war, being neither excessively jingoistic nor deeply gloomy. Often, he was controversial and 'fell foul of the civilian (but not the military) censor for his eyewitness writing from the Somme.' His brother, Maurice, the first Cabinet Secretary, also educated at Rugby with a distinguished military and civil service career said of him that Donald had a gift of saying what he wanted to say but couldn't.⁶⁹ Maurice in his career appears to conform far more closely to the stereotype of the public schoolboy but still had sympathy with the views of his brother. Another Old Rugbeian R. H. Tawney, the distinguished economic historian, social reformer and proponent of adult education, was greatly influenced by

---

63   Hew Strachan, Introduction to Edmund Blunden, *Undertones of War* (London: Penguin, 2010), p. xii.
64   Uppingham School Roll p. 219, p. 225 Obituary G.F. Shove, *The Times*, 8 August 1947, p. 7 and Obituary R.S. Shove *The Times*, 3 February 1966, p. 17. The 'Apostles' is a Cambridge undergraduate intellectual society. Members have included G M Trevelyan, Bertrand Russell and John Maynard Keynes.
65   John Bew, *Citizen Clem: A Biography of Atlee* (London: Riverrun, 2017), p. 87.
66   Ibid., p. 71.
67   Ibid., pp. 6, 21.
68   Daniel J McClean, *Rugbeians in the Great War* (Yorkshire: Pen and Sword, 2019) p. 22.
69   Ross Davies, *'A Student in Arms': Donald Hankey and Edwardian Society at War* (Farnham: Ashgate, 2013), pp. 1-3.

two teachers at the school. The first, his Headmaster was John Perceval (who had been the first Headmaster of Clifton and later Bishop of Hereford) and was a campaigner for higher education for women and workers. J. L. Paton, a classics teacher who was known for leading a simple life organised, taught classes for local working men in his spare time.[70] Public schoolboys were the subject of a variety of influences. They were capable of thinking for themselves far more than they have often been given credit for. Some of them became war poets so it is important to consider their work, in understanding their involvement in the Great War

Poetry and Memoirs

Our understanding of the poetry of the Great War is to a large extent influenced by the impact of Wilfred Owen, Siegfried Sassoon, Robert Graves amongst others. For many their encounter with the war is through their works, as well as others such as Pat Barker and Stephen MacDonald, and not history.[71] Not all of the British poets of the Great war had a public school education. Wilfred Owen, writer of *Dulce et Decorum est* was educated at the Shrewsbury Borough Technical School.[72] Yet this poem is most commonly associated with public school involvement in the Great War with its reference to Horace and by implication that old boys' views had been shaped by their classical education. Horace's words 'Dulce et Decorum est pro patria mori' often appear on memorials to public schoolboys but the association of the poem with public school involvement seems to be more by implication than any specific evidence. Peter Parker, for example, in *The Old Lie* provides no specific evidence of the connection. Owen's bitter conclusion to the poem may have been a reflection on the address by Lieutenant Colonel William Shirley, the commanding officer of the 2nd Battalion of the Artists' Rifles Own joined in October 1915. A cultured, energetic and intelligent man who had served in the pre-war Indian Army he emphasised to the new recruits the importance of total commitment in serving the country. His address was peppered with quotations from John Ruskin to support his point. He recited Horace's words, already familiar to Owen with the reflection that living for one's country would be of much greater use and less problematic than dying for it.[73] The best poetry is a deeply personal and powerful statement of what the poet strongly believes. Owen was reflecting on the futility of losing life in war (possibly with Shirley's words in mind) when he wrote *Dulce et Decorum est* and not just reflecting on the public school junior officers he served with. The poem includes a graphic description of the death of a soldier, too slow to put his gas mask on. The random nature of a soldier being unfortunate enough

---

70   McClean, *Rugbeians in the Great War,* p. 84.
71   Nigel Jones, Introduction to Arthur Graeme West, *Diary of a Dead Officer* (London: Greenhill Books, 2007), p. 7.
72   Dominic Hibberd, *Wilfred Owen* (London: Phoenix, 2003), p. 45.
73   Hibberd, *Wilfred Owen*, p. 215.

to be caught in an attack leaving the front line for rest is bitterly commented on in the closing lines of the poem 'The old Lie: Dulce et Decorum est /Pro patria mori.' Using Horace was a device for Owen to express his anger that the loss of life in war could be so random and unfair. It is a powerful phrase but it can be argued that this is not what Horace was saying. The next line by Horace in his ode says that life catches up with everyone eventually. It has been argued, Horace was saying one should live one's life with courage and integrity never running away from trouble. While in military life this may involve giving your life, the brave course of action (as Shirley suggested) is often likely to be to face up to the problem and not throw your life away needlessly.[74] The public schoolboys called on to translate Horace would have translated his ode in this light and not just in terms of 'Dulce et Decorum est pro patria mori.'

Owen is known for the bitterness of his poetry but his style evolves and changes over time. Not all of his poetry was so bitter and as every poet's style may change, so do the concerns of each poet. The public school war poets all had different concerns and influenced different people. Vera Brittain did not become a pacifist until 1937 and during the war it was Rupert Brooke's poetry with its 'romantic spirit of patriotic idealism' which influenced her most.[75] Sorley's poetry is less romantic than Brooke's but not as angry as that of Owen. Robert Graves's (Charterhouse) poetry is concerned with comradeship, while Sassoon's moved from the romanticism of Graves to a deep anger against the war as personified in *The General*. The war poets were men with strongly held opinions who did not always agree. Graves disapproved of Sassoon's use of poetry as propaganda.[76] In a more conciliatory spirit Blunden appreciated Owen's anger but it was not the approach he wanted to take.[77] If they had their doubts about the war the public school war poets were not pacifists and on the front line fought as bravely as their comrades; Sassoon and Blunden were both awarded the MC, with Sassoon being known as 'Mad Jack' for a bravery almost to the point of recklessness. The work of these public school educated poets suggests an education in the classics produced men with strongly held individual views.

Many of the public school poets would write their memoirs after the war which, as with their poetry, would take differing views as a result of their own differing attitudes and experiences. Blunden believed that each book would resonate with an audience according to its own circumstances.[78] British society of today, which has not experienced a major conflict since 1945, understandably has a deep antipathy to the horrors of the Great War. It is understandable that Graves's *All Quiet on the Western Front*

---

74 Harry Eyres, *Horace and Me: Life Lessons from an Ancient Poet* (Paperback edition, London: Bloomsbury, 2014), p. 82.
75 V. Brittain, *Verses of a VAD 1918* (Paperback edition, London: Virago, 2008) p. x.
76 Hibberd, *Wilfred Owen*, p. 369 and Jean Moorcroft Wilson, 'Siegfried Sassoon (1886-1967)', *The War Poets Association* <http://www.warpoets.org/conflicts/great-war/siegfried-sassoon-1886-1967/> (accessed 23 January 2020).
77 Strachan, Introduction to *Undertones of War*, p. xvi.
78 Ibid., p. xv.

with a direct and brutal approach should strike a chord with a modern audience. The book, however, should be treated with caution as it has enough factual errors for it to be more fiction than memoir. Both Blunden and Sassoon disliked it for this reason. Graves's deliberately brutal approach was in contrast to Blunden's more nuanced style in *Undertones of War*. For Blunden, war 'contained horror and humour, waste and honour, boredom and intensity, intellectual isolation and profound comradeship.' He did not believe it was possible to write a book which would be properly understood by both those who had been members of the armed forces during the war and those who had not. Blunden suggested his book was meant to be understood by those who had served.[79] This is a problem the reader encounters with any memoir, whether or not they agree with the views and sentiments in it. They were not there and can look in through a literary window with no context to set it in without further reading and research. The author writes about their own particular circumstances and is not always privy to the wider circumstances. Blunden admitted in the 'Preliminary' to the first edition that the experience he wrote about was 'very local, limited, incoherent.'[80] Decisions to attack could be inexplicable to Blunden on the front line but entirely understandable within the wider situation. He disapproved of the attack on 29-30 June 1916 by the 11th Royal Sussex against a salient near Neuve Chapelle, suffering 120 casualties. He could not see its wider purpose which was to discourage German troop movements in anticipation of the offensive on the Somme (which commenced on the next day).[81] The memoirs of the war poets are to be read as small contributions to a greater picture. They also need to be read alongside the memoirs of other public schoolboys who served.

Not all the memoirs of the public school war poets were bitter and critical of the war. For example, as has already been discussed, Blunden in his memoir took a different approach to Graves. It is clear he was traumatised by the war, critical of some of the decisions taken by the high command but did not express anger in the way Graves did. Other memoirs, published and unpublished, expressed different emotions. The poet and regular army officer, Julian Grenfell (Eton) in his letters home expressed a joy about war and killing Germans which to the modern reader can seem barbaric.[82] For him war was something he loved but he was able to look beyond his own happiness and in the same letter expressed a deep compassion for the local residents; whom he describes as having no food and leaving their houses, carrying their children and taking everything they could.[83] He recognised the bravado expressed in his letters could be misunderstood. In a letter, he described the death of several Germans. Realising that his triumphalism would be misunderstood he implored his mother not

79 Ibid., pp. vi-vii.
80 Blunden, *Undertones of War*, p. xii.
81 Strachan, Introduction to *Undertones of War* p. xii.
82 Keegan, *The Face of Battle*, p. 274.
83 Letters of Julian Grenfell, October 1914, *Herts Memories* <https://www.hertsmemories.org.uk/content/herts-history/diaries-and-letters/hertfordshire-voices/the_letters_of_julian_grenfell_1914/the-letters-of-julian-grenfell-october-1914> (accessed 24 January 2020).

to publish his letters they would be seen as egotistical and deeply unpleasant.[84] Graham Greenwell (Winchester) in *An Infant in Arms: Letters of a Company Officer 1914-1918*, although not being as openly enthusiastic about war as Grenfell. saw it as an adventure while recognising it was easier for a young man to face up to the trials of war.[85] Guy Chapman (Westminster) was more critical of the war but recognised that the conflict had made him. In his personal reminisces Harold Howitt (Uppingham) said of the war: 'I suppose in retrospect that a large part of the time – say 99%, or any other shot at a percentage – had been fun, and only the balance Hell.'[86] For Charles Douie (Rugby) in *The Weary Road* there had been no sense of disillusionment.[87] The accounts written were also vulnerable to the facilities of memory. Blunden did not write his memoir until 1928 and Howitt until 1967; time plays tricks with the mind hence why any individual work should not be taken as definitive. However, the views of public schoolboys about the war should not be seen as an expression of romantic idealism, even Grenfell with his love of war was filled with compassion for the civilian. Some were more sceptical and damaged by the war than others and in the case of Graves veered towards fiction. It can be debated whether Graves's work constitutes fiction but fiction as a genre has played an important part in shaping an understanding of public schoolboys during 1914-18.

Public School Fiction

Public school fiction, like other genres of history such as historical fiction (Pat Barker is just one example), has had a powerful effect on people's perceptions of the public schools. This was something the public schools were inevitably sensitive about. In February 1917, the former Master of Marlborough (Basil Willson who had recently left the school to become Dean of Bristol) gave an address about public schools saying that there were many mistaken ideas often based on *Tom Brown's Schooldays*.[88] Tom Brown had proved to be a useful way of identifying a public schoolboy as a 'Christian Gentleman'.[89] Given this stereotyping of the public school boy it is necessary to consider examples of this fiction to examine how much this literature reflected the schools the authors drew on in their individual novels and to what extent they presented the public school boy as a romantic idealist.

When Thomas Hughes started writing, in 1856, *Tom Brown's Schooldays*, he initially did so to set out the qualities he would look for in choosing a school for his eight-year-old son. Over time it emerged into a reverent tribute to Thomas Arnold, his

---

84 Ibid., November 1914.
85 Seldon and Walsh, *Public Schools and The Great War*, p. 226.
86 Uppingham School Archives (hereinafter USA), Reminisces of Harold Gibson Howitt, p. 52.
87 Seldon and Walsh, *Public Schools and The Great War*, p. 225.
88 *The Malburian*, Vol LII No. 7725 19 March 1917, pp. 31-33.
89 Tozer, '"To the Glory that was Greece"', p. 115.

Headmaster at Rugby. Its influence lies in its immense popularity. Published in 1857, by 1890 there had been more than 50 editions including translations into French and German.[90] As discussed above, Pierre de Coubertin drew on it as one of his influences, misinterpreting it as true representation of Arnold's use of sport as part of an education. He confused fiction with reality as Arnold's main concern was with and using education to provide a moral training for boys. *Tom Brown's Schooldays* reflected Hughes's love of sports because he saw it as teaching 'courage, cooperation and loyalty'. He did not anticipate that they would lead to the games cult for which public schools have incurred so much criticism.[91] His book was influential, especially on the middle classes seeking an education for their sons but was not intended to be a template to describe all public school life. Ronald Knox (Eton) the Roman Catholic priest and theologian while having little sporting ability, enjoyed his time there despite his headmaster, Edmond Warre, being a keen sportsman.[92] The modernist architect Oliver Hill went to Uppingham from 1901 to 1904 when the cult of games was at its height. Considering cricket to be a waste of time, with some trepidation, he asked the Headmaster, Selwyn, for permission to spend one afternoon sketching and exploring the countryside instead. To his great surprise permission was granted not only for one afternoon but the rest of his time at the school. Further support came from his unconventional Housemaster, Hockliffe (see above) who encouraged his architectural interests.[93] As Hill's experiences showed, Tom Brown was not always representative of public school life, its success meant that it spawned many imitators which encouraged the idea it was representative of life at the schools. Other books, however, set school life in a different light.

In contrast to Hughes's good natured, cheerful and optimistic tale, Rudyard Kipling's *Stalky and Co* (first published as a book in 1899) had a hero who was ingenious and crafty.[94] As much as *Tom Brown's Schooldays* was not a precise representation of life at Rugby, *Stalky and Co* did not precisely represent the United Services College (USC) at Westward Ho!, where Kipling was educated, and which in general he found an agreeable experience. The purpose of the school was to prepare its boys to run the empire or to be army officers. It was a cut-price Haileybury.[95] The real USC was not military in tone, not especially religious, its headmaster was not in holy orders and not an especially devoted Christian, fagging did not exist and the cane was not deployed. However, Kipling's 'the college' is presented as being tougher and more barbaric, with

---

90 Tozer, *The Ideal of Manliness,* p. 214.
91 Isobel Quigly, *The Heirs of Tom Brown: The English School Story* (London: Chatto & Windus, 2018). p. 53.
92 Ibid,, p. 52.
93 Vanessa Vanden Berghe, 'Oliver Hill and the Enigma of British Modernism during the Inter-War' (M.Phil thesis, East London, 2013), pp. 15-16.
94 Ibid., p. 43, 116.
95 Quigly, *The Heirs of Tom Brown*, p. 112, 115.

the cane being a favoured means of punishment, than USC actually was.[96] There are no romantic reminiscences about the classics; their teacher King was the enemy to Stalky and his friends, feelings reciprocated by King: 'The Fifth Form had been dragged several times in its collective life, from one end of the school Horace to the other. Those were the years when Army examiners gave thousands of marks for Latin, and it was Mr King's hated business to defeat them.'[97] The school in Kipling' stories are not devoted to producing romantic idealists but boys preparing for a set career. In *Stalky and Co* the lecture by an old boy on patriotism, is treated with disgust by the pupils. Kipling appears to be saying that while others may be taken in by such sentiments public school boys will not be.[98] The later Stalky stories tell of the same individual who is ingenious and crafty but now serving the Empire using these attributes to regularly extract himself from trouble.[99] Stalky becomes a man not possessed of a romantic vision of protecting the Empire but using an education at school to do a job within it. Kipling was a far superior writer to Hughes and immensely popular at the end of the 19th Century and at the start of the 20th Century. His stories appear to have been closer to the realities of public school life than those of Hughes. Stalky does not care for games, and cricket in particular, and games are not presented in a favourable light. Another of English literature's greats, P. G. Wodehouse, also produced a book which took the opposite view to Hughes on games.

Like Kipling, Wodehouse greatly enjoyed his time at school describing Dulwich as 'Heaven.'[100] However, he was not besotted with the school after he left and although he kept in touch with Dulwich, his relationship with it was not governed by an excess of sentiment.[101] Despite his naivety, which damaged his reputation during the Second World War, Wodehouse had a well-tuned ability to poke fun at institutions and present another side of a fashionable view. In 1909 his *The Swoop!, or How Clarence Saved England*, a send up of invasion literature, appeared. Books such as William Le Queux's *The Invasion of 1910*, which had originally appeared as a series in the *Daily Mail* were playing on a fear of invasion by Germany. In *The Swoop!* England is invaded by nine different armies; as the English elites are more interested in a cricket match to respond, the country is saved by a boy scout called Clarence. In *Mike: A Public School Story* (the first part of which appeared in 1909) Wodehouse parodies public school life. Mike is at the Wrykyn where he excels at cricket but neglects his academic work. His father sends him to Sedleigh, a school with an excellent reputation for getting the academic best out of boys, after Mike ignores warnings that if he does not improve, he will be withdrawn.[102] Like *Stalky*

---

96   Ibid., p. 113.
97   Kipling, *Stalky and Co.*, p. 157.
98   Quigly, *The Heirs of Tom Brown*, p. 124.
99   Ibid., p. 117.
100 Robert McCrum, *Wodehouse: A Life* (London: Penguin, 2005), p. 25.
101 Quigly, *The Heirs of Tom Brown*, p. 166.
102 McCrum, *Wodehouse*, p. 83.

and Co, in *Mike* it is not about those who are precocious at games and prosper. Neither is brawn the predominant feature in the winning of an argument. Unlike *Tom Brown's Schooldays* those who are articulate and brilliant in conversation win through.[103] In the years from the publication of *Tom Brown's Schooldays* in 1857 to the first appearance of *Mike* in 1909 public school fiction a less reverential view of games developed. The appearance of *The Loom of Youth* in 1917 moved the genre into an approach which was far more negative about public school life. The critic, Isobel Quigly sets *The Loom of Youth* apart in the public school genre because it is the only school story written by a boy.[104] Alec Waugh's novel is perhaps best known for its references to homosexuality. In reality, these references were very discrete and easily missed. However, for his pains in writing the book, Waugh was expelled along with his father from the Old Shirburnian Society. In his introduction to the novel Thomas Seccombe suggests the book is much more about the dominance of games and the aristocratic status of those best at them at public schools, 'The Tyranny of the Bloods'.[105] The real scandal it presents is one of the mediocrity and dishonesty. It is not that the school is immoral, it is that it is amoral. There is a low level of cribbing with boys hoping to get by rather than win prizes. The classics, and especially Horace, are treated with scorn. The Housemaster leaves the prefects to run the house, which they fail to do in a fair and just manner. The commander of the OTC is mediocre and its drill is repetitive. It is hardly the environment which will produce the romantic idealist. Not surprisingly, the book, which although only about one school but sought to present a negative picture of all public schools, was widely criticised within the public school movement.[106] Edward Lyttelton, capable of viewing public schools with a critical eye, thought it was simply untrue.[107] A public school prefect, under the penname Jack Hood, published a rebuttal of *The Loom of Youth* in 1919.[108] *The Mill Hill Magazine* took a more balanced view, disliking the exaggeration and sneering but thought at the heart of it was a 'kernel of truth' which merited thought and consideration. At Sherborne, teachers and others who had been poorly disguised in Waugh's novel were hurt by his belittling tone and many wrote to tell him so. William Hayman who was at the school from 1917 to 1921 recorded some lengthy and thoughtful notes about the book. Describing it as a vivid account, having characters who seemed to live and an autobiographical style which gave it authenticity he believed it was a story of 'a small set of boys in School House, their motives and their actions.' Every house at Sherborne was a 'closed community' and boys in each one would have had different experiences. Waugh, he says, was a

---

103 Quigly, *The Heirs of Tom Brown*, p. 173.
104 Ibid., p. 197.
105 Ibid., p. 202.
106 Jack Hood, *The Heart of a Schoolboy* (London: Longmans, Green and Co., 1919), p. 2.
107 Quigly, *The Heirs of Tom Brown*, p. 199.
108 Hood, *The Heart of a Schoolboy*.

member of a small unpopular group 'several of whom were "pretty bad lots."'[109] By 1914 the public school movement had become more diverse and the criticisms that were made of Sherborne could not necessarily be applied to other schools. The book, however, struck a nerve and damaged the reputation of the public schools.

Conclusion

Public schools in literature swung from the optimism of Thomas Hughes in 1857 to the negativity of Alec Waugh in 1917. This fiction is a mixture of real school life, propaganda and polemic. As the 19th century progressed the picture painted by Hughes held less credibility. The individual in fiction with a romantic vision became less prevalent and games were presented in a less positive way, as depicted by Wodehouse and Kipling. The attitudes of public schoolboys, as expressed in their memoirs, varied according to personal standpoints. Not all of them were disillusioned in tone, not all of them were gung-ho and many had views which were more pragmatic and there was no single point of view among them. The classics and sport were often in conflict with each other and the teaching of the classics in the years before the war often concentrated on the technical aspects such as grammar. Ideology and ethos are not enough to explain the involvement of public schoolboys in the Great War. The evidence suggests that the romantic idealist identified in scholarly works was not the product of public schools in the years leading up to 1914. To obtain a better understanding of this involvement it is necessary to consider the development of the schools they underwent to in the years between 1868 and 1914.

---

109 SSA, William Rollo Lenden Hayman (1902-1983) notes about his time at Sherborne School (Abbeylands) 1917-1921.

2

Public Schools in the Victorian Age

As already noted, public schools have been viewed as being monolithic with little differences between them. This can be partly attributed to the Clarendon Commission's setting out a template for what made a good public school. However, it cannot be assumed that all schools chose to follow this template unquestioningly. Even by the close of Victoria's reign in 1901, schools were diversifying from this standard model and different approaches were developing. Differences included the way powers were given to senior boys, the importance attached to games and the increasing number of schools which emphasised science (and not classics) within their curricula. Although during Victoria's reign, links between the army and the public schools were developed, they were initially limited to a small number of schools. By the time the Second Anglo-Boer War (1899-1902) broke out substantial differences had developed between the army and the schools despite the schools taking practical steps to support the war effort. While the army's performance in the Boer War was criticised so too was the contribution and attitude of the public schools

Age of Educational Reform

To understand the nature of public schools during Victoria's reign, it is necessary to examine their reform and development from the late 1860s. As society became more industrialised, the necessity for a reform of education, to meet the needs of the economy, was recognised.[1] The passing of the Public Schools Act in 1868, the Endowed Schools Act in 1869 and the Elementary Education (Forster) Act in 1870 represented a substantial reform of the educational system. The Forster Act set out to ensure all children in England between five and 12 received a basic education and the reforms to secondary education of 1868 and 1869 set down the principle that it

---

1   Colin Shrosbree, *Public Schools and Private Education: The Clarendon Commission, 1861-64 and the Public Schools Acts* (Manchester: Manchester University Press, 1988), p. 35.

should be funded through fees. After the enactment of the Reform Act of 1832 the middle classes were politically more influential. One of their major concerns was the standard of public schools. Their concerns mainly revolved around the improper use of the endowments set up to run the schools and the poor teaching of the classics.[2] The structure of many of the endowments was anachronistic, which gave rich opportunities for them to be misused. In 1818 the Brougham Commission's investigation of the abuse of charities accused the Warden and Fellows of Winchester of deviating from the original intentions of the founders and pursuing their own interests.[3] Similar criticisms were made of other public schools. The Clarendon Report of 1864 addressed the governance and quality of education at the nine leading schools in the country. These were seven boarding schools: Eton, Charterhouse, Harrow, Rugby, Shrewsbury, Westminster, and Winchester, and two day schools (St Paul's and Merchant Taylors). The report formed the first of a two-stage approach to the reform of secondary education. Although legally similar to many other English grammar schools they had been identified as the leading schools for educating the sons of the aristocracy and gentry.[4] The decision to investigate these schools first, rather than all endowed schools, was made to reduce political and religious controversy which would have hindered reform.[5] That Clarendon's report was designed to address all secondary education is demonstrated by its collection of evidence from schools other than those being investigated. It was particularly interested in developments relating to the teaching of modern studies and science alongside the preparation of boys for Civil Service entrance examinations. Evidence was requested from the City of London School, Cheltenham, Marlborough and Wellington who the Commission believed particularly excelled in at least one of these subject areas.[6] The report proposed several changes to the curriculum. It recommended that mathematics, a foreign language, music, drawing, history, geography, English composition and natural science should be included in the curriculum alongside the classics, where Arnold's approach of using them to teach moral values was to be adopted. Another Arnold's innovations, the prefect system as part of the schools' system of discipline, was endorsed. Its recommendation that that entrance should be by competitive exam led to the exclusion of poor but gifted local scholars in favour of the more prosperous classes.[7] It meant that the schools became the preserve of the affluent middle classes, whose parents could afford the tuition required to pass an academic and competitive

---

2 Ibid., p. 24.
3 James Sabben-Clare, *Winchester College After 600 Years, 1382-1982* (Southampton: Paul Cave, 1981), p. 7.
4 Gillard D (2018) *Education in England: A History* <www.educationengland.org.uk/history> (accessed 6 February 2020) and Shrosbree, *Public Schools*, p. 86.
5 Shrosbree, *Public Schools*, p. 50.
6 Ibid., pp. 91-92.
7 Gillard D (2018) *Education in England: A History* <www.educationengland.org.uk/history> (accessed 6 February 2020).

exam.[8] Parliament, when it passed the Public Schools Act made one more significant innovation when it decided that headmasters, and not the governing bodies, would have control over matters of internal management and the curriculum.[9] Initially, it meant that that many headmasters who were classicists could resist innovation in the curriculum but in the longer term, it also gave headmasters to make their own innovations to their curricula. Parliament's decision to establish a Commission to negotiate revised statutes with each individual school further enhanced their power to dictate the nature of the changes to be made.[10] It was a further block on achieving Clarendon's proposed reforms.[11]

Clarendon set the tone for the investigation of a further 782 grammar schools, as well as some proprietary and private schools. The Taunton Commission addressed how the endowed schools, not covered by the proposals of the Clarendon Commission, were to be reformed. The availability of the endowed schools, which the middle classes favoured, was patchy and, when available, their quality was distinctly variable.[12] Taunton was asked to give special consideration to the way endowments were and should be used to fund the schools within its remit.[13] It concluded that this there were significant gaps in the provision of secondary education because of an uneven geographical distribution of and large variations in the quality of the endowed schools with the endowments being used inflexibly.[14] It mimicked many of Clarendon's proposals which favoured the middle classes.[15] To address the inflexible use of endowments the Endowed School Commission (later absorbed into the Charity Commission) was created with the power to create new schemes for endowed schools.[16] Underlying the Commission's (ESC) approach to drafting new schemes for the endowments was its decision to categorise each new scheme into one of three grades: in first grade schools children would stay until 18 or 19 and Greek and Latin would be taught (the schools which became part of the expanded public school movement); in second grade schools children would stay until 16; at third grade schools children would stay until 14.[17] In exercising its powers, the ESC exercised them in favour of the middle classes with the first grade schools receiving the lion's share of

---

8   Shrosbree, *Public Schools*, pp. 9-10.
9   Ibid., p. 117.
10   Ibid., p. 189.
11   Ibid., p. 118.
12   Ibid., p. 49.
13   David Allsobrook, 'An Investigation of Precedents for the Recommendations of the Schools Inquiry Commission 1864-1867 With an Analysis of Reasons for the Failure of the Endowed Schools Act, 1869' (PhD thesis, Leicester, 1979), p. 425.
14   Gillard D (2018) *Education in England: A History* <www.educationengland.org.uk/history> (accessed 6 February 2020).
15   Allsobrook, Schools Inquiry Commission, Appendix I.
16   Gillard D (2018) *Education in England: A History* <www.educationengland.org.uk/history> (accessed 6 February 2020).
17   Allsobrook, Schools Inquiry Commission, Appendix I, pp. 1-2.

funds.[18] In doing so the public schools were established as providers of secondary education to the affluent middle classes. To be successful, Headmasters and schools had to respond to the needs of this group.

The Public Schools, 1869-1901

It is important to understand the influence of headmasters in developing schools with their own unique approaches. Headmasters fought hard to maintain their vision is demonstrated by St Paul's, which had a long dispute with the ESC and its successors, not settled until 1900. The resistance of Thring at Uppingham to the ESC's attempts to prescribe how a public school should operate was typical of how headmasters ensured their school was unique. . He objected to the approach of the ESC which set out a template which endowed schools only had to conform to, to achieve success

To Thring the ESC was as a government device to interfere in the way individual public schools were run.[19] At his initiative, the HMC was formed (its first meeting was hosted by Thring at Uppingham). In the years before 1914, the HMC played an important role as a mouthpiece for headmasters keen to resist government intervention. Membership was widespread and included the Clarendon Schools, who had initially been excluded Despite the basic operating model, based on Arnold's approach, there was no one size fits all way schools were run. The dominant position of the headmasters meant that all schools were unique in their approach. The differing approaches of two headmasters at Uppingham demonstrates this. It also illustrates how following a formula was not enough. Thring placed checks on the role of the prefects so that their powers were appropriately restricted.[20] For Thring games were important only so far as they helped a boy's self-confidence. This would not be the case for all boys; some would achieve this through other activities such as gymnastics and carpentry.[21] Although his successor, Edward Selwyn, in many ways followed Thring's educational approach, he made changes designed to make the school more attractive to parents at a time when competition between schools had become fiercer. His changes, in 1889, to the curriculum included Greek becoming optional and science being made compulsory in the lower forms.[22] However, his introduction of compulsory games and house colours led to his downfall. In contrast to Thring, he granted the leading games players special privileges and an elevated importance within the

---

18   Gillard D (2018) *Education in England: A History* <www.educatione<ngland.org.uk/history> (accessed 6 February 2020).
19   A B Gourlay, *A History of Sherborne School* (Sherborne: Satwells, 1971), pp. 129-131 and Bryan Matthews, *By God's Grace* (London: Whitehall Press, 1984), pp. 97-98.
20   Mangan, *Athleticism*, pp. 45.
21   Malcolm Tozer, *Edward Thring's Theory, Practice and Legacy: Physical Education in Britain Since 1800* (Newcastle upon Tyne: Cambridge Scholars Publishing, 2019), pp. 189-190.
22   USA.

school but failed to intervene when some of them abused their position.[23] C R W Nevinson, the celebrated war artist, described their behaviour:

> It is now the fashion to exclude the 'hearties' from accusations of sexual interest or sadism or masochism; but in my day it was they, the athletes and above all the cricketers, who were allowed these traditional privileges. Boys were bullied, coerced and tortured for their diversion, and many a lad was started on strange things through no fault nor inclination of his own.[24]

The suggestion of homosexuality and the prevalence of bullying led to the number of boys at Uppingham declining from 450 in September 1903 to 380 in September 1906.[25] A significant number left within two years of joining the school. In 1903, eight percent left in their first year and 14 percent in their second. In 1905, the figures were seven percent and nine percent respectively.[26] The decline in numbers cannot be explained by other factors such as the economic situation, the British economy was in recession, as after Selwyn's departure numbers rose again. It is far more likely that boys were withdrawn because parents were concerned about morality and bullying in the school and the cult of games getting out of control. The trustees had a difficult relationship with him and the drop in pupil numbers was a significant factor in them ending his headmastership in December 1907.[27] As powerful as headmasters were their position was not unassailable. Parents would not blindly support a school, if the way they were run led to moral problems. Parents had more important considerations, beyond the playing of games, in the selection of a school for their sons. The ending of practices such as patronage, the purchasing of army commissions in 1871, and the phasing in of competitive entrance by examination for bodies such as the Indian Civil Service was an opportunity for public schools. What attracted parents was their ability to prepare pupils for these exams. It was not so much that the schools imparted 'a distinctive and valuable set of values' in the eyes of parents but that the educational services provided were a means to provide their sons with a status.[28] For example, as Sheffield explained, to be an officer one had to be a gentleman.[29] By passing entrance exams to the Army the status of gentleman was met. It was the ability to help their sons achieve this which made public schools attractive to parents. Public school ethos was not, of itself, enough to attract pupils.

By the end of Victoria's reign, parents were taking an increasingly utilitarian approach to their sons' education. While parents might desire for their sons to be

---

23 Matthews, *By God's Grace*, p. 233.
24 C R W Nevinson, *Paint and Prejudice* (New York: Harcourt, Brace and Company, 1938) p. 12.
25 Matthews, *By God's Grace*, p. 128.
26 Ibid., p. 131.
27 Ibid.., pp. 128-129.
28 Honey, *Tom Brown's Universe*, pp. 151-152.
29 Sheffield, *Officer-man Relations*, p. 112.

gentlemen, they also wanted them to have the means to be able to afford to be so. Selwyn had responded to this demand by reforming Uppingham's curriculum. In some cases, he introduced other classes with some reluctance. Business, Army and Engineering classes were introduced at the request of parents although Selwyn was sceptical about their benefits. He viewed classes to prepare boys for Sandhurst and Woolwich entrance examinations as little more than cramming classes.[30] Other headmasters introduced army classes in response to parental demand; at Winchester, the Army Class was only taught the bare minimum to enable its pupils to obtain a cadetship.[31] However, although providing an Army Class was a necessity a career in the army was not the only one sought by the parents of boys. Boys entered other careers and the schools had to cater for these as well. The HMC minutes from 1899 to 1913 show that for many headmasters classics remained an important part of the curriculum (as discussed in Chapter 1 they were a requirement for entry to Oxbridge)

However, by the end of Victoria's reign not all schools followed the traditional classics based model. Cheltenham and Rossall placed more emphasis on the Moderns.[32] Cheltenham, as an army school, placed an emphasis on the Moderns which tied in more with the army's views about the type of education it wanted its cadets to have.[33] The school was being used to prepare boys for a military career at least 10 years before the purchase of army commissions was abolished, subsequently the value of schools as a means of passing these exams increased.[34] Other schools adapted to meet parental demands, Tonbridge, a founder member of the HMC, developed a science based curriculum. Alfred Earl was appointed in 1884 as Head of Science, over the next 34 years created a highly regarded science department.[35] The success of this approach is demonstrated by the university courses followed by Tonbridgians 1918-24. Out of 217 boys who went on to university 52% studied science based subjects, the equivalent figure for Radley in the same years is 26%.[36] While the dominant position of headmasters was important in setting the tone of a school, governing bodies also played an important role, as demonstrated by Uppingham's decision to remove Selwyn. At Oundle, Frederick Sanderson made substantial changes to the school's curriculum which resulted in the school being known for its emphasis science and engineering. It was a review carried out by the governing body which led to Sanderson's appointment and the change in the school's fortunes. In 1876, taking advantage of the reforms proposed by Taunton, the Grocers Company, which governed the school decided to split the existing school into a public school (which retained the name of Oundle) mainly for boarders serving the professional and middle classes and a modern school

---

30 *Uppingham School Magazine* (hereafter USM), February 1919, pp. 10-11.
31 Sabben-Clare, *Winchester College*, p. 60.
32 Bishop and Wilkinson, *Winchester and the Public School Elite*, p. 23.
33 This topic will be discussed fully in Chapter 3.
34 Honey, *Tom Brown's Universe* p. 151.
35 H.B. Orchard, *A Look at the Head and the Fifty* (London: James and James,1991, pp 45-6
36 David Walsh, 'Tonbridge Curriculum' email correspondence, 29 January 2021.

for the sons of local farmers and tradesmen. After initial success the number of pupils at Oundle rapidly declined as the parents of boys with little aptitude for the classics removed their sons to other schools.[37] The review concluded that even the older public schools were having to broaden their curricula in response to the demands of parents and Oundle could not afford to ignore these demands.[38] It decided Oundle should be self-funding and that it would be 'a first grade public school giving prominence to modern subjects and providing high classical education for boys intended for a university career.'[39] Once this decision had been made Sanderson's qualifications for the post of Headmaster were obvious. He had been successful at Dulwich in establishing the science and engineering classes; boys at Dulwich after receiving a general education were allowed to stay by their parents to receive a scientific education relevant to their future life in business and led to an increase in the number of boys at and the continuing prosperity of the school.[40] Sanderson revision of Oundle's curriculum was in accordance with the governing body's requirements. The opportunity to study the classics was not removed but the opportunities to study modern languages, science and engineering became an integral part of the school. The aim was to prepare boys on the modern side for careers in occupations such as the Army, Civil Service, science, manufacturing and engineering.[41] The changes were attractive to parents, especially those in industry and the professions. An analysis of admissions between 1892 to 1922 demonstrates that Sanderson was drawing from parents based in the industrial and manufacturing towns of the north and London in the South.[42] Sanderson disliked the cult of games, his success demonstrated that they were not an essential element of a public school for a substantial group of parents.[43] The success of Sanderson's approach is measured in the growth of the school. From the low point at the time of Sanderson's appointment by 1914, the number of boys at the school had risen to over 350 from 102.[44]

Other schools were established by groups to meet the needs of those they represented. Epsom College, which opened in 1855, was established by the Medical Benevolent Society (a predecessor of the BMA) to provide hospital accommodation for impoverished doctors and their widows and a school for the sons of doctors, fees were charged but support was provided for the orphans of doctors and the sons of impoverished doctors.[45] As with many other public schools the hospital was phased out and

---

37 Palmer, 'Sanderson', pp. 31-32, 40-41.
38 Ibid., p. 42.
39 Ibid., pp. 45-46.
40 Richard. J. Palmer, 'The influence of F.W.Sanderson on the development of science and engineering at Dulwich College, 1885-1892', *History of Education*, 6: 2 (1977) pp 121-130, p. 129.
41 Ibid., pp. 97-98.
42 Ibid., p. 167.
43 Ibid., p. 167.
44 Ibid., p. 128.
45 Alan Scadding, *Epsom College: A Celebration Benevolence and Excellence 150 Years of the Royal Medical Foundation of Epsom College* (Privately Published: Epsom, 2005), p. 9.

education became the sole activity. To fund education for doctors' sons, in 1862, places were made available for the sons of non-medical parents but they were required to pay higher fees.⁴⁶ The focus of the school remained to prepare boys to read medicine and in the years that followed several scholarships for boys to go to medical schools were established, which meant that science featured prominently in the school's curriculum By 1871, a Chemistry Laboratory and Lecture Room had been opened.⁴⁷ The emphasis switched to promoting medicine as a career rather than supporting doctors and entrance exams were introduced for those applying for scholarships and the sons of doctors were no longer be given preference in the allocation of spaces.⁴⁸ Under Reverend T. N. Hart-Smith, Headmaster from 1889, the school's science facilities were substantially expanded but all boys were required to also study a classical, literary or modern language subject.⁴⁹ The recognition of its curriculum as meeting the requirements of the Preliminary Scientific Exam, under which pupils were deemed to have met the standards required to pass the first year of a degree course, demonstrates the status of its science teaching.⁵⁰ Of the entrants to the school from 1901 to 1914, 26 percent went on to have careers in medicine.⁵¹ A snapshot comparison in 1907 with two leading public schools demonstrates Epsom's dominance as a source of doctors. Shrewsbury was more successful than Epsom in Oxbridge entrance with 10 of the 67 pupils (15 percent) who entered the school that year being successful compared to Epsom's eight percent (5 of 60 pupils). However, in that year, none of Shrewsbury's pupils are recorded as having pursued a career in medicine. For Epsom, the comparable figure is 17 (28% of its entrants). When compared to Winchester the comparisons are equally dramatic. In 1907, 104 pupils entered Winchester of which 54 (52 percent) entered Oxbridge but only 3 took up medicine. Between 1901 and 1914 45 percent of Winchester's pupils went on to Oxbridge, where a classical education was required, compared with eight percent for Epsom. The comparable Oxbridge figures for two other schools, Sherborne and Uppingham, are 18 percent and 17 percent and relatively few entered medicine. Table One shows a similar pattern for success in army entrance examinations.

---

46   Scadding, *Epsom College*, p. 31.
47   Ibid., pp. 38-39.
48   Ibid., p. 48, 54, 59.
49   Ibid., p. 79.
50   Discussion with Liz Manterfield of Epsom College Archives, 4 July 2019.
51   The figures which follow are based on analysis of ECA, Epsom College Register 1889-1914 and *Shrewsbury School Register Vol. I. 1798-1908* (Shrewsbury: Wilding, 1928) *The Sherborne Register Fourth Edition* (Privately published: Sherborne, 1950) *Uppingham School Roll 1824-1905* Third Issue (Privately published: London 1906) *Uppingham School Roll 1853-1947 Seventh Issue* (Privately published: London, 1948) *Winchester College A Register for the Years 1901 to 1946* (London: Edward Arnold, 1956).

Table 1 Success Rates for Army Entrance 1901–1914

School	Percentage entering Regular Army
Epsom College	5%
Sherborne	11%
Uppingham	7%
Winchester College	21%

These comparisons of Epsom's against other schools, together with the evidence for Oundle and Tonbridge, demonstrate schools sought to meet the needs of different groups and as a result they varied in their approach both to the curriculum and sports. Shrewsbury (a Cavendish school) was known for the quality of its teaching of the classics.[52] As a result, it was a leading provider of civil service entrants where the examinations required an education which included the classics. However, even a classics based school needed to respond to parental demands. It was slow to do so and not until 1889 (over 20 years after the Public Schools Act had come into effect), were there were classes for the Army and Civil Service examinations together with an advanced science class and science and mathematics was taught throughout the school. Like other schools these innovations were a response to the demands of existing parents. A decline in numbers in the late 19th century only started to recover in the early 20th century.[53]

The importance of what was expected by parents in the priorities of a school can also be seen in the development of Lancing, founded by Reverend Nathaniel Woodard in 1848,[54] Woodard took a conservative approach and when the school was established the emphasis was on the classics with no science teaching.[55] However, Woodard's High Church beliefs made the school unattractive to many parents who believed it made the school unmanly.[56] The arrival of Reverend Henry Walford (who had been in Arnold's Sixth Form at Rugby) as Headmaster, led to changes which made the school more conventional; games became compulsory and masters were appointed to raise the standard of games.[57] The school's historian has argued that despite the rise in importance of games, the range of games played widened which reduced the risk of the cult of games taking hold.[58] Like all schools it was forced to introduce the teaching of the moderns, despite a preference for the classics.[59] Lancing's High Churchmanship meant its educational and religious approach made it unique.

---

52 Leach, *A School at Shrewsbury*, p. 76.
53 Ibid., p. 73.
54 Mangan, *Athleticism*, p. 3.
55 Ibid., pp. 36-37.
56 Ibid., pp. 40.
57 *Ibid.*, pp. 40-41.
58 Basil Handford, *Lancing College: History and Memoirs* (Chichester: Phillimore, 1986), p. 131.
59 Handford, *Lancing College*, p. 106 and p. 133.

Lancing was not the only school where the religious ethos acted as a powerful counter to the cult of games and the danger of militarism, as the Non-Conformist Mill Hill and Roman Catholic Stonyhurst demonstrate. The values and status of the communities they served and represented had led to an educational approach which varied from the model applied at other public schools. Stonyhurst, a Jesuit school, set out to serve more than the privileged but regarded the middle class as being a valuable tool in achieving this. By winning the support of the better off the Jesuits would be able to subsidise their whole system of education.[60] Established in France, when a Roman Catholic education was banned in Britain; it moved to England in the early 19th century when new laws allowed Roman Catholics to open schools in England.[61] By joining the HMC in 1900, it marked a further development of the diversity of the public school. Stonyhurst differed from other public schools. It operated a Playroom system where boys were grouped by age instead of all ages Houses.[62] Secondly, Power was not devolved to the prefects and power was firmly in the hands of a small group of masters who organised, supervised and participated in games with the boys.[63] This approach of 'constant watchfulness' limited the ability of boys to bully each other.[64] The educational approach of a Jesuit boarding school varied in other ways from that of the hypothetical public school. Classics were taught but were not at the heart of its approach. Instead, the emphasis was on an education in faith and training boys to be Catholic leaders. Sport played little part in moral education and Stonyhurst had a strong tradition of drama as an alternative to games.[65] Despite these differences in approach from other schools (and in particular the lack of importance placed on games) it is important to note that there were similarities. Stonyhurst boys, as with other public schools, were trained to be leaders and its old boys considered it to be a public school as opposed to a Catholic school.[66] Although different in its approach a Jesuit education promoted the idea of patriotism.[67] Christian denominations shared a belief that the country must be protected from invasion. The industrial revolution led to many Non-Conformists becoming commercially successful and, like Catholics, had a significant investment in the British way of life. Mill Hill's founders established it to provide the sons of Non-Conformists with a good education which would otherwise be difficult to obtain outside Anglican schools.[68] Mill Hill opened in 1807 (and became a member of the HMC in 1872)[69] and set out to emulate the best features of

60 Mangan, *Athleticism*, pp. 58-59.
61 I D Roberts, 'Jesuit Collegiate Education in England, 1794 1914' (MEd dissertation, Durham,1986), p. 3.
62 T E Muir, *Stonyhurst 1593-1993* (London: James & James, 1992), p. 22.
63 Mangan, *Athleticism*, p. 147.
64 Muir, *Stonyhurst*, p. 32.
65 Mangan, *Athleticism*, p. 64 and p. 103.
66 Honey, *Tom Brown's Universe* p. 287.
67 Mangan, *Athleticism*, pp. 64-65.
68 Braithwaite, *"Strikingly alive"*, p. 21.
69 Ibid., p. 88.

the Clarendon schools but innovated in four areas: science, music, small class sizes and modern languages.[70]

By the end of Victoria' reign public schools varied in their educational approach and sought to appeal to different groups of parents. While headmasters were important figures in setting the direction of their schools there were other important influences. Governors played an important part in setting the direction of the schools as well as the groups behind the foundation of the schools. Not all parents wanted a classical education for their sons. The ability of schools to provide them with knowledge and skills which would help them pursue a career in business or the professions became increasingly important. At many schools the level of importance attached to games was not as high as has been suggested Parents sought value for money which included the happiness of their sons and an education to help them in their careers. Most were 'reasonably solvent but certainly not wealthy' and sought value for money[71] Classics, militarism and a love of games were not essential requirements for many of them.

From Crimean War to Boer War

From the 1860s public schools slowly started to become a source of junior officers. As the dominance of Eton in the late 19th Century officer corps, discussed in the last chapter, showed relatively few schools were drawn on. Only with the advent of the Boer War did a wider public school involvement develop. The Crimean War (1853–1856) exposed severe flaws within the British Army. Demands for enquiries into these failings led to a Royal Commission being established in 1856 to consider of the abolition of the system of purchase of commissions in the army. Little change came out of the report, but it did start a debate and campaign for reform. Prominent among the reformers was Sir Charles Trevelyan, a civil servant, who argued that that replacing purchase with competitive entry would open the army's officer corps up 'to the professionalising influences of the middle class, would widen the pool of candidates and improve its quality.'[72] Reform was slow but the entrance requirements for junior officers was kept under review by the Council of Military Education (CME), established in 1857. It consulted a small group headmasters (Eton, Harrow, Winchester, Westminster, Rugby, Charterhouse and King's College) as to what could be expected of 17-year-old boys which led to a proposal for an entrance examination.[73] Links between the army and public schools were strengthened by decisions to admit candidates at a later age and base the entrance examination on the classical syllabus The decision to favour the classics was criticised in parliament as discouraging the

---

70 Ibid., p. 9.
71 McCrum, *Wodehouse*, p. 26.
72 Worthington, 'Antecedent Education and Officer Recruitment', pp. 63-65.
73 Ibid., p. 68.

study of sciences.[74] However, as the schools were not prepared to compromise on their syllabi the army took the view it was better to recruit public school boys as they had the qualities to lead men.[75] Once the purchase of commissions was abolished in 1871 entrance examinations became the main way of gaining a commission in the army and from the 1880s onwards the HMC was regularly consulted by the army and Civil Service Commissioners about their content.[76] Both the army and the Commissioners were keen to ensure a continuing supply of candidates from the public schools. Public schools were, therefore, able to maintain a strong hold over the entrance examinations by holding out the threat that any innovations to the syllabus would damage the relationship between the army and public schools. In the years before the Boer War the public schools held the whip hand in discussions about the army entrance examination because of the army's belief of the importance of tone and character as preparation for a commission. Although by the time the war broke out the schools the army drew its officers had widened, it was still dominated by the top 10 army schools who contributed 66 percent of officers.[77]

While the schools were reluctant to adjust their curricula they started to offer their boys basic military training. This was not an explicit effort to support the army but a patriotic response. The military threat from France had led to the formation of the Volunteers in 1859. Schools started to establish their own Corps, which were attached to local Volunteer units with the first ones being established at Eton, Harrow, Rugby, Rossall, Felsted, and Hurstpierpoint in 1860.[78] The development of the Corps was gradual. By the outbreak of the Boer War at least 39 schools had established Corps.[79] Although supported by the War Office it provided no central guidance on what training they should undertake, their aim was to produce soldiers for the Volunteers rather than officers for the Regular Army. Lacking central guidance, the development of Corps activity was gradual. The first Public Schools Camp first held in 1889 by four schools was slow to establish itself before gaining the support of a large number of schools[80] Only with the outbreak of the Boer War did the growth of the school Corps movement start to accelerate.[81] It was a response to a threat rather than an explicit act of militarism

The public school response needs to be seen within the context of wider concern British society to the threat to British prosperity and security, posed by early Boer

---

74   Ibid., p. 140.
75   Ibid., pp. 144-146.
76   Ibid., p. 163.
77   Halstead, *A School in Arms*, p. 32
78   Haig-Brown, *The OTC and the Great War*, p. 5, C R L Fletcher, *Edmond Warre D.D., C.B. C.V.O. Sometime Headmaster and Provost of Eton College* (London: John Murray, 1922), p. 98 and Derek Winterbottom, *The Tide Flows On: A History of Rossall School* (Rossall: Rossall School, 2006), pp. 21-22.
79   Haig-Brown, *The OTC and the Great War*, p. 5.
80   Ibid., pp. 1, 10
81   Ibid., p. 5

success. The 'Black Week' in December 1899 when Britain suffered three defeats in seven days provoked alarm and thousands responded by answering an appeal for volunteers to serve in South Africa. One of the most immediate responses was at Uppingham where the Headmaster, Selwyn, responded to the crisis in February 1900 by making it compulsory for every boy to pass a shooting test. No boy was allowed to participate in inter-house competition and was ineligible for a school prize until he had passed the test.[82] Selwyn's critics have labelled this as militaristic but the Afrikaner farmers had deployed superior musketry skills. In addition, the deployment of more troops to South Africa left only 17,000 troops in Britain and left the country feeling vulnerable to an attack by France, who it was believed might be about to launch an invasion. In this air of crisis, the Prime Minister, Lord Salisbury, gave a speech in March 1900 which spoke of the value of rifle clubs in helping to resist an invasion.[83] His speech probably reflected the public mood rather than being a pro-active response. In February 1900, the HMC Committee agreed that boys over 15 should be enrolled for basic military training which included musketry.[84] In its call for volunteers to fight in South Africa the government lay down a number of requirements including that any man volunteering should be a first class shot.[85] Public schools rather than being militaristic were responding to the need for volunteers. However, they found themselves blamed for some of the army's failures.

The criticisms made of the army's performance in the war were numerous. Leo Amery said junior officers 'possessed quite enough natural intelligence to make a good soldier, if that intelligence had been given training to improve it and free play to develop it' but the system 'stood in the way of all real progress.'[86] Kipling's criticism of 'muddied oaths' and 'flannelled fools' was a direct criticism of the of what he saw as a public school obsession with athletic prowess.[87] William Elliot Cairnes laid the blame for the failure of the officers on 'the faults of the system.'[88] Cairnes was a Captain in the Royal Irish Fusiliers, a respected writer on military affairs and went on to be the Secretary to the Committee on the Education and Training of Officers.[89] For him at the root of the problem lay a monotonous daily routine and poor training where all originality of thought was discouraged and which merely encouraged officers to spend

---

82 Matthews, *By God's Grace*, p. 244.
83 David G Morgan-Owen, *The Fear of Invasion Strategy, Politics and British War Planning* (Oxford: OUP, 2017), p. 37.
84 Worthington, *Antecedent Education and Officer Recruitment*, p. 242.
85 Ian Beckett, *Britain's Part-Time Soldiers: The Amateur Military Tradition 1558-1945* (Barnsley: Pen and Sword Military, 2011), p. 202.
86 Leopold Stennett Amery (ed.), *The Times History of the War in South Africa, 1899-1902, Vol. II.* (London, Sampson, Low, Marston and Company, 1909), p. 36.
87 Peter Donaldson, "We are having a very enjoyable game': Britain, Sport and the South African War, 1899-1902', *War in History* 25: 1. pp. 4-25.
88 W. E. Cairnes, *An Absent-Minded War: Being some reflections on our reverses and the causes which have led to them* (London: John Milne, 1900) and *The Times*, 4 January 1901, p. 6.
89 *The Times*, 22 January 1902, p. 15.

time on the sporting field.⁹⁰ These were criticisms which were shared others, including G. F. R. Henderson.⁹¹ Others argued part of the problem could be attributed to the poor quality of general education received by officers and that losses in South Africa could be attributed to public school playing fields.⁹² The education provided public schools was heavy criticised. Army classes were said to be too large and discipline within them was poor and that a classical education was irrelevant to the educational requirements for junior officers.⁹³

The Army appears to have arrived at this conclusion at the start of the Boer War and made changes without consulting with the HMC. Faced with the need to expand rapidly, it revised the entrance requirements for militia officers. The effect of this was to make it considerably easier for a boy to gain a commission. Exam requirements were adjusted so that there were no compulsory subjects and a boy was able to concentrate on papers best for him. The new arrangements were permanent and not to the public schools' advantage. They meant boys could leave at 17 and gain commission when they were 18 and a half as opposed to those who went to Sandhurst and who would not gain a commission until they were 20.⁹⁴ It meant that boys would not enter the Army class and leave school earlier. This was a major concern for schools as boys leaving earlier and not taking part in the classes schools were providing for their sixth forms would have a severe effect on income. The HMC protested at the loss of its unofficial veto but received short shrift from the War Office. It responded that the changes had been welcomed by parents and boys and pointed out that if boys left early the schools only had themselves to blame for not being attractive enough. *The Times* reflected the views of many, in its report on the HMC meeting, when it observed of the schools: 'You have had these young men up to seventeen, it might be retorted. What have you been doing with their minds?' If the schools were to be viewed as meeting the educational requirements of the army, they needed to demonstrate that the accusation that they produced boys who only cared for sport and who had no sense of industry was 'a malicious libel.'⁹⁵ For all their support for the army by offering basic military training it was to be on their terms, ignoring the needs of the army. This rift between the Army and the schools did not heal itself after the end of the Boer War

---

90   Cairnes, *An Absent-Minded War*, pp. 6-7.
91   Sir Neill Malcolm, *The Science of War: A Collection of Essays and Lectures 1892–1903 by the late Colonel G. F. R. Henderson CB* (London: Longmans, Green and Co., 1912), passim.
92   Worthington, 'Antecedent Education and Officer Recruitment', p. 200.
93   Ibid., p. 201.
94   HMC, Report of the Twenty-Seventh Meeting of the Headmasters' Conference December 1899, pp. 37-46.
95   *The Times*, 24 December 1900, p. 7.

Conclusion

The public school reforms of 1868–1869 were designed to meet the requirements of the upper middle classes and led to a significant expansion of the movement. The revised approach adopted the methods of Arnold in how a school should be run. It gave the headmasters the scope to run their schools as they saw fit. A new Headmaster could significantly alter the priorities of a school, as Selwyn did, However, there were other factors which were important in the development of individual schools. Governing bodies played an important role in the direction of a school. This could be in a negative way by the dismissal of a failing headmaster or the positive decision to select a headmaster who would set out to achieve the educational priorities set by the governors. The educational approach was also affected by the bodies and groups behind the foundation of individual schools. The values of different Christian denominations were an important influence as were the priorities of professional interest groups, such as doctors. While many headmasters may have favoured classics, they had to pay heed to the requirements of parents; their priorities were for their sons to pass the entrance examinations for the army and civils service or develop skills which would be useful in business. As a result, greater provision of Army and Business classes developed alongside more teaching of science. Schools which focussed on the teaching of the classics were forced to adopt to these requirements to remain attractive to parents. Although Clarendon had developed a hypothetical model for the operation of schools by the end of Victoria's reign there were many variations from this model. At many schools games did not enjoy a cult status and the classics enjoyed a lower priority. The army increasingly turned away from the idea that the teaching of the classics was an essential preparation for the development of officer cadets. Despite the development of Corps at the schools there was increasing friction between the schools and the army. The army recruited from a small group of schools where it had strong connections rather than because it valued public school ethos. When the Boer War came it recruited boys to the expanded army before many headmasters considered they had completed their education. The social status of public schoolboys was considered to be more important rather than a militaristic approach.

3

A Lack of Common Purpose:
The Army and the Public Schools, 1901–1914

> *It was widely believed that there was a direct connection between the ethos of public schools … and the ability to lead men in battle.*[1]

Discussion about public school involvement in the Great War has revolved around the belief that the values and ethos they inculcated in their boys made a commission the expected rank of public school old boys.[2] There is no doubt that there was a strong sense of patriotism within the public schools in the years before 1914, as there was in much of the rest of the British population. Neither can it be contested that when war came the public schools were a significant source of junior officers. It would be wrong, however, to conclude that this meant the relationship between the public schools and the army was always harmonious in the pre-war years. There were strong differences about the correct approach to educating boys in preparation for Sandhurst and Woolwich. Tensions also arose from the differing priorities and interests of the school and army. The Boer War came as a rude shock to the British Empire in terms of its military preparedness. Both the army and the public schools agreed that changes were required but disagreed about what was required and how they would be executed.

Growth and Evolution of Public Schools 1901-1914

Many schools underwent change to address changes in parental expectations. Winchester changed its approach to one with the aim of not forcing a boy into a mould but building up his character and ability.[3] It promoted an intellectual approach in which it was the case that while games were important and the cult of games

---

1   Sheffield, *Officer-man Relations*, pp. 119-120.
2   Barnett, *The Collapse of British Power*, p. 227.
3   Sabben-Clare, *Winchester College*, p. 10.

was present, it was never principally a sporting school and there was a tolerance of the non-athlete.⁴ Other schools catered for different educational requirements and their development demonstrates how the public school movement became more diverse in its approach. Christ's Hospital's purpose was to provide the children of the less well off with an education. Its boys' school moved out of the City in 1902 to Horsham, to give its pupils considerably better facilities and sought to make itself more like a public school. Games became compulsory every afternoon, a house system was adopted, and a Corps established. Despite these changes, the cult of games did not take hold.⁵ Given the less privileged background of its pupils, the curriculum had a more vocational flavour than schools such as Winchester and Shrewsbury. In the years leading up to 1914, the subjects taught included Classics, Mathematics, French, Science, Drawing, Music and 'Commercial'. The practical inclination of the syllabus was further supported by the opening of a Manual School in 1910. As a school while still teaching the classics it also had a strong emphasis on more practical topics to cater for the needs of its pupils. The nature of public schools was influenced by government moves to oversee education more closely. The 1902 Education Act was a response to concerns that Britain's secondary education system was lagging behind those of the USA and Continental European countries and was not meeting the needs of industry and a universal system of secondary education was required.⁶ Amongst its provisions, County and County Borough councils were to be responsible for considering and supplying their local secondary education needs. The Act did not set out to provide secondary education for all, but it did substantially increase the state provision of secondary education. The number of schools receiving state support rose from approximately 500 in 1904-1905 to more than 1,000 by 1913-1914; in the same period the number of pupils rose from 64,000 to 188,000.⁷ As a result, public schools faced greater competition from the state schools. By 1914 many public schools (such as Sherborne) had developed their teaching of the moderns in response to this and the demands of its middle-class parents. The power of the government to influence public schools increased through the ability of national and local government to make grants. The Perse, Bradford Grammar School and Oakham were some of the HMC members who received them on the condition that they offered 25 percent of their places to children from Elementary Schools and permitted inspections by the Board of Education. The Board was able to push some public schools towards syllabi more closely aligned to the needs of industry. It also attempted to supervise public schools not in receipt of a grant but met with resistance from Headmasters and governing bodies determined to protect their independence. In 1908 Mill Hill's

---

4   Ibid., p. 120. Ibid., pp. 93-94, 99-100.
5   Humble, 'Leaving London', p. 158.
6   Roy Lowe, 'Education, 1900–1939' in Chris Wrigley (ed.), *A Companion to Early Twentieth Century Britain* (Oxford: Wiley-Blackwell, 2009), pp. 424-437.
7   D Gillard (2018), *Education in England: A History* <www.educationengland.org.uk/history> (accessed 6 February 2020).

Court of Governors resolved to work with 19 other schools to resist an attempt by the Board to inspect schools under powers it claimed it had inherited from the Charity Commissioners.[8] Another request by the Board was rejected in 1912 on the grounds it did not have the power to demand the specified information.[9] Other schools, not in receipt of grants resisted attempts by the government to monitor and control them. Epsom rejected a request by the Board to provide audited accounts and other specified information, in 1910.[10] Winchester, until 1918, resisted Board inspections instead, like many other public schools permitting inspections by the universities.[11] Other schools co-operated. Christ's Hospital, which was not in receipt of a grant, allowed the Board to inspect it. As a result of the Inspectors' recommendations, amendments were made to the timetable and curriculum which increased the importance of the moderns and practical subjects.[12] Despite resistance to direct intervention, many public schools moved away from curricula based on the classics. By 1914, the idea that all public schools were homogeneous and producing boys who were brainwashed by being taught the military exploits of heroes from the classics and the playing of games was not sustainable. Board of Education pressure and parental requirements meant that most schools were obliged to move away from this approach.

Officer Recruitment from Boer War to Great War

In the aftermath of the Boer War, the army's preference for recruiting boys for its officer corps from a small group of schools appears to have continued. From 1905 to 1908 Bedford, Charterhouse, Cheltenham, Clifton, Eton, Haileybury, Harrow, Marlborough, Rugby, Wellington College and Winchester between them provided 55 percent of the entrants to Woolwich and Sandhurst.[13] However, as has already been discussed, the army had serious concerns about the relevance of the public schools' curricula to its requirements. In response, in April 1901, St John Broderick, the Secretary of State for War, established the Committee on the Education and Training of Officers to investigate the education given at Woolwich and Sandhurst and whether changes were required to the way cadets were admitted. The committee's chairman was a cabinet minister, Aretas Akers-Douglas, two MPs, two representatives of the military and two HMC representatives (Warre of Eton and Walker of

---

8   MHSA, Minute Book Vol. 11 30 September 1908, pp. 364-366.
9   MHSA, Minute Book Vol. 12 1 February 1912, p. 171 and 27 March 1912, p. 181.
10 ECA, Finance Committee Minutes 28 September 1910 and ECA, Council Minutes 30 June 1911 pp. 6-7.
11 WCA, Report of the Headmaster for the School Year ending August 1918, p. 4.
12 Christ's Hospital Archives (hereinafter CHA), Treasurer's Annual Report Year Ending 31 March, 1911 and CHA, Report of the Boy's School Year Ending 31 December 1910, p. 6.
13 A B N Churchill, 'Army as a Profession, The (lecture)', *Journal of the Royal United Services Institute*. 54: No 1 (1910). pp. 168-198.

St Paul's) made up the rest of the committee. Its military secretary was Cairnes who had already published a trenchant critique of officer recruitment.[14] The report made several recommendations for reform of officer training and supported the approach of public schools being the primary source of officers. The HMC, even though it had two representatives on the committee, was cautious in its response. Warre, in his report to the HMC, proposed that it waited until the Government had appointed an Inspector-General of Military Education who would have a significant influence on the syllabus for army entrance. As it had been recommended that an Advisory Board be set up which would include HMC representatives he was hopeful that 'the views of the Conference will not be ignored.' On the proposed structure of examination papers, he remained concerned that it promoted cramming (and unwelcome competition from crammers) rather than the acquisition of knowledge.[15] Broderick in his response to the report in March 1903 chose to delay any decisions on the syllabus by announcing that he would appoint an Advisory Board to work with the recently appointed Director-General of Military Education and Training. He was in favour of recruiting officers from public schools and universities but believed that further work was needed in respect of schools. His main regret was boys were leaving at 17 to join the army and lose what he believed was a valuable part of public school training over the next two years.[16] Warre's recommendation that the HMC await the appointment of the Advisory Board appeared to have paid off when it recommended a system which made it considerably easier for a boy from a public school to pass a competitive examination than a candidate from the crammers.[17]

If this was to the satisfaction of the HMC then the proposals for the place of Greek and Latin in the curriculum were distinctly less palatable. Under the new scheme which followed the Akers-Douglas report all potential cadets would not be able to sit a competitive examination to Sandhurst or Woolwich unless they had a Leaving Certificate or a Qualifying certificate. Leaving Certificates were to be granted by a number of bodies which included the Oxford and Cambridge Schools Examination Board, the body which inspected most public schools. Leaving Certificates allowed the candidate to sit an unlimited number of competitive examinations whereas a Qualifying Certificate only applied to one competitive examination. If unsuccessful in a competitive examination a candidate had to obtain another Qualifying Certificate before sitting a competitive examination again. Public Schools, which were able to offer Leaving Certificates, had an immense advantage over the crammers whose candidates sat for the Qualifying Certificate. Despite this considerable advantage the HMC was not content. The structure of the Leaving Certificate made it possible for a boy to be successful without taking either Latin or Greek. It made it likely

---

14 Worthington, 'Antecedent Education and Officer Recruitment', pp. 202-203.
15 HMC, Report of the Thirtieth Meeting of the Headmasters' Conference December 1902, pp. 57-62.
16 Mr Brodrick, P. Debs, Vol. 119, 9 March 1903, columns 132-140, Commons.
17 Worthington, 'Antecedent Education and Officer Recruitment', p. 225.

the classics would be ignored as boys would be tempted to take the easiest option for them. Taking a classics-free route would debar a boy who was unsuccessful from Oxbridge and 'the learned professions.'[18] It is unlikely that many boys who attempted to enter the army would have, if they were unsuccessful, wished to follow the route of Oxbridge or the professions. The public schools were more interested in bending the syllabus desired by the army to something more closely tied in with their own interests, regardless of the army's requirements. Neither the Army Council nor the Advisory Board was receptive to the objections of the HMC, also rejecting the threat that if implemented the proposals would lead to the end of Army Classes. In their view their proposals would attract a better quality of public schoolboy into the Army. The ability of a candidate in the classics was not viewed as being an essential attribute to being a successful officer. A classical education, which included military exploits from ancient history, was unattractive to the army.

Used to getting its own way in the past the HMC now found itself carrying less weight with the army, who although keen to recruit from the public schools, was in the aftermath of the Boer War keen to improve the quality of its junior officer corps. The reforms which had followed the Boer War had, even within tight spending restrictions under the Liberal Government, led to significant reform of and greater efficiency in the British Army.[19] The result was a fighting force which, although small in size, in 1914 despite substantial losses acquitted itself well in helping to stop the Germans from being able to quickly knock out France out of the war. Andrew Duncan has argued that the officers who led their men in 1914 thought seriously about how they would use technology on the modern battlefield and how they would fight and move in combat. The training which equipped officers to achieve focussed on practical skills and practical knowledge. The purpose of military education was to give officers the required professional skills. All cadets who arrived at the military colleges were expected to have a general education which equipped them to develop these professional skills. A competence in Latin and Greek may help to develop an officer's problem-solving skills but they were not essential. Equally relevant were subjects such as French, German, the sciences, English and History. The relevance of sciences is perhaps more obvious but English was important because any officer needed to be able to communicate effectively, foreign languages to widen their understanding of military powers who they would fight alongside or against, and History so that the skills learnt could be used to analyse military history for important tactical and strategic lessons which could be applied to current military problems.[20] The army like many other parts of Edwardian society was having to adapt to a more complex world where

---

18 HMC, Report of the Committee of the Headmasters' Conference for 1904, pp. 94-96.
19 Trevelyan, *A Shortened History of England*, p. 503.
20 Andrew Duncan, 'The Military Education of Junior Officers in the Edwardian Army' (PhD thesis, Birmingham, 2016), pp. 218-219.

specialism was becoming increasingly necessary. It was these innovations which the leadership of the HMC opposed.

The emphasis on the moral tone of a public school education became less relevant. Schools such as Dulwich, Epsom and Oundle made more of an impact with their emphasis on science and engineering, while still according the classics an appropriate importance for those boys who were intellectually inclined towards them. Public schools served a variety of educational requirements and there was inevitably a tension between meeting each of them completely. To survive they needed to attract enough fee-paying boys. Failure to provide an education which met both a need for an appropriate scholastic, as well as a moral, training could lead to a decline in a school's fortunes. Selwyn's departure from Uppingham demonstrated that a lack of balance could lead to serious problems; under him, the overemphasis on games led to a poor moral tone (not the intended effect of playing games) and to parents withdrawing their sons. Oundle had to reduce the emphasis on the classics and introduce science and engineering, to attract more parents.

The army required a general education which was more relevant to its needs and which the public schools were not providing. Its own requirements placed less importance on a classics-based education. Broderick's successor as Secretary of State for War, Arnold-Forster, regarded an emphasis on classics as giving an unfair advantage to certain public schools. Others disagreed, Lyttelton, Headmaster of Eton and no fan of the way the classics were taught, strongly believed in the importance of the classics because they taught a boy how to think. Opinions within the government were also divided. The Civil Service Commissioners, who administered and advised on the entrance examinations, believed that officers should be recruited directly from the public schools.[21] Their approach for civil service examinations was firmly based on the view that a complete education included the classics. However, the army wished to teach boys to think but in a way which was more geared to the technical requirements of fighting a war. This increasing specialisation placed a strain on the relationship between the army and the public schools. However, the size of the army was kept under tight control in the years before 1914 and its recruitment needs were not such that it was a significant source of opportunities for the public schools. During 1908, 417 cadets entered Sandhurst and Woolwich.[22] An analysis of the entrants to a selection of public schools (using their School Rolls) in the year 1904-1905, from which it is most likely the successful entrants were drawn, demonstrates the relative importance of the army as a source of opportunities. At Sherborne, a school classified as I in Honey's categorisation but not known as a leading army school, 28 percent of its boys for that year entered Oxbridge while four percent entered the Regular Army. For Uppingham, a school with many similarities to Sherborne, the figures were 26 percent and three percent. At Winchester, a Clarendon school known for

---

21 Worthington, 'Antecedent Education and Officer Recruitment', pp. 223-238.
22 Duncan, 'The Military Education of Junior Officers', p. 224.

its academic achievement, and as an army school, the figures were 48 percent and 20 percent respectively. Epsom known for supporting the medical profession, sent nine percent each of its boys to Oxbridge and the army, while 39 percent of its entrants for that year eventually entered the medical profession. No figures for the total entry during that period to HMC schools are available but if the entry analysis for these four schools is aggregated, the respective figures are 30 percent for Oxbridge and 10 percent for the Regular Army. While this is not a scientific sample there is no reason to assume they are not a representation (if not a precise one) of the overall situation.[23] The 1909 HMC conference touched on another reason why entrance to the army was relatively low. Speaking about the army entrance exams the Reverend S. R. James, Headmaster of Malvern, argued that the absence of a 'living wage' for army officers discouraged many from considering the army entrance examinations.[24] The figures show that the number of boys entering the military colleges was such that there was a limit to how much effort many public schools would make to support their boys in army entrance exams. At times there were attempts to encourage boys to pursue other careers. The father of Archibald Wavell was told his son, who had won a scholarship at Winchester, was too good for the Army Class by the then Headmaster, Reverend W. A. Fearon. Wavell's father, an army officer himself who wished his son to pursue the same career, briskly dismissed the advice but it is indicative of the importance given to an army career by public schools.[25]

The reforms following the Boer war which led to the professionalisation of the British Army changed its requirements and led to there being less of a common purpose between it and the HMC. Between 1904 and 1910 there continued to be friction about entrance conditions. This was made worse by the tendency for individual schools to resist government attempts to regulate and direct them after 1902. Once again, at its 1905 meeting the HMC passed a resolution objecting to the proposed changes to the entrance examinations. The objections it had raised at the 1904 meeting had been dismissed out of hand by the Army Council in March 1905 which had said it was not prepared to accept any of the HMC's proposed changes. The new rules 'should be allowed to have a fair trial'.[26] The HMC's concern was that that the curriculum for the army would be 'divorced' from those of any 'other educational authority.'[27] A further sign of the tensions with the army was that the schools had also objected to the publication of a list by the Army Council of those schools which were permitted to issue Leaving Certificates. The Army Council replied that it would go ahead whether

---

23   Figures based on analysis of ECA, Epsom College Register, *The Sherborne Register, Uppingham School Roll 1853-1947* and *Winchester College: A Register*.
24   HMC, Report of the Thirty-Seventh Meeting of the Headmasters' Conference, December 1909, p. 92.
25   R H Kiernan, *Wavell* (London, George G Harrap & Co., 1945), p. 50.
26   HMC, Report of the Thirty-Third Meeting of the Headmasters' Conference December 1905, pp. 98-103.
27   HMC, Report of the Committee of the Headmasters' Conference for 1905, pp. 94-96.

or not the HMC objected. It also reiterated its stance about the new syllabus saying that it needed to be given a 'fair trial.'[28] The issue of army entrance examinations became the subject of regular discussions at HMC conferences. The 1909 conference discussed a report from its 'Army Council Examination Sub-Committee' which set out a number of concerns, including proposals to reduce the military colleges entry age by six months, to end qualifying exams and to rely solely on competitive examinations.[29] The 1910 conference opposed these but participants expressed concerns about the inadequacies of public school training At the meeting, comments about the inadequacy of officer pay were voiced but also doubts were expressed about the value of a public school education. J. E. King of Clifton doubted whether the loss of the last year of education at the schools had the detrimental effect other headmasters were suggesting. He also reflected on whether removing the organisation of games and training from boys to masters had deprived the former of valuable management training. This was perhaps overly nostalgic as delegation of the management of games to boys could create other problems. The Reverend W. C. Compton of Dover warned that public schools had to recognise there was a danger they would be seen as having an 'axe to grind.'[30] It is noteworthy that there was no discussion about whether a public school met the technical requirements of the army. The minutes of the meeting of the representatives of the HMC with the Army Council on 10 January 1910 contain no discussion about the army's technical requirements.[31] If the headmasters were oblivious to this as a problem they were in for a rude awakening when on 24 January 1911 they met Richard Haldane, Secretary of State for War who informed the headmasters that he proposed to reduce the entry age to 16 and a half for Woolwich and 17 for Sandhurst and to end the Army Qualifying Examination to address the problem of the 'serious shortage of officers in the army.' Haldane explained that he believed the shortage was the result of the 'deficient preparation of candidates' and the curriculum at the military colleges would be extended to include the subjects 'neglected in the Public Schools and other preparing establishments.'[32] Haldane's views should not have come as a surprise to the headmasters. He was a proponent of National Efficiency; in 1902 he had expressed the opinion that the commercial status of the country was dependent on education. Education had two purposes; 'the imparting of culture for

28 HMC, Report of the Committee of the Headmasters' Conference for 1906, pp. 94-96.
29 HMC, Thirty-Seventh Meeting of the Headmasters' Conference, December 1909, pp. 88-94 and Report of the Committee of the Headmaster's Conference Committee for 1909, pp. 145-146.
30 HMC, Report of the Thirty-Eighth Meeting of the Headmasters' Conference, December 1910, pp. 54-63.
31 Report of the Committee of the Headmaster's Conference Committee for 1910, pp. 120-121.
32 Report of the Committee of the Headmaster's Conference Committee for 1911, pp. 96-97.

culture's sake …and the training of captains of industry on the other.'[33] Even though these views related to training to support commerce it would not have taken a leap of imagination to realise Haldane would also hold similar views about training those who led the army. After this rude shock for the HMC, the Army Council offered an olive branch. The 1911 HMC meeting was sent a letter inviting all member headmasters and the head of their Army classes to visit Sandhurst to witness 'the work in progress' at the RMC. It was explained that the Army Council was exploring how co-operation between it and its principal source of officers might be 'facilitated.[34] It was implied, this was just one of the steps it wanted to take to improve co-operation. From 1911 until 1914 the HMC reports and minutes suggest a far more harmonious between the army and the HMC. The 1912 HMC Committee Report refers to two meetings with the General Staff at the War Office where subjects included the timing of examinations, detailed discussions about the content of the syllabus and a presentation on the advantages for Woolwich cadets who could speak two modern languages.[35] In 1913 two more meetings took place at the War Office but the committee's report does not provide any details of what was discussed.[36] The War Office became more pro-active in its approach to recruiting from the public schools. In 1910 Major Maxwell Earle was appointed to the War Office as the staff officer responsible for army examinations (which included those for the military colleges).[37] In his own memoirs he described how the army was short of candidates and he spent a lot of time lecturing at Public Schools and universities.[38] Analysing the figures for Epsom, Sherborne, Uppingham and Winchester (see above) it appears there was mixed success in increasing public school recruitment. For Winchester the level of recruitment rose by 38 percent and for Uppingham the level doubled. Winchester as an army school was an obvious place to seek more recruits (especially as a significant number of its pupils were the sons of army officers) but the increase for Uppingham reflects a decision by the army in 1910 that it needed to broaden its recruitment base from the traditional army schools.[39] However, for Epsom and Sherborne there was no real increase in recruitment levels. Epsom can be explained that as a school with a strong reputation for medicine the army was already recruiting as many as it could from the school. In the case of Sherborne, it was known as a classical school unlike Uppingham which had developed a strong reputation for science. Despite Haldane's commitment to address issues such as poor pay for army officers, Bowman and Connelly have argued that to

33 Richard Burdon Haldane, *Education & Empire: Addresses on Certain Topics of the Day* (London: John Murray, 1902), p. x.
34 HMC, Thirty-Ninth Meeting of the Headmasters' Conference, December 1911, pp. 32-33.
35 Report of the Committee of the Headmaster's Conference Committee for 1911, pp. 110-112.
36 Report of the Committee of the Headmaster's Conference Committee for 1912, p. 138.
37 War Office List, 1911.
38 The National Army Museum, 2016-10-23, Colonel Maxwell Earle Papers.
39 Sheffield, *Officer-man Relations*, pp. 97-98.

be an officer in the pre-war army a private income was required.⁴⁰ There were some improvements to officer pay but these were not sufficiently radical enough. The figures suggest that despite all the obstacles Earle faced he was able to make some progress in increasing officer recruitment aided by more co-operation between the schools and the army. Some of this success can be attributed to him being well suited to this work. In 1919 Lord Gorell, who established the Army Educational Corps, described Earle as 'a regular Guardsman of forceful character, liberal mind and warm friendliness to the educational work we are attempting.'⁴¹ Clearly this helped in improving a difficult relationship.

In the years immediately after the Boer War there were a series of disagreements between the army and the War Office about the recruitment of army officers from public schools. Some of this stemmed from the specific technical demands of the army which the schools felt unable to meet because of the requirements of Oxbridge and the Civil Service Commissioners, where the classics were a key requirement. While Latin or Greek (but never both) could be taken as part of the entrance examinations the classics were not viewed as being essential for the general education of army officers. It is unlikely that many of those who entered the army from the public schools were profoundly influenced by the deeds of military heroes from ancient history. If the schools were militaristic, they did not allow that to get in the way of promoting their own interests. Their Corps and OTC activity could be seen as being militaristic, but as will be argued this is an oversimplification.

From Military Training to Officer Training

The motion passed by the HMC Committee in 1900 to give boys over 15 military training had been proposed by Dr Warre, Headmaster of Eton, who followed this up by submitting a detailed scheme to the War Office in March 1900 which proposed that public schools would become an officer training and recruiting ground for the army. In essence, the proposal was that legislation was passed which was similar to the Volunteer Act and would outline the basic training requirements for the School Corps. The Corps would be separated from the Volunteers and known as Instructional Corps which would be directly controlled by the War Office. Cadets would obtain certificates of efficiency and proficiency which could be used to support their entry into the regular or auxiliary forces. To support this, he requested government funding.⁴² The funding was requested for the provision of Sergeant-Instructors, arms and

---

40   *The Times*, 15 March 1911, p. 8 and Timothy Bowman and Mark Connelly, *The Edwardian Army: Recruiting, Training, and Deploying the British Army, 1902-1914* (Oxford: Oxford University Press, 2012), passim.
41   Jim Beach, *Lord Gorell and the Army Educational Corps 1918-1920*, (Cheltenham: Army Records Society, 2019), p. 8.
42   Worthington, *Antecedent Education and Officer Recruitment*, pp. 243-244.

ammunition, ranges and grants for those certified as efficient and proficient. This was to be provided to all HMC schools, a number of which did not yet have Corps. Taught for three years, the syllabus would include subjects such as strategy, tactics, projectiles and explosives. If accepted, the Corps at the schools would have supplanted the role of Sandhurst with it becoming a military university and staff college becoming a postgraduate college. In a broadly sympathetic biography of Warre, C. R. L. Fletcher (an Old Etonian) believed that Warre had pushed his luck with his proposals for statutory funding and in effect the replacement of Sandhurst by the public schools.[43] Not surprisingly, this somewhat artless attempt at a land-grab by Warre met with a lukewarm response from the War Office. Replying in May 1900 Lansdowne, the Secretary of State of War, supported the principles behind the memorandum but did not believe legislation was appropriate. This was on the grounds of the expense involved and that the public would be hostile to the idea of compulsory military training in the schools. So as not to pour too much cold water on the idea, Lansdowne proposed that Warre's scheme be discussed at the next meeting of the HMC.[44] To try and gain public support Warre put his idea to influential army officers in a lecture at the Royal United Services Institute (RUSI) in June 1900. The response at the meeting to his proposals was broadly favourable although there was disagreement over the details of the scheme including by Major Hoare of Haileybury who spoke on behalf of a number of School Corps COs.[45] As suggested, Warre's proposals were put to the December 1900 meeting of the HMC which agreed to form a committee to consider how their School Corps could be best organised to participate in the national defence. It was agreed that a committee be formed consisting of Warre, Lyttelton (then of Haileybury but who would eventually succeed Warre at Eton) and Gow of Westminster, plus four to seven officers who commanded corps in public schools who would be nominated by the HMC committee. The committee would consider the best way to organise the Corps within the schools.[46] Superficially, the decision indicated a desire by the schools to co-operate with the army, but when considered alongside the objections to the revised examinations for Militia officers (discussed above) it represented a strong desire by them to resist any encroachment by the army on the education of boys. One of the objections to the new scheme for Militia examination had been that they allowed the army to provide a technical education for officers at an earlier age.[47] The HMC was keen to play a part in national defence but on terms which coincided with

---

43 Fletcher, *Edmond Warre*, pp. 267-269.
44 Worthington, *Antecedent Education and Officer Recruitment,* pp. 244-245.
45 Rev. Hon. Colonel E Warre, 'On the Relation of Public Secondary Schools to the Organisation of National Defence', *Royal United Services Institution, Journal,* Vol 44: 273, pp. 1237-1268
46 HMC, Report of the Twenty-Eighth Meeting of the Headmasters' Conference, December 1900, pp. 51-54.
47 HMC, Report of the Twenty-Eighth Meeting of the Headmasters' Conference December 1900, p. 51.

its own agenda and not necessarily the needs of the army. It viewed the reorganisation of the Corps at school and their removal from the control of the Volunteers as an opportunity not to be missed to strengthen its hold on the provision of officer cadets.

The committee's report recommended that the School Corps should be separated from the Volunteers and become a separate Corps of Military Instruction.[48] The appointment of Warre and Walker to the Akers-Douglas Committee whose terms included the supply of potential officers put further discussion on hold until the 1902 meeting. In the event, the idea of a compulsory School Corps was not considered until the 1904 meeting. A motion to agree to compulsion was watered down to one instructing the HMC committee to consider its desirability. Most headmasters were in favour of 'the efficiency and development of the cadet corps' but this did not mean that they supported compulsion. The Headmaster of Winchester had reservations about the cost to the schools and more importantly that compulsion would create a distaste for volunteerism on which home defence rested.[49] The public schools' alleged militarism had its limits. The following year, however, it was decided to seek guidance from the military authorities on how best to train all boys in elementary drill and the use of arms. However, it came with the rider that there would need to be financial support to train boys to use rifles.[50] It was the army's need to address a shortage of officers in the reserves which led to the creation of an Instructional Corps which would be known as the OTC. Since 1903 a series of committees under Sir Edward Ward (Permanent Under Secretary of State, War Office) had been considering this problem but progress had been painfully slow. In July 1906 the Army Council asked Ward to establish yet another committee to consider the various options for creating a reserve of officers. The committee was small and consisted of representatives of the War Office, the Universities and the headmasters. The Reverend A. A. David, Headmaster of Clifton (an army school), was invited by the War Office to represent the headmasters.[51] The committee identified that there was a shortfall of officers of 4,419 in the Regular Army while the Auxiliaries (Volunteers etc.) were 3,914 below establishment. It considered how Russia, Germany, France and Japan had addressed the problem of having a sufficiently strong reserve of officers in the event of war. By the time it took evidence, based on the written questions it had submitted to each witness, it is clear the committee had formed a clear view of the approach to dealing with officer shortages. Between 1 November 1906 and 25 January 1907 evidence was taken from 28 witnesses, six of whom were school Corps Commanders: de Haviland of Eton, Hoare of Haileybury, Hawkesworth of Rugby, Jones of Uppingham, Collett of Wellington and Carus of Stonyhurst. Also interviewed, were the Headmasters of

---

48   HMC, Report of the Committee of the Headmasters' Conference for 1901, p. 5.
49   HMC, Report of the Committee of the Headmasters' Conference for 1904, pp. 28-46.
50   HMC, Report of the Thirty-Third Meeting of the Headmasters' Conference December 1905, pp. 45-47.
51   Worthington, *Antecedent Education and Officer Recruitment*, pp. 253-256.

Bedford (King) and Westminster (Gow).[52] The reasons for the selection of witnesses by Ward in most cases are obvious. With the exception of Jones and Carus the witnesses were either from Cavendish schools (Westminster), schools which since 1900 had provided a substantial number of cadets to the army (Bedford, Eton, Haileybury and Wellington) or fell into both categories (Rugby). From the point of view of the War Office these were considered to be the leading schools. Why Carus and Jones were invited to give evidence is not immediately obvious. Carus was CO of Stonyhurst, a leading Roman Catholic school but not known for sending cadets to the military colleges. The reasons for the attendance of Jones are more obvious. He was the only school Corps CO to have served in the Boer War. Since 1898 he had been CO of the Uppingham Cadet Corps. Before he arrived at Uppingham he had already developed a reputation for his work with the cadet corps at Bradfield.[53] Jones was commissioned into the Leicester Volunteers in March 1899 and within a year took leave of absence from Uppingham to serve in South Africa, following the Black Week. Letters to his brother, Edgar Montague Jones who in 1902 became Headmaster of St Albans School and established an OTC contingent at the school in 1908, show that he took a strong interest in the work of the School Corps. The two brothers appear to have developed a working relationship with Hoare at Haileybury (which was 16 miles from St Albans). Hoare was one of the founding members of the public schools camp in 1889 and Haig-Brown credits him with having 'first place amongst school-master soldiers and not a little of the praise for the evolution of the OTC'.[54] Hoare was influential and it is likely he became aware of the Uppingham CO's ideas through Edgar, who later said that the scheme for the OTC was agreed after the two brothers and Hoare of Haileybury went to see Haldane, the Secretary of State for War in 1907 to set out their proposals.[55] It is unlikely that the relative upstart from Uppingham would have been heard by the authorities without the support of Hoare.

Throughout his time in South Africa, he wrote to his brother promising to 'make himself heard' on the subject of school cadet corps.[56] He was in regular correspondence with his Headmaster, Selwyn, who had kept him up to date with discussions at the HMC and Warre's scheme which he dismissed as 'absurd.' Edgar's letters to Herbert have not survived but it appears there was regular correspondence about training schoolboys.[57] From January 1901 Jones was writing to Edgar with his ideas about how to improve the cadet corps. These revolved around making the corps a more interesting experience and improving the quality of the training; corps 'must

---

52 *Interim Report of the War Office Committee on the Provision of Officers (a) For Service with the Regular Army in War and (b) for the Auxiliary Forces Minutes of Evidence (Hereinafter Ward Committee Evidence)*, Cd. 3205 (London: HMSO, 1907), pp. 3-4.
53 St Albans School Archive (Hereinafter SASA): E Montague Jones: Military Matters.
54 Haig-Brown, *The OTC and the Great War*, pp. 1-2.
55 SASA: E Montague Jones: Thirty Years as a Headmaster.
56 SASA: E Montague Jones: C H Jones correspondence, 9 June 1900.
57 Ibid., 30 November 1900.

have more than square drill.' All boys should be allowed to attend the shooting range and it must not be reserved for 'crack shots.' NCOs should only be appointed if they had passed an examination. In the school library there should be a section for military books which would include technical references and infantry and cavalry drill. He proposed that schools should establish a military history prize only open to corps members. However, the corps was not to be a closed society; there should be a school corps committee which would include at least one representative of 'Non-corps people.' At its discretion the school corps should invite non-members to meetings. For example, a history master could be invited to talk about a famous battle or war. All this would not be possible unless the 'Schoolmaster Captain' made 'himself as efficient as possible.' He recognised his ideas needed further development but they formed the basis of his proposals for the OTC.[58] His experience in South Africa had convinced him of the need to reform training for schoolboys.

These ideas, however, formed the core of his approach which he summarised in his evidence to the Ward Committee:

> We train them all though with the idea of their eventually becoming officers, and we take them a good way along the course towards that end. They have, of course, to begin with drills in the ranks and then they become corporals and sergeants, and we then make them drill the company, set piquets and outposts, and develop them as far as possible in the duties of junior officers.

The seed of the idea to form what became the OTC came from Warre, but a comparison of Jones's detailed suggestions to the committee with the final scheme for the OTC strongly suggests that his evidence was highly influential.[59]

By 1 December 1906 Ward had taken evidence from the final public school representative, Carus, and was able to put his proposals to the HMC. At the 1906 HMC on 20 and 21 December a letter from Ward was read inviting the HMC to appoint a sub-committee to meet with his committee to discuss the proposals on a date after the middle of January 1907.[60] Ward was keen to move quickly to address the shortage of officers in the reserves. Only six days after the last evidence had been taken, on 31 January 1907, the Ward Committee met with the HMC representatives. Ward set out the details of his proposals and in a spirit of conciliation, not always evident in the past, stated he wanted to consult with the HMC about details, (especially the financial arrangements) relating to the schools. The HMC representatives asked several detailed questions about how the scheme would work. Ward made it clear that the whole purpose of the meeting was to resolve these difficulties. Most importantly, the

---

58 Ibid., 19 January 1901.
59 See Halstead, *A School in Arms*, pp 137-139.
60 HMC, Report of the Thirty-Fourth Meeting of the Headmasters' Conference, December 1906, pp. 91-92.

headmasters wanted to know what instructional support they would receive from the War Office if their Corps were separated from their local Volunteers. For example, Bedford was an engineering corps and relied a great deal on its local Volunteers to provide training for its cadets.[61] After agreeing the scheme with the HMC, Haldane announced it to Parliament in February 1907. The committee's proposals were designed to streamline the system of Training Corps at both schools and universities. To ensure there were enough officers in the event of war it proposed that gentlemen could become officers by being attached to a unit for a period of a year, after which they would retain a liability of service with a regular recall annually or biennially.[62] In return they would receive pay during their periods of attachment.[63] After completing their minimum period of service gentlemen would become officers in the Special Reserve. In a country where military service was not compulsory the committee recognised that a year's service would not be especially attractive to young men starting a career. It therefore proposed that earning a certificate of proficiency from the school corps (Certificate A) would entitle the holder to exemption from four months of the one year's service. Passing another certificate of proficiency in the University Corps (Certificate B) would provide a further exemption of four months Similar exemptions would be offered to those joining the Territorial Force (now known as the Territorial Army) as officers.

These proposals provided incentives for young men to become officers and achieve the valued status of a gentleman. Equally important was the way the corps would be organised. All the 'University and School Corps' were to be organised into a single body, the OTC. They were to be placed under the direct control of a department of the War Office which would oversee the running of and examinations for the OTC.[64] Importantly, it was made clear that the headmasters would be responsible for the management of their corps much of which would be delegated to the master who was the school's contingent CO. Ward recognised that as 'the ruler of the school' the headmaster needed to be afforded administrative control of their contingent. However, the War Office would control the training programme for all the school contingents. Only military qualifications and not general education would count in the award of certificates.[65] The War Office would provide financial support for the OTC which would be based on the number of 'efficient' cadets.[66] Efficiency would be measured by the number of cadets over 15 who had met criteria which included a minimum level of attendance at parades and training camp and the unit passing an annual inspection.[67] This was an improvement on the previous arrangements for the school corps. Under

---

61 *Ward Committee Evidence*, p. 90.
62 Ibid., p. 6.
63 Ibid., p. 15.
64 Ibid., p. 7.
65 Ibid., p. 96.
66 Ibid., p. 10.
67 *Regulations for the Officers Training Corps* (London: HMSO, 1912), pp. 19-20, 29.

the previous system the corps were attached to local Volunteer units which had discretion about what support and training the corps were provided with. Instead, under the War Office, the training for all cadets was standardised and the schools had a defined standard to meet to ensure funding, one which tied in with the requirements of the army. From 1908 the regulations were regularly revised to make sure they were in line with the army's approach to training which became more professional as part of its response to the Boer War. By 1912 the papers for the Certificate A examination at the schools were based on *Field Service Regulations (FSR), 1909* and *Infantry Training, 1911* which laid down how the British Army would fight in battle.[68] The aim was that those who studied for them would have the basic skills to be a junior officer on being called up.

The scheme was welcomed at the December 1907 meeting of the HMC. The Reverend David who moved the motion supporting the scheme did not believe there could be any arguments about this. In addition to no longer being at the whim of the Volunteer Units to which School Corps were attached the separation from them would mean that boys would no longer repeat their training, if they joined the Volunteers after they left school, for which many boys had been a disincentive. The introduction of the concept of efficiency would enable the schools to measure whether they were meeting the required standards. David pointed out that the scheme was underpinned by two principles: the boys would be trained to be officers and the training in the OTC would be part of a continuous and progressive programme which would start when a boy was 15 at school and end when he was 22 and with the Auxiliary forces. It was emphasised that the OTC would be voluntary for schools to join and undertaken in the boys' spare time. Previous motions from the HMC had proposed compulsory training but given previous differences of opinion within it this was not a major concern.[69] In any event, the idea of compulsory military education was politically unacceptable. From the point of view of the schools the OTC enhanced their position as the primary source of officers for the army. This point was reinforced when the OTC regulations came into effect and provided that those with Certificate A would receive 200 marks in the entrance examinations for Woolwich and Sandhurst.[70] This may partly explain the improved recruitment from Winchester and Uppingham discussed earlier. The training scheme was not as extensive as that proposed by Warre but by 1912 the examination consisted of two written papers, the first being common to all arms, the second was arm specific, while the last test was an oral examination. The training was to be practical with no military theory included.[71]

68 *Field Service Regulations (FSR), 1909* (London: HMSO, 1909) and *Infantry Training, 1911* (London: HMSO, 1911).
69 HMC, Report of the Thirty-Fifth Meeting of the Headmasters' Conference, December 1906, pp. 35-36.
70 *Regulations for the OTC*, p. 22 and TNA WO 92/9034.
71 *Ward Committee*. p. 7.

The first written paper was based on the *Field Service Regulations, 1909* and for the infantry (as in the case of many schools) the second paper was based on *Infantry Training, 1911*. The oral test covered drill, the tactical handling of a section, musketry regulations where the cadet was also required to be familiar with his rifle 'as a weapon', military law and tactics.[72] The scheme did not guarantee a supply of officers but it did provide a means to for replenishing their ranks. As Worthington has argued, it was militaristic but as its purpose was defensive (to protect the country in event of war) it was not an espousal of militarism by the schools.[73] That the scheme did not lead militarism can be seen by the OTC's failure to provide officers for the Special Reserve, one its primary objectives. Haldane reported in March 1912 that of the nearly 18,000 who had left the OTC (Schools and University) only 283 had taken commissions in the Special Reserve with a further 500 having passed their Certificate A and Certificate B examinations.[74] There were good reasons for this. The syllabus for Certificate A was demanding, required coaching outside normal school activities, and passing was not guaranteed. In addition, to be eligible a cadet had to be deemed to be 'efficient', the conditions for which were substantial.[75] He also must have completed the musketry training and been passed physically fit. Within a busy school life these requirements were not easy to achieve. Alan Haig-Brown, who was CO of the Lancing OTC, commented that those involved in the OTC at schools had 'been watched with a jealous eye to see that they did not encroach an inch upon the claims of work or the necessities of games.'[76] Although the scheme was voluntary for schools to join, each one took a decision as to whether joining should be compulsory for its boys. In 1911 Mill Hill, a Non-Conformist school, with a suspicion of the cult of games and militarism decided to form an OTC. This was on the proviso that membership was voluntary. Having consulted with Lancing and University College School it was concluded there was no danger of militarism as although other schools found it encouraged boys to think of the army as a profession it did not encourage the 'jingo' spirit. The committee considering the matter was firmly of the view that the Headmaster would not allow the OTC to foster 'a spirit of aggression among the boys.'[77] At Uppingham, where games had a high status, it was voluntary and the top games players often chose to opt out of the OTC.[78] Winchester did not make the OTC compulsory and instead of joining boys could

72 *Regulations for the OTC*, pp. 41-47.
73 Ian Worthington, 'Militarization and Officer Recruiting: The Development of the Officers Training Corps', *Military Affairs,* Vol. 43 No. 2 (Apr. 1979) pp. 90-96.
74 Spiers, *Haldane*, p. 191.
75 Regulations for the OTC 1912, pp. 19-20.
76 Haig-Brown, *The O.T.C. and The Great War*, p. 62.
77 MHSA, Minute Book, Vol., 12-13 July 1910 pp. 94-97.
78 Halstead, *A School in Arms*, p. 50.

opt to undertake a couple of extra hours work a week instead.[79] Lancing claimed to be the first public school to achieve 100 per cent voluntary membership.[80] However, in an interview Ernest Millard who was at the school from 1911 to 1914 recalled that although membership was not compulsory everyone joined.[81] Where membership was voluntary but the contingent had a high percentage of the school enrolled it is likely the alternative was considerably less attractive. Even before the advent of the OTC, schools were using this approach. At Bedford, all boys who did not join the OTC were required to do gym which was designed to be less interesting than the Corps; this was also the case at Wellington.[82] In times of peace the OTC was not such a pressing concern to many boys and levels of enrolment depended on pressure applied to them to join. Levels of enrolment varied from school to school. When war came it would be different and many public schoolboys, whether or not they had been members of the OTC, quickly volunteered.

Although there was now an integrated programme and funding dependent on the level of efficiency achieved, in the early days of the OTC the training was variable in quality. The Army took action to address the problem and during the holidays of Christmas 1909 and 1910 and Easter 1912 120 masters were attached to regular battalions to learn company drill.[83] The annual inspection system was robust and not merely a rubber-stamping exercise. In the summer of 1914, the inspecting officer of the Fettes contingent complained about its slovenliness, whereas the Uppingham contingent was strongly praised in July 1914 by its inspecting officer.[84] Some schools were stronger in some areas of the OTC syllabus than others. At Lancing Haig-Brown placed a high priority on drill which it was said greatly improved the *esprit de corps*.[85] This did not mean other areas of training were deficient; Millard also enjoyed rifle shooting and the tactical lectures but found the field days boring.[86] He believed the OTC was the basis of the army at war. John Murray Rymer-Jones who was at Felsted from 1910 to 1914 thought that he had not learnt a lot from the OTC and felt Certificate A was easy (this was not the experience of all boys). The main advantage to him was the discipline gained from drill.[87] Greenwell, educated at Winchester from 1910 to 1914, said that everyone, he was at school with, found the OTC boring.[88] For boys like Greenwell who planned to go to Oxbridge, this is not surprising. George

79 Sabben-Clare, *Winchester College*, p. 169.
80 *Lancing College War Memorial* <http://www.hambo.org/lancing/view_man.php?id=132> (accessed 19 February 2016).
81 IWM 14985: Millard, Ernest (Oral History).
82 *Ward Committee Evidence*, pp. 18, 34.
83 E M Teagarden, 'Lord Haldane and the origins of the Officer Training Corps' *Journal of the Society for Army Historical Research*, 45: 182 (1967), pp. 91-96.
84 Seldon and Walsh, *Public Schools and The Great War*, p. 26 and USA.
85 Handford, *Lancing College*, p. 134.
86 IWM 14985, Millard.
87 IWM 10699, Rymer-Jones, John Murray (Oral History).
88 IWM 8766, Greenwell, Graham Hamilton (Oral History).

Harbottle, educated at the Leys from 1907 to 1910, a school with a Methodist background and reservations about compulsory military service, thought well of his time in the OTC. He was not fond of the drill but described the field days as 'grand fun.' Field day tactics were taught ahead of them 'on the blackboard by the master in charge of the OTC'.[89] From this brief survey it can be seen that although the OTC created standards for providing military training the quality of different contingents varied and dependent on the quality of the masters running them. Boys who were members of these contingents had differing views on their quality but some of this can be accounted for by their individual characters and intellectual ability.

Conclusion

If public schools were militaristic this took a distant second place to the pursuit of their own educational interests. The public schools were keen to be the primary source of officers, which was a point of view the army shared. The army viewed the public schools as a good source of officers but there were a series of disagreements with the public schools about how this was to be achieved. After the Boer War the army became more assertive about its requirements and less beholden to the schools in complying with their vision about what formed a proper education for the officer cadet. As the army became more professional a talent for classics became less important and it became more interested in ability in modern languages and scientific subjects. The HMC, under a leadership firmly wedded to the classics, resisted attempts by the army to admit cadets at a younger age. They were reluctant to compromise as an ability at classics was more important for a larger group of pupils than those entering the military colleges. The situation was resolved partly by the army holding out an olive branch to the schools in 1911 and between then and 1914 the two parties worked together more closely. The formation of the OTC also contributed to the reduction of tensions. Warre's attempt in 1900 to take over the officer training role from the military colleges had been the start of a difficult relationship between the army and the public schools. The establishment of the OTC to help provide officers for the reserve also set out the training to be provided by public schools and the expected standard. It cemented the position of the public schools as the primary source of officers for the regular army and auxiliaries. The training in the OTC was part of an integrated scheme for the training of officers based on understanding parts of the *FSR*. Schools were given the role of basic training under the direction of the War Office. Headmasters were given overall responsibility for the running of their school contingents, but effective control rested with the War Office. The result of more clearly defined roles for each party and more harmonious relations between them contributed to an increased level of recruitment from some but not all schools. The ability of the schools to provide a basic military

---

89   IWM 9474, Harbottle, George, (Oral History).

training became more important than the teaching of Horace and other ancient Greek and Roman writers. Success at recruiting officers for the reserve was limited but after the outbreak of the war the boys who had undergone OTC training would make an important contribution to the war effort.

Oakham OTC at Rugely Camp in August 1914, so rapid was army mobilisation that the school's cadets were left to cook for themselves. (Oakham School)

St Albans School, site of the school library in the 1914 which was requisitioned by the army as a military prison. (James Halstead)

Oundle Munitions Workers, summer 1915. Apart from munitions production being part of regular school life, school holidays were also devoted to production. (Oundle School)

Sherborne OTC Band 1915. Many public schools had corps bands. (Sherborne School)

Uppingham OTC Camp c.1916. The obvious exhaustion of the boys demonstrates the demanding nature of their training. (Uppingham School)

Inns of Court OTC Training Trenches. Some 13,000 yards of excavated works was where Eton, Harrow, Westminster, Berkhamsted and Merchant Taylors OTC contingents took part in military exercises. (James Halstead)

Edmund Blunden with fellow Christ's Hospital Old Boys. The photograph depicts the famous 'Feast of Five' at St Omer in 1917. Blunden (front right) is in the company of four Old Blues all serving with the Royal Sussex Regiment. Two were killed within a few months and a third committed suicide in 1924. (Christ's Hospital)

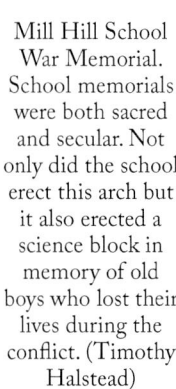

Mill Hill School War Memorial. School memorials were both sacred and secular. Not only did the school erect this arch but it also erected a science block in memory of old boys who lost their lives during the conflict. (Timothy Halstead)

4

Building from Scratch:
Public Schools and the New Army, 1914–1915[1]

Mobilisation for war is for every Power a ragged business. We have our peace establishment of Regular officers. There is practically no deficiency there. But when we pass to mobilisation we want a great many more officers.[2]

When Britain declared war on 4 August 1914 it is generally acknowledged that the mobilisation of the British Expeditionary Force was a well-planned and executed exercise, the details of which had been set out in the 'War Book' which had been prepared by the Government in the years leading up to 1914. The highly-detailed plan laid down the administrative arrangements for the actions to be taken by each government department in the event of war.[3] The clearest demonstration of the success of the 'War Book' was the speed with which the railways were mobilised so that the regular army could be transported to the south coast prior to deployment to France. The plan specified that the troops were to be sent to Southampton to be embarked and the detailed timetable allowed for troop trains to arrive at the port every twelve minutes for sixteen hours each day. By 31 August 1914, 670 trains had carried nearly 120,000 soldiers to the port.[4]

However, while the plan successfully addressed the immediate problems of mobilising for war it did not address the long-term strategy required to sustain or develop the British Army beyond deployment. The pre-war government's view was that

---

1   This is a revised and expanded version of idem., '"A Ragged Business": Officer Training Corps: Public Schools and the Recruitment of the Junior Officer Corps of 1916' in Spencer Jones (ed.), *At All Costs The British Army on the Western Front 1916* (Warwick: Helion, 2018). I am grateful to Dr Jones for his permission to include it.
2   Lord Haldane, P. Debs., 1912 Volume 11, 13 May 1912, columns 984-6, Lords.
3   David French, *British Economic and Strategic Planning 1905-1915* (London: George, Allen and Unwin, 1982), p. 82.
4   Christian Wolmar, *Engines of War: How Wars Were Won & Lost on the Railways* (London: Atlantic Books, 2010), p. 155.

Britain's main contribution would be at sea, which would include a naval blockade of Germany, but a comparatively low level of involvement on the continent. Britain would support the war through its economic strength and by providing financial and logistical support to its allies. The appointment of Lord Kitchener as Secretary of State for War on 5 August 1914 led to a radical change in the government's policy. He quickly disabused the cabinet of the notion that the war would be a short one and informed them that a large army to fight on the continent would be needed if the war was to be won. To lead this new army, it was necessary to identify and recruit suitable men as junior officers. At the outbreak of the war the British Army had 24,896 officers but by November 1916 this had grown into an officer corps of 122,352.[5] The vast majority of this expanded corps were new junior officers. During Kitchener's term of office, it was necessary to find *at least* 30,000 officers to lead the infantry battalions which he had created. This figure took no account of replacing the casualties suffered or the officers needed for other parts of the army such as the Royal Engineers, Royal Artillery and the Army Service Corps.[6] With no detailed plans or mechanisms in place to initiate such an expansion it was inevitable that the process of recruiting junior officers would be, as Lord Haldane predicted, a "ragged business."

The composition of the Junior Officer corps at the start of 1916 was mainly the result of an ad hoc system of recruitment which was inevitable after Kitchener's change of policy. Inevitably, carrying out such a rapid expansion from such a low base of preparedness would require a great deal of improvisation. However, by 1916 it became clear that being the *alumnus* of a public school was not a guarantee of a commission. To understand the capabilities of the junior officer corps in 1916 it is necessary to study the system which produced them. Although by the beginning of 1916 a more coherent and formal system for recruiting junior officers had evolved, the officers who served in the opening of the Battle of the Somme were primarily products of the early, *ad hoc* approach to recruitment. This improvised approach means that the expansion of the junior officer corps cannot be solely explained by factors such as drawing on young men with experience of serving in the OTC of the leading public schools; it is more nuanced than that. The expansion of the junior officer corps was complex. This chapter examines the role of the public schools and their old boys in the expansion of the army. Although the importance of the OTC in this expansion rose as the process became more organised it was not the sole factor. Although far from perfect an *ad hoc* approach proved to be successful in building from scratch the junior officer corps of a citizen army.

---

5   *Statistics of the Military Effort of the British Empire During the Great War* (London: HMSO 1922), pp. 30-31.
6   Peter Simkins, *Kitchener's Army: The Raising of the New Armies, 1914-1916* (Barnsley: Pen and Sword, 2007), p. 212.

A Low Base

In the years before the war there were several factors which had constrained the preparation of the British Army for war. Both long term and short-term political factors led to the army being, until 1914, a relatively small body. Up until the start of the 20th Century it was not necessary for Britain to have a large army. A standing force of continental proportions was not required by the British government, which could rely on its command of the sea for defence. In the event of war, the island geography of Britain and its naval mastery provided an insurance policy which would buy time. If faced by a sudden attack by powerful enemies, Britain would have time to build up the necessary land forces to achieve victory.[7] Further, the Royal Navy could simultaneously protect the maritime trade routes upon which the prosperity of the Empire depended whilst denying them to any enemy. Therefore, it is not surprising that Britain devoted its resources to supporting its navy, assigning relatively little to the army. In addition, especially amongst Liberals, the legacy of Cromwell and James II in the seventeenth century continued to cast a shadow. Following the removal of James from the throne in 1688 the basis on which the army existed, funded and governed itself was set out by the Mutiny Act passed in 1689 and annually renewed. The events which followed the English Civil War had left British parliamentarians with a fear of military dictatorship. Even after the end of the Napoleonic threat in 1815 both the main political parties endeavoured to keep army expenditure as low as possible.[8] Such constitutional and political luxuries were the privilege of an island nation with a strong navy; the countries of mainland Europe with substantial land borders were not in the same position and conscription was a necessity.

The landslide victory won by the Liberal Party in 1906 gave them the opportunity to implement a peace dividend after the Boer War.[9] To fund the planned programme of radical social reforms the well-off needed to be taxed more heavily, and savings had to be found elsewhere. The army, with its ambivalent relationship with politicians, was a natural target. Its annual budget was reduced and restricted to £28m per annum and this remained the case until 1914. In contrast, annual expenditure on the navy rose, in response to the German threat, and was £46.3m just before the outbreak of war.[10] It was within the constraints of expenditure and political suspicion of the army that Haldane the new Secretary of State for War had to act. Haldane, a Liberal

---

7   Michael Howard, Introduction in Michael Howard (ed.) *Soldiers and Governments: Nine Studies in Civil-Military Relations* (London: Eyre & Spottiswoode, 1957), pp. 13-14.
8   Robert Blake, 'Great Britain The Crimean War to the First World War' in Michael Howard (ed.) *Soldiers and Governments: Nine Studies in Civil-Military Relations* (London: Eyre & Spottiswoode, 1957), pp. 27-28.
9   Niall Ferguson, *Empire: How Britain Made the Modern World* (London: Penguin, 2004), p. 287.
10 Simon Batten, *Futile Exercise? The British Army's Preparations for War 1902-1914* (Warwick: Helion, 2018), pp. 208-209.

Imperialist in a party split between imperialists and radicals, was concerned about the German threat to the British Empire and used his considerable skills to address it, while working under these political constraints. He was a proponent of National Efficiency and despite the stringent financial limitations, his pragmatic approach and a considerable ability to manage available resources efficiently allowed him to make considerable progress. He concentrated on building a small professional army and developing the Territorial Force (TF) and Special Reserves (SR) to provide ready access to additional trained men in the event of war.[11] The creation of the OTC was part of this reform with one of its key purposes bring to feed recruits into the TF and SR. This allowed the development of an OTC training programme which was integrated into that of the army as a whole. As discussed in the previous chapter, cadets in the Junior OTC received training which equipped them to gain commissions as junior officers in the SR and TF relatively quickly provided, they passed the Certificate A examination. This was a notable improvement from the situation which Britain had found itself in during the Boer War when it recruited 'suitable gentlemen' as officers but left them ill-equipped to perform the role.[12]

Haldane's reforms were limited by the political circumstances of the day. He preferred to achieve consensus rather than push for radical changes. Although the reform of the OTC was a positive development it only provided a small number of officer candidates for the army. As Kitchener recognised at the start of the war Haldane's reforms did not place the British Army in a position where it could make a significant military contribution to victory. In August 1914 Britain not only needed to expand its army rapidly, but on a scale far greater than it had ever done in the past.[13] The public schools and their old boys would play an important part in this expansion.

Building the New Army

When Kitchener assumed the post of Secretary of State for War in 1914, he in effect tore up Haldane's approach to growing the army to fight the war. The TF was sidelined and no longer a key part of feeding men into the army. Instead it was decided to create a new army through a massive expansion of existing regular regiments; the men would be provided by a nationwide call for volunteers. This sudden change of approach meant that there was no mechanism in place to recruit and train the junior officers in sufficient numbers to lead this new army and, in effect, it was necessary to start from scratch. Until 1910 the army had drawn its officers from a relatively small social group consisting mainly of "families with military connections, the gentry and peerage and

---

11 Spiers, *Haldane*, p. 191.
12 John Mason Sneddon, 'The Company Commander', in Spencer Jones (ed.) *Stemming the Tide: Officers and Leadership in the British Expeditionary Force 1914* (Solihull: Helion, 2013), p. 317.
13 Simkins, *Kitchener's Army*, p. 40.

to some degree the professions and clergy".¹⁴ The army despite its differences with the HMC had succeeded in building a professional junior officer corps but this was small in number and not large to provide all the leaders the army now required.

This sudden change in policy meant that there was no defined approach to the recruitment and training of officers. At the outbreak of the war the OTC contingents were at their summer camps but these were rapidly disbanded as the army personnel attending and running the camps were mobilised. Public schools reacted as each thought best. The Headmaster of Winchester, Montague Rendall, quickly set about organising a replacement OTC camp, between 31 August and 14 September, with the agreement of the War Office. Attended by 500 OTC cadets and old boys it was run mainly but not exclusively by officers from the College's OTC.¹⁵ The accounts of the different school magazines whose OTC contingents participated vary, but it is clear from analysing them that there were substantial contingents from Winchester (150) and Sherborne and Rugby (60 each) together with smaller attendances from other schools including Bradfield, Charterhouse, Clifton, Eton, Harrow, and Marlborough.¹⁶ For many schools the short notice had meant that they were unable to send a large number of participants. There was a variety of activities which, *The Shirburnian* reported, were wider in their scope than a summer camp would normally allow: 'We had Signalling, Physical Drill, Trench-digging, in addition to Close Order Drill and Route-marching; there were lectures on foreign armies, on hygiene, and outposts, and the fortnight added considerably to everyone's military efficiency in numerous ways.'¹⁷ *The Wykehamist* reported that nearly all those who had attended the camp and subsequently applied for a commission had been awarded one.¹⁸ The magazines of other attending schools were equally positive but Greenwell who attended recalled the relatively wide age range of those who attended and the problems this presented. Amongst those who attended was the 35-year-old Raymond Asquith, son of the Prime Minister. Like many of the older men who had no OTC experience either at school or university he struggled with drill.¹⁹

The volunteering for service by older *alumni* of the public schools was matched by similar enthusiasm from those still at school. Greenwell who had laughed at Guy du Maurier's *An Englishman's Home* and its idea of war with Germany had no doubt he should serve after leaving Winchester in 1914. At Winchester many boys had left far earlier than normal because of the 'special gravity of the crisis.' An unusually large number (112) of boys had left at the end of the summer term, at least 95 of whom

---

14   Sheffield, *Officer-man Relations* (PhD thesis, London, 1994), p. 3.
15   WCA, Report of the Head Master for the year 1914, p. 3.
16   *The Shirburnian,* Vol. XXVII., No. 11. November 1914, p. 416 and *The Wykehamist*, No. 534. October 1914, p. 345.
17   *The Shirburnian,* Vol. XXVII., No. 11. November 1914, p. 416.
18   *The Wykehamist*, No. 534. October 1914, p. 345.
19   IWM 8766, Greenwell.

had joined the army.[20] At Marlborough 50 boys who had been expected to return had joined the army.[21] In November 1914 the *Mill Hill Magazine* reported that 320 of its old boys were already serving (90 of whom had been in the OTC).[22] This was particularly remarkable for a school where militarism and joining the army, in peace time, had been discouraged.[23] Only at Christ's Hospital where only the relatively few Grecians (boys preparing for Oxbridge or the professions) were allowed to stay beyond 17 (whereas for many other public schools it was 18 or 18 and a half) was the effect of the war on leavers minimal. In 1914, when boys were able to join the army when initially they were 17, they do not appear to have joined immediately after leaving school. In 1913 140 boys had left and in 1914 the equivalent figure had left with no more than two joining the army. Even in 1915, 152 had left of whom only 16 had joined the army.[24]

The effect on teaching staff at the schools was also significant. At Marlborough by November 1914 two staff had left to serve in the war[25], at Christ's Hospital by the end of 1914, nine teachers (nearly 25 percent of the total) and the bursar were on active service,[26] at Winchester seven masters had temporarily left for active service in 1914,[27] while at Sherborne three masters had joined the army.[28] This was despite the War Office strongly stating that teachers should stay with their schools unless their headmaster could spare them 'from scholastic and O.T.C. work. Under no circumstances should the training of the contingents suffer.'[29]

It is important not to see this vigorous response to the outbreak of war solely in terms of the public schools. The response of public school boys was not a militaristic one underpinned by their education in the classics. Theirs was a response reflected across all parts of British society. Between 4 August and 12 September 1914, 478,893 men enlisted. The British feared a domination of Germany by a militaristic German Empire which they believed to be 'a blustering international bully.'[30] However it is important not to confuse this response as hysteria or jingoism. Those who enlisted were driven by 'a sense of well-considered duty and necessity' which created an obligation to serve.[31] An examination of the town of Winchester (as opposed to just the

20 WCA, p. 3, Report of the Head Master for the year 1914, pp. 2-3.
21 *The Marlburian*, Vol. XLIX., No. 740. October 8th 1914, p. 133.
22 *MHM*, Vol. xlii., No. 3. November 1914, p. 102.
23 Braithwaite, *"Strikingly alive"*, pp. 135-136.
24 CHA, Reports of the Boy's School Year Ending 31 December 1913, p. 1; 1914, p. 1 and 1915, p. 1.
25 *The Marlburian*, Vol. XLIX., No. 740. October 8th 1914, p. 133.
26 CHA, Report of the Boy's School Year Ending 31 December 1914, p. 1.
27 WCA, p. 3, Report of the Head Master for the year 1914, p. 2.
28 SSA, Headmaster's Report to the Governors for 1914, pp. 6-7.
29 TNA WO 293/1/189: Employment of Officers of Junior Division O.T.C. in T.F. or other Units, 13 September 1914.
30 William Philpott, *Bloody Victory: The Sacrifice on the Somme* (London: Abacus, 2010) p. 20.
31 Catriona Pennell, *A Kingdom United: Popular Responses to the Outbreak of the First World War in Britain and Ireland* (Oxford: Oxford University Press, 2014), p. 159.

College) illustrates this. In 1914 the residents of Winchester from all social backgrounds supported the war effort both through charitable giving and voluntary work. Of the 568 men from the town who volunteered in August and September 1914, 73 percent were from a working class background.[32] In Hertfordshire the Scouts over 14 (the minimum working age) were quick to respond providing a 24 hours a day cover for the army, fire brigade, police, ambulance service and local council.[33] This was typical of an impromptu and impressive response, both in voluntary and military terms to the advent of war throughout the country. The spontaneity of this response was typical but, like officer recruitment, lacked effective control and direction.

British society and the army were unprepared to fight a war in the way envisioned by Kitchener so it is not surprising that the development of an approach to recruiting officers was haphazard and rapidly evolving. On 10 August an appeal was made for 2,000 officers; *The Times* contained an announcement from the War Office that it required 2,000 unmarried men for commissions in the regular army. It asked for men who were, or had been, cadets in university OTCs or had a good general education.[34] The War Office also wrote to potential candidates; Philip Howe, the Old Uppinghamian (OU), who had graduated from Sheffield University and served in its OTC contingent, received a letter inviting him to apply for a commission. The policy of the War Office to recruit gentlemen as officers was clear but somewhat simplistic.[35] On 12 August the formation of the New Army was announced in the press.[36] The applications for commissions to the War Office far exceeded the 2,000 initially requested on 10 August.[37] Major J.G. Dooner, who was responsible for the OTC, explained to the December 1914 meeting of the HMC the effect on the War Office of the 14,000 applications for commissions which had arrived in the first post after the New Army was announced. Only able to review 150 applications a day it had taken nearly three months for the War Office to weed out unsuitable candidates.[38] Those applying for commissions in response to the initial call for volunteers had simply ignored the statement that it was directed at members of the OTC. Stripped of the OTC membership requirement the criteria were general in nature. Candidates should be aged between 17 and 30, single, physically fit and have a good education.[39] In order to speed up the recruitment of officers, the power of nomination was devolved from the War Office

---

32 Derek Whitfield, 'To what extent and why did the voluntary ethic characterise Winchester's response to war in 1914 and 1915?' (MA dissertation, Birmingham 2015).
33 *Everyday Lives in the War, Research in Brief – Scouting in the First World War* <https://everydaylivesinwar.herts.ac.uk/2015/04/scouting-in-the-first-world-war-contributed-by-frank-brittain-county-archivist-for-hertfordshire-scouts/> (accessed 30 April 2020).
34 *The Times*, 10 August 1914, p. 5.
35 Christopher Moore-Bick, *Playing the Game: The British Junior Infantry Officer on the Western Front 1914-18* (Solihull: Helion 2011) p. 19.
36 Simkins, *Kitchener's Army*, p. 40.
37 Ibid., p. 213.
38 HMC, Report of the Headmasters' Conference December 1914, pp. 60-62.
39 TNA WO 293/1/70: Temporary Commissions, 12 August 1914.

to the battalion commanding officers. While membership of the OTC and especially possession of Certificate A remained important in the War Office's selection of candidates, this was unlikely to meet the demand for officers. Not every OTC member had attempted Certificate A and, of those who had, not all had passed. At Uppingham by the time war broke out 499 OTC cadets had been eligible to attempt Certificate A. Of these it is estimated 103 sat the papers of whom 69 had passed (i.e. 13.4 percent of those eligible).[40] Uppingham appears to have been a relatively strong unit so the participation and pass rates are likely to have been higher than many schools but extrapolating this pass rate, to the total number of Junior OTC members who had enlisted by March 1915, implies in the region of 5,600 of them had passed Certificate A. Even this optimistic estimate was not enough to meet the army's requirement for officers. The Lieutenant Colonels who were an important part of officer recruitment in the early months cast their nets wider than the OTC.[41] The evidence suggests that even the War Office's general specification for suitable candidates, whether or not they were members of the OTC, was placed to one side and it led to men with a variety of backgrounds being granted commissions. Battalion COs were left to judge for themselves what constituted a suitable candidate (and gentleman). Their recommendation for a commission was almost always accepted by the War Office. In these circumstances there was inevitably a combination of factors which led to a successful application for a commission. This included membership of the OTC, the sort of school attended, having the right connections and sometimes even bribery.

That many of the men who attended the camp organised by Winchester received commissions reflects this overwhelming and urgent need for junior officers to lead the New Army. Even OTC members who knew they would be favoured in the selection of cadets were prepared to take short cuts to get a commission. Greenwell, who attended the camp, asked a neighbour, Sir Beachcroft Towse VC, to assist him and as a result the latter's contacts at the War Office, Greenwell's commission was gazetted on 1 October 1914. In reality, he said, he had already been carrying out officer duties for a month.[42] This arrangement did have some logic. An instruction from the War Office on 11 September 1914 said cadet officers from the OTC would be ordered to join their battalions immediately (before their name appeared in the Gazette) to act as instructors to recruits. This it was hoped would compensate for the shortage of NCOs.[43] It is likely that this instruction was the formalisation of a practice which already existed. The army urgently needed men to train the new recruits and those with OTC experience were pressed into service as quickly as possible. Others were granted commissions on the basis of previous military experience outside the OTC

---

40 Analysis based on USA, Junior Division Officers Training Corps Uppingham School Contingent and Files of R. Sterndale-Bennett (1910-1921).
41 HMC, Report of the Headmasters' Conference December 1914, pp. 60-62.
42 IWM, 8766, Greenwell.
43 TNA WO 293/1/152: Officers from O.T.C. to Act as Instructors to Recruits, 11 September 1914.

and local connections. Captain William Satterthwaite, educated at Uppingham from 1893 to 1895, and a director of a silk spinner, had been a member of the Volunteers between 1902 and 1907. In September 1914 he applied for a commission with the 2/5th Kings Own where he was known to many of the men he commanded.[44] Others were granted commissions despite having no previous military experience. Raymond Asquith, who was one of the older men who struggled with drill at the camp attended by Greenwell was gazetted as a Second Lieutenant in the Queen's Westminster Rifles in December 1914.[45]

Connections of various types were often important in speeding up the process of gaining a commission. The father of Arnold and Cyril Christopherson, W.B. Christopherson, a doctor at Barts, used legal connections to help his sons to gain commissions. On 9 December 1914, H.W. Host of 6 Grays Inn Square wrote to him to report that a James Roche had arranged for Colonel Ommaney of the 12th Service Battalion, Welsh Regiment to sign the required forms and make the necessary arrangements for the two men to be gazetted to his regiment.[46] This was, no doubt, a mutually acceptable agreement; Christopherson had gained his sons a commission and the status that went with it, and Ommaney had dealt with part of the responsibility devolved to him of finding officers for his battalion.

Local connections were also used to attempt to recruit officers. The Sedbergh magazine of November 1914 included a notice from the 3rd (Special Reserve) Battalion the King's Own Regiment, based in peacetime at nearby Lancaster, inviting applications for commissions. It also offered reductions in probationary training for holders of Certificate A (and B). Demonstrating the variations in approach to recruiting officers, the notice set an age range of 17 to 25 (and not 30 as the War Office had done in August).[47] Local connections were often tenuous but used to gain commissions quickly; Oscar Hornung who had left Eton to read history at Cambridge and was living in Essex went to his nearest barracks believing joining a reserve regiment was the best way to get to the front and was one of many to gain a commission on 15 August 1914. Like Greenwell he waited a month to have his commission in the 3rd Essex gazetted although he was already serving.[48]

OTC experience helped but in the rush to appoint officers, it is difficult to identify even an informal methodology. Analysing the recruitment of cadets from the Junior OTC demonstrates how any attempt to apply a model to junior officer recruitment and explain it in terms of being the *alumnus* of a public school is flawed. By March 1915, at least 16,000 former cadets from Junior OTC contingents had been

---

44   Ellen War Memorial (Volume One) cited in Email, Shaun Corkerry, 8April 2020.
45   *London Gazette*, Supplement 29027, 1 January 1915 p. 132.
46   TNA WO 339/17833: Lieutenant Arnold Bayley Christopherson. The Welsh Regiment.
47   *The Sedberghian*, Vol. XXXV., No. 5. November 1914, p. 218.
48   *Eton College Chronicle*, No. 1537. 22 July 1915, p. 852 and E.W. Hornung, *'Trusty and Well Beloved' The Little Record of Arthur Oscar Hornung, Second Lieutenant 3rd (attached 2nd) Essex* Regiment (Privately published, 1915), p. 1.

awarded commissions. However, the proportion of candidates who enlisted and were granted commissions varied a great deal. At Harrow, the 370 former cadets had all been granted commissions whereas in the case of Wellington School in Somerset only 43 of the 105 who had enlisted had won commissions. Indeed, the 10 leading schools which contributed the most officers to the army before the war (Charterhouse, Cheltenham, Clifton, Eton, Haileybury, Harrow, Marlborough, Rugby, Wellington College and Winchester) provided 38 percent of OTC cadets who held a commission by March 1915. In total, they provided just under 21 percent of all OTC cadets recruited during the period demonstrating that the cadets of the ten leading schools were far more likely to be awarded commissions; 94 percent of the cadets from the ten leading schools were awarded commissions by March 1915. The cadets from these schools were a known quantity to the army and as Greenwell showed likely to have strong connections with the army, therefore it is no surprise it significantly drew on these schools for cadets.

Further analysis reveals that 59 schools had had over 75 percent of their former OTC cadets accepted for commissions by March 1915. These 59 schools made up 36 percent of the 166 schools with OTC contingents in March 1915, but provided 67 percent of the cadets from the Junior OTC who gained commissions by March 1915. In other words, just over one third of the OTC contingents had provided more than two thirds of OTC officers. The table below shows a sample of 13 schools with an OTC during the Great War. From this sample can be seen the dangers of taking a one-size-fits-all approach to understanding the contribution of the OTC and public schools to providing officers for the new army. Of the 166 schools with OTC contingents in March 1915, 90 were members of the Headmaster's Conference (HMC) and generally recognised as public schools. Of the 59 schools where over 75 percent of their cadets had been awarded commissions by March 1915, only 44 of them were members of the HMC. In other words, less than half of the public schools had converted the vast majority of their OTC cadets into officers by March 1915. Indeed, of the 59 OTC contingents which had had done so, 25 percent were not members of the HMC at all. In other words, there was a not a straightforward prejudice within the army towards those contingents with a public school background.

Table Two summarises the contribution of officers to the army with a selection of schools with different backgrounds who had Junior OTC contingents. 11 of the 13 schools were members of the HMC. Two of the schools, Eton and Shrewsbury, were Cavendish schools (considered to be one of the nine original public schools with Eton also being a leading army school). Oakham, Oundle, Tonbridge and Uppingham were originally endowed grammar schools which the Taunton Commission had investigated and been reformed as a result of the Endowed Schools Act. The remaining HMC schools were all founded in the 19th Century and formed part of the expansion of the public school network and were not in Honey's group of the 22 leading schools. Of the two schools which were not members of the HMC, Worksop was one of the group of boarding schools established by Woodard, of which Lancing was at the head.

Table 2 Enlistment Analysis – Selection of Junior OTC Contingents[49]

	Former Cadets Officers at Aug 14	Commissions Aug-14 to March 15	Serving in the Ranks March 15	Total Enlisted to March 15	Commissions to March 15	Officers as % of Total
Eastbourne College*	70	53	230	353	123	34.8%
Epsom*	17	53	47	117	70	59.8%
Eton*	145	850	13	1,008	995	98.7%
Grimsby Municipal College	0	25	0	25	25	100.0%
Lancing College*	59	143	41	243	202	83.1%
Mill Hill*	6	62	350	418	68	16.3%
Oakham*	46	65	17	128	111	86.7%
Oundle School*	29	197	75	301	226	75.1%
Shrewsbury*	30	198	67	295	228	77.3%
Stonyhurst*	21	79	27	127	100	78.7%
Tonbridge*	74	176	131	381	250	65.6%
Uppingham School*	61	215	74	350	276	78.9%
Worksop College	2	55	98	155	57	36.8%

*Member of the HMC in August 1914

The figures reinforce the uneven nature of the early stages of officer recruitment. By the end of the war the ratio of old boys who had become officers would be far higher for many schools, but the figures to 1915 demonstrate the unevenness of recruitment. Tonbridge and Uppingham were similar in background and ranking (both Honey Class I) and yet had significantly different ratios of OTC cadets who had become officers (65.6 percent vs 78.9 percent). Eastbourne and Lancing were both Class II schools but the ratios for cadets becoming officers varied even more dramatically (35.8 percent vs 83.1 percent). Epsom (Class III) with an officer ratio of 59.8 percent and Oundle (Class IV) whose comparative figure of 75.1 percent both appear to have performed better than Eastbourne. The two schools Mill Hill and Stonyhurst who were not Anglican further demonstrate this diversity in the early stages of the war. Mill Hill with a non-militaristic tradition had 16.3 percent of its cadets become officers by March 1915 despite its strong response to the outbreak of the war while Stonyhurst (like Mill Hill unclassified by Honey) had 78.7 percent of its cadets become officers.

Review of some the of schools in this group in more detail demonstrates some of the factors which led to the apparent uneven performance in providing officers. Grimsby

---

49 The table and accompanying commentary are based on analysis of Haig-Brown, *The O.T.C. and The Great War*, pp. 97-106.

Municipal College OTC demonstrates that the selection of officers went beyond relying on the top 'army' schools. Its cadets provided many officers to the local Pals battalion, the 'Grimsby Chums'. The elevation of these cadets to commissions was in response to the unique character of the Pals battalions and the unusual circumstances of Grimsby. Its Principal and CO of its OTC contingent, Ernest Stream (a former Volunteer) along with the Town's Mayor, Alderman Tate, was the leading figure in establishing the Chums.[50] Grimsby, a fishing town, had only expanded in the 1850s with the arrival of the railway and was to all intents and purposes a new town. As a result, there was a limited tradition of wealthy local men sending their sons away to public school. Some of the town's wealthy Non-Conformists sent their sons to Mill Hill. Consequently, many of the town's young men were educated locally, continued to live in Grimsby and did not have a background which the army would normally have expected of a gentleman (and junior officer). The nature of the Pals battalions was that they were based on a shared background, such as a regional identity or common place of work. It was natural, therefore, for the Pals officers to come from the same background. The existence of an OTC in Grimsby provided an obvious source of officers for the Chums. All 25 cadets from the college's OTC had gained commissions by March 1915, almost certainly because they were judged to have an adequate mix of skills and local background to make them suitable officers. Officers for the Chums were also drawn from Worksop College.[51] As will be noted from Table 2, by March 1915 only 36.8 percent of its OTC cadets had become officers. While Worksop's old boys provided some officers to the Chums the importance of local connections is demonstrated by all of the Municipal College's cadets having gained a commission by March 1915.

Although the national OTC had been designed to provide common and integrated training for potential officers it is clear from the example of Stream and others that dynamic leadership was important in providing effective training. The CO of Lancing College OTC, Alan Haig Brown, was a leading figure in the OTC movement and in 1915 published *The O.T.C. and The Great War* which celebrated the movement's contribution to the war. He was CO of the College's OTC from its formation in 1908 to 1915 when he left to serve with the army. At Lancing, it is claimed that the contingent was the first one where every boy was a member on a voluntary basis.[52] As noted in the previous chapter, it is likely the alternative to joining the OTC was less attractive but there is no doubt that Haig Brown was an inspiring figure.[53] In many schools, such as Winchester and Uppingham, where there was more choice about joining their OTC contingent, many chose not to.[54]

---

50 *Grimsby Evening Telegraph*, 14 July 2014, p. 19.
51 Peter Chapman (2015) 'Grimsby Chums', 3 July 2015 correspondence.
52 Lancing College War Memorial Lieutenant Colonel Alan Roderick Haig-Brown DSO <http://www.hambo.org/lancing/view_man.php?id=132> (accessed 31 December 2016).
53 Handford, *Lancing College,* p. 134.
54 See Chapter 3.

The recruitment of officers from a restricted range of OTC contingents points to their reputation and efficiency being an important factor. The War Office carried out annual inspections of all OTC contingents; this was not just a cursory examination but a thorough exercise to confirm their efficiency. As noted in Chapter Three, the unflattering inspection report in the summer of 1914 for the Fettes contingent demonstrated that these reports were not bland and uncritical (in contrast Uppingham's report for 1914 was complementary). From these reports, the War Office developed a strong impression as to which were the best contingents. The reputation and background of the school was not the only factor in judging its efficiency. Oakham, just under 87 percent of whose cadets had become officers by March 1915, had no military tradition and was far from a typical public school. Although a founder member of the HMC in 1869 it had then left the organisation, as its fortunes waned at the same time as nearby Uppingham expanded under Thring. It had only been readmitted into the HMC in 1911 after the school's decline was halted by the awarding of direct grant status so that it became Rutland's grammar school as well as a boarding school. The OTC at Oakham was only established in 1911; unlike many other schools it had not established a rifle corps. Nearby Oundle had established one in 1903 after the Boer War, which had then become part of the OTC in 1908. The Headmaster of Oakham had decided in 1911 that the interesting training provided by the OTC made it a useful addition to the school's curriculum; the same year he had also increased the amount of Army Class work at the school.[55] That 111 of its 128 cadets who had enlisted had gained commissions by March 1915, when many other schools with a longer military tradition lagged behind, indicates that Oakham's OTC contingent and its Army Class was highly regarded. Eastbourne College had established a Corps in 1896 and had an Army Class but as the table shows only 34.8 percent of its OTC cadets had been granted commissions by March 1915.[56]

Nevertheless, the reputation of a school still played an important part in its success at providing men to take up commissions. Oundle under Sanderson had gained a reputation for its emphasis on the sciences and bringing the best out of every boy.[57] In early 1915 Cecil Lewis was interviewed for a commission by Captain Lord Hugh Cecil. The latter clearly held Sanderson in high esteem and the connection was of great assistance in gaining Lewis a commission, despite being underage.[58] This reputation rubbed off on other old boys from Oundle; boys who had not served in the OTC, although they may have served in the Rifle Corps, were clearly attractive to recruiters because of the school's reputation. By March 1915 Oundle had provided 301 former OTC cadets to the army, of whom 226 had gained commissions. The figures for Oundle show that many who had not served in the OTC had enlisted and become

---

55 *Grantham Journal*, 5 August 1911, p. 2.
56 Haig-Brown, *The O.T.C. and The Great War*, p. 5 and IWM 9275, Heath, Charles Philip (Oral History).
57 Palmer, *The Life of F. W. Sanderson*, pp. 365-366.
58 Cecil Lewis, *Sagittarius Rising* (London: Penguin, 1977), pp. 18-19.

officers. By November 1914, 440 men had enlisted. A year later, in November 1915, the figure had risen to 657; 45 of whom had been killed in action.[59] The recruitment figures for Uppingham demonstrate that many who served had no OTC experience. This included those who had preferred sport to the OTC, such as George Horridge who was at school from 1908 to 1912 after the OTC had been established. Others such as Hugo Burnaby who had been an Imperial Yeomanry officer during the Boer War, had made the mistake of applying formally to the War Office for a commission. He was rejected on the grounds of his age, 40, but not deterred he successfully applied directly for a commission to the Durham Light Infantry.[60] Charles Mott, a 44-year-old solicitor at the outbreak of war, had no military experience but was as determined as Burnaby to serve. Being told he was too old did not deter him and using a contact at the War Office he secured a commission with the Army Service Corps (ASC).[61] Only 37 percent of those from Uppingham who served in the Great War had been OTC cadets, yet more than 77 percent of OUs who joined the army became junior officers. It is clear that junior officers were drawn from a wider catchment than merely the OTC. Indeed, by February 1916 and the introduction of conscription, an impressive 77 percent of all the OUs who served in the war had already enlisted.[62] At Oundle by November 1915 64 percent of those who served in the war had already enlisted.[63]

The development of the junior officer corps by the end of 1915 suggests that there was some sort of unofficial approach to officer recruitment, if not a formally documented one. It would appear that although the army did use some criteria in the recruitment of many officers this was not set in stone. More nuanced judgements were also made about the suitability of men to be officers. The case of St George's, Harpenden illustrates how this could work. Founded in 1907, St Georges was the first co-educational boarding school and in 1914 was not yet a member of the HMC. It did not have an OTC contingent, instead having a Cadet Corps unit; the Cadet Corps was designed to prepare men to be soldiers whereas the OTC was designed to prepare men to be officers. Therefore, it would appear St Georges was unlikely to be a good source of officers, especially as it was a relatively small school. However, during the war, of the 106 boys who served 59 (56 percent) became officers.[64] To place some context on this, of those old boys from Wellington School, Somerset, which had an OTC contingent before the war, only 39 percent were awarded commissions.[65] By the end

---

59 Palmer, *The Life of F. W. Sanderson*, p. 219.
60 Halstead, *A School in Arms*, p. 76.
61 John Mott email corrspondence, 'OUs in WW1', 7 January 2015.
62 Halstead, 'The First World and Public School Ethos: The Case of Uppingham School', pp. 222, 224.
63 Figure based on analysis of *Oundle Memorials of the Great War MCMXIV-MCMXIX* (Privately published: Oundle, 1920) and Palmer, *The Life of F. W. Sanderson*, p. 219.
64 Based on analysis of *The Great War 1914-1919: Old Georgians' Roll of Honour and Record of Service* (Privately published: undated).
65 Based on analysis of Asher C. J. Pirt MA, *WSS Old Boys and the Great War 1914-1918* (Watchett: Privately published, 2013).

of 1915, at least 24 Old Georgians (41 percent of those gazetted during the war) had been granted commissions.[66] Examination of officer files for Old Georgians suggests a variety of reasons for this decision. In some cases, it was because they were members of a University OTC. Some had brief experience of service in another school's OTC contingent. Others still were chosen simply because they had the right background. Old Georgians nearly all had a professional or middle-class background.[67] The boys of Wellington, Somerset were drawn from an agricultural background.[68] In addition to the more professional and commercial background of its pupils, St Georges had a distinctive educational ethos. The front page of its first prospectus in 1907 contained a long extract from Thring of Uppingham's educational ethos.[69] At the heart of Thring's approach to education was an aim to bring out the best in every boy so that they possessed independence, inquisitiveness, and self-confidence.[70] Men who displayed these qualities were attractive material to the army.[71] One of these men was Phillips Muirhead, who was awarded a commission in October 1914 after enlisting the month before. It has been suggested that Muirhead did not care for being in the ranks and that strings were pulled to get him a commission.[72] However, if strings were pulled it appears that it was easy to pull them to great effect. A letter from the Royal Horse Artillery, Woolwich (the signature is indecipherable) makes enquiries about whether his application is likely to be successful. The writer describes him as being 'an intelligent fellow well above the normal gunner.' As further support the letter points out that Muirhead had been captain of the St Georges rugby team and had also played for his county. Sporting ability was a further qualification which could only help him to find a way through the heavy load of commission applications the War Office was handling.[73]

Sports qualifications were not the only path to a commission, especially as the war proceeded. Arthur Francis Scroggs had seen a short period of service with the St Pauls OTC; but the use of Form MT393 (which was for men who had not served in the OTC) to apply for a commission demonstrates it was not long enough to count. His file recommends him for a commission on the grounds that he was a mathematician

---

66 Based on analysis of *The Great War 1914-1919 Old Georgians' Roll of Honour and Record of Service*, St Georges School Archive (SGSA).
67 Storrie, *"Here I am; Send me"*, p. 1.
68 J. de Symons Honey, *Tom Brown's Universe: The Development of the Victorian Public School* (London: Millington, 1977), p. 68.
69 SGSA: 1907 Prospectus.
70 Halstead, 'The First World and Public School Ethos: The Case of Uppingham School', p. 227.
71 There is an indirect connection to Uppingham. A major figure in the governance of St Georges was Canon Hardwicke Rawnsley (one of the founders of the National Trust) who was an OU and protégé of Thring. See Malcolm Tozer, *The Ideal of Manliness: The Legacy of Thring's Uppingham* (Truro: Sunnyrest Books, 2015), passim.
72 Storrie, *"Here I am; Send me"*, p. 44.
73 TNA WO 339/17988: Lieutenant Phillips Quincy Muirhead, Royal Field Artillery.

and had a scholarship to Merton. With this background, he was granted a commission in the Royal Garrison Artillery where mathematical ability was a much-needed skill.[74]

Other Old Georgians were able to draw on social connections and enrol with the socially exclusive Artists' Rifles. The Artists' Rifles, which rapidly became an OTC unit, had to use unconventional methods to select men. When war broke out the regiment searched the London telephone book for men with socially acceptable addresses. The men identified were sent handwritten invitations to join the regiment. However, the response was overwhelming and large crowds gathered outside the barracks. Unable to handle the volume of enquirers, some NCOs changed into civilian clothing and mixed with the crowds, giving out written invitations to those who appeared suitable to attend an interview the next day. The rest were left to look elsewhere.[75] Given the elite background of the Artists the vast majority of the men recruited were quickly awarded commissions.

By December 1914 the devolved system of recruitment was leading to some battalion COs to pursue their own interests ahead of the need of the army to recruit men to be junior officers. The 16th Public School Battalion (PSB) lost many new recruits who with their educational background were recognised as potential officer material by other battalions and were offered commissions with them. For the CO, Lieutenant Colonel Hall, like other COs his main object was to assemble an effective fighting unit which he could take to France at the earliest opportunity. Fearing his battalion would never to get to the front because of the high turnover Hall tried to block this by declining to forward to the War Office applications to become officers; some candidates were forced into desperate measures to gain a commission. Charles Lawson was only successful because he found a replacement by visiting a recruiting office and giving the Recruiting Sergeant ten shillings for his next recruit![76] The delegation of recruitment also meant there was no formal assessment of men to assess their aptitude to be officers and occasionally men who gained commissions fell short of the mark and had to be removed. Maurice Ellinger of the 9th Service Battalion of the Sherwood Foresters was allowed to resign his commission after two attempts at suicide by drug overdose on 6 and 9 November 1914. The original intention had been to remove him from the regiment on the grounds he was unlikely to be an efficient officer, but after lobbying from his father the army agreed to allow him to resign on grounds of ill-health to protect his career.[77] Nevertheless, it is noticeable how few officers were removed or allowed to resign because they were not up to the job.

---

74   TNA WO 339/72553: Lieutenant Arthur Francis Scroggs, Royal Garrison Artillery.
75   Barry Gregory, *A History of the Artists Rifles 1859-1947* (Barnsley: Pen and Sword, 2006), pp. 122-123.
76   Steve Hurst, *The Public Schools Battalion in The Great War* (Barnsley: Pen and Sword, 2007), pp. 27-28.
77   *London Gazette*, 29 December 1914, p. 11145. The Sherwood Foresters, Nottinghamshire & Derbyshire Regiment.

A More Formal Process

When the HMC met in December 1914, it is clear that they wished to offer whatever co-operation they could rather than quibble about the War Office's approach, in contrast to the at times fractious relationship between the two bodies. Lyttleton of Eton remarked that from his dealings with the War Office it was 'in a state of very great confusion and overwork' which had been 'overwhelming.'[78] The view of the Chairman that this was not the time to 'cavil' at how the War Office was conducting itself. It was a view from which there was no dissent. Cases such as that of Ellinger were causing concern to the headmasters and this was raised with Major Dooner. He responded saying that the War Office was keen to have the views of headmasters and OTC COs about candidates. It wanted them to have 'the opportunity of putting forward any candidates they thought ought to have Commissions, and at the same time calling our attention to any candidates they thought ought not to have Commissions.' Dooner was sympathetic to the headmasters' concerns. Unfortunately, a system to provide headmasters with a list of candidates for them to comment on their suitability appeared not to have worked.[79] It was not only the problem of unsuitable old boys gaining commissions which concerned the meeting. Such was the pressure on the recruitment system that many suitable candidates were enlisting because of the delays in reaching a decision about awarding them a commission.[80] A choice made easier by the existence of socially elite units such as the PSBs. The priority of many of those volunteering was to serve in whatever way they could as quickly as possible. Getting to the front was more important than becoming an officer. This enthusiasm flew in the face of Dooner's already stated view that he did not want boys to enlist; it was more important they became officers. He recognised that the existence of the PSBs, and other socially elite battalions, was one cause of this problem and had stated that he was he was in favour of disbanding them. However, this was not the unanimous view of everyone in the War Office.[81] The problem was still upmost in the minds of headmasters at the HMC meeting of 1915. Forming *corps d'elite* was leading to old boys being wasted unnecessarily. A. L. Francis, Headmaster of Blundells, reported that in one action the socially elite Liverpool Scottish more men had been lost 'than could be replaced by one entry for Woolwich and Sandhurst.'[82]

What was clear that the War Office had been forced, by the sheer volume of applications to be an officer, to devolve, to battalion COs, its power to appoint officers as a temporary expedient. As an improvised system it had created many anomalies and enabled guidance from the War Office to be often ignored but it nevertheless produced an impressive number of suitable candidates. By the end of 1914 the War Office had cleared its backlog

---

78 HMC, Report of the Headmasters' Conference December 1914, pp. 49-50.
79 HMC, Report of the Headmasters' Conference December 1914, p. 58.
80 HMC, Report of the Headmasters' Conference December 1914, p. 54.
81 HMC, Report of the Headmasters' Conference December 1914, pp. 52-53.
82 HMC, Report of the Headmasters' Conference December 1915, p. 73.

and reclaimed control of officer recruitment. As discussed above, in the case of Oundle and Uppingham a significant proportion of their old boys who became officers had not served in the OTC. This was the case for many of the public schools. However, the War Office regarded the OTC as an important source of future junior officers and from the point of view of the public schools providing suitable candidates from their contingents was their primary concern. Major Dooner had made it quite clear that high importance was placed on the OTC as a source of officers for the whole war.

As a result, the OTC became more prominent in the announcement of commissions in the *London Gazette*. From early 1915 these announcements often reported that the candidate was an OTC cadet or ex-cadet. For example, taking two days, on 9 April 1915 the *Gazette* announced that 52 cadets or ex-cadets were to be temporary Second Lieutenants and on 25 June 1915 59 names were announced.[83] Those who had served in the OTC already had an advantage, as Greenwell had observed of the camp organised by Winchester. The integrated programme meant that they already had other advantages over other new officers. The summary of the syllabus for the training of new officers issued by the War Office on 20 August 1914 laid down subjects which would already be familiar to OTC cadets.[84] This gave OTC cadets a significant advantage. Hugh Peachey, who had served in the Boer War and volunteered again in 1914, discussing the examinations he needed to pass to confirm his commission, observed that not one man over 30 had passed yet but 'schoolboys and Sandhurst cadets have it at their fingertips' when it came to passing them.[85] To reinforce, this the Artists Rifles became an OTC contingent responsible for training candidates from TF courses for commissions. As an incentive, all those attached to this unit would receive the pay and allowances of a Second Lieutenant.[86] Shortly afterwards, other senior OTC contingents such as the Inns of Court were also given the responsibility of providing this month-long course.[87] However, the option of joining a battalion directly remained, although by December 1915 some but not all headmasters were strongly encouraging their boys to join the Inns of Court OTC before joining another unit.[88]

The resumption of control of officer recruitment by the War Office, therefore, did not mean that there was complete consistency in the way men were accepted for a commission. In 1914 there had been many cases where men who did not meet the medical criteria were still gazetted. Roland Leighton, after being refused a commission on the grounds of his poor eyesight, was able to gain a commission in the Worcester Regiment through connections he had developed.[89] Delegating officer

---

83 *London Gazette,* 9 April 1915 pp. 3454-3455 and 25 June 1915 p. 6174.
84 TNA WO 293/1/160: Elementary Training of Young Infantry Officers, 20 August 1914.
85 London Metropolitan Archives, F/PEY 261, *Peachey Papers*, Letter to Steph October 1914.
86 TNA WO 293/1/29: Artists Rifles formed into an Officers Training Battalion, 31 December 1914.
87 Lewis-Stempel, *Six Weeks*, p. 53.
88 HMC, Report of the Headmasters' Conference December 1915, pp. 50-52.
89 Don Farr, *None That Go Return* (Solihull: Helion, 2010), pp. 61-62.

recruitment to battalion COs made it easier to circumvent requirements but even in 1915 candidates who did not meet the medical criteria were granted commissions. Ronald Barnes (later Lord Gorrell), educated at Winchester and Harrow, was refused a commission in 1914 on account of his poor eyesight. In 1915 eyesight requirements had been relaxed by the army so he tried again for a commission. He passed his medical which he described as an 'awful swindle.' The medical officer gave him plenty of opportunity to memorise the board before testing him.[90] If medical requirements were ignored so were age requirements. Frederick Jackson Widdowson, although not educated at a public school, had taught at Christ's Hospital since 1902 and been CO of its Corps and OTC until 1909.[91] Aged 47 in 1915, which was well outside the age criteria for officers, he was gazetted to the Durham Light Infantry on 24 September to his former rank of Captain in the Royal Sussex Regiment.[92] Even in late 1915 there was a shortage of officer material and a man with a public school connection was valuable enough for the normal rules to be waived, and him to leave the school at short notice.[93] A system of volunteering while being in sympathy with pre-war political consensus was not geared up to serving the needs of total war where resources needed to be directed more efficiently and effectively.

During 1915 the Director of Military Training (DMT), Sir Frederick Heath-Caldwell, estimated that 45,000 'young officers' had received training.[94] Until the end of 1915 the demand for officers outstripped the supply of candidates and shortcuts continued to be taken to appoint junior officers. Only at the end of 1915 was it considered that there was a sufficient reserve of infantry officers. As a result, it was ruled that temporary commissions in the infantry would only be given to men who had served in the ranks or been through the Artists' or Inns of Court OTC.[95] From February 1916, the introduction of Officer Cadet Battalions (OCB) and conscription provided a greater element of quality control for new officers. Men could no longer apply directly for commissions and either had to come from the ranks or the OTC. All the cadets in an OCB underwent a four-and-a-half-month training course with a commission only being granted if the course was successfully completed. This was, however, the formalisation of a system to identify gentlemen (temporary or otherwise) to lead the army. It would not be until the Second World War that the British army introduced aptitude tests for officer candidates.

---

90 Beach, *Lord Gorrell*, pp. 4-5.
91 *The Blue*, Vol. XLIII., No. 1. October 1915, p. 2 and p. 13.
92 John Venn, Alumni Cantabrigienses: *A Biographical List of All Known Students, Graduates and Holders of Office at the University of Cambridge, from the Earliest Times to 1900* (Cambridge: Cambridge University Press, 2011), passim. p. 458; and *London Gazette*, 24 September 1915, p. 9442.
93 *The Blue*, Vol. XLIII., No. 1. October 1915, p. 13.
94 *The Times*, 20 September 1945 p. 7 and Lancing Maj General Frederick Crofton Heath-Caldwell CB Royal Engineers and Royal Air Force 1858-1914 <https://www.jjhc.info/heathcaldwellfc1945> (accessed 6 May 2020).
95 HMC, Report of the Committee of the Headmasters' Conference for 1915, p. 147.

Conclusion

In popular culture, the perception of the First World War junior officer is coloured by characters such as *Blackadder's* the Honourable George Colthurst St. Barleigh, who is portrayed as a parody of the public school officer, being brave but profoundly stupid. He cannot wait to encounter Germans but lacks the skills to be an effective leader, as Captain Blackadder is not slow to point out. This chapter argues that this is a gross distortion of many young men who became junior officers. Those who had service in the OTC had received training which was integrated into the army's wider scheme. Within the OTC scheme the army appears to have concentrated on recruiting from the most efficient contingents. Men gained commissions not only because of their background but also because of the effectiveness of their OTC training and general education. However, from 1916 it became clear that being the *alumnus* of a public school was not the guarantee of a commission.

It was the recruitment and training activities of 1914 and 1915 which built the junior officer corps which was in place at the start of 1916. The lack of preparation for total war in 1914 meant that there was no adequate system for rapidly recruiting and training Kitchener's New Armies. To build a citizen army quickly a great deal of improvisation was required. However, despite appearances, the approach to recruiting officers was not entirely unstructured. The evidence suggests that the more efficient OTC contingents were favoured as a source for the recruitment of officers, especially up to March 1915. The army wanted gentlemen to be officers but as the case of St Georges demonstrates, was prepared to exercise some flexibility in finding suitable men. There was no specific formula up to that point which led to a totally unquestioning recruitment of public school boys and cadets from the OTC. Guy Chapman compared his development as an officer up to the middle of 1916 as being forced to grow 'like a plant in a hot house.'[96] Training of officers was unsystematic and often took place on the job. As 1915 progressed and some order was brought to affairs a more formal approach to recruitment and training developed. The men who took on commissions in 1914 and 1915 were still relatively raw in 1916. However, in the 'hot house' they had developed skills which would form the basis, with the greatly improved training from 1917, of the men who led the British army to victory in November 1918.

Public schools had played an important part in building the junior officer corps of January 1916. While providing many men to lead in the army from the start of the war they also increased their commitment to the preparation of their boys to be officers. As with the recruitment of the officer corps this was improvised at the start of the war. However, between 1914 and 1918 it became more closely integrated into and closely directed by the Army. The evolution of this training is examined in the next two chapters.

---

96 Chapman, *A Passionate Prodigality*, pp. 138-139.

5

Drawing on Their Own Resources: Public School OTCs, 1914-1915

For the first two years of the war, a lack of support forced the public schools to fall on their own resources. The War Office (for the purposes of this and the following chapters, the War Office refers to the General Staff at the War Office, which oversaw the OTC) was overstretched and one of its immediate priorities was to train and prepare Kitchener's New Armies. With this lack of resources, it was happy to devolve junior officer training to the OTC contingents of the public schools. By using the OTC in this way, the War Office drew on those schools which had contingents. A significant minority of schools with OTC contingents were not HMC members (and by definition not public schools). Those HMC members who did not have a contingent were viewed by the War Office in a different light to those which had one. In the early stages of the war, the OTC was treated as a resource which would produce cadets almost ready to be officers and who could be used in other *ad hoc* tasks such as training the New Armies. This was a significant change to its pre-war purpose as it no longer acted as part of a progressive training scheme for potential officers. The provision of training for New Army officers was initially lacking and then haphazard; with officers and cadets often being used to provide training. This withdrawal of pre-war support, in August 1914, to the OTC was made worse by a lack of useful guidance to the Junior OTC contingents on the training they should be undertaking and it was only at the end of 1915 that the War Office was able to begin using the OTC in the manner it had intended before the war. From the end of 1915, it gradually began to provide the OTC with more meaningful guidance and useful support. The introduction of conscription in January 1916 gave the War Office far greater control over the recruitment of officers and the allocation of manpower. With these new powers and a temporarily adequate supply of junior officer reserves, the War Office no longer needed to unquestioningly accept OTC cadets as being suitable junior officer material.[1]

Kitchener had warned the Cabinet when recommending the creation of the New Army that it would take three years for it to reach a stage before it could make a

---

1   HMC, Report of the Committee of the Headmasters Conference for 1915, p. 147.

significant contribution to winning the war. Building the New Army required considerable resources and it was inevitable that other activities, such as the OTC, would suffer as a result and have to draw on their own resources in 1914-15. The result was an inefficient use of the OTC. Learning new military skills often arose from the OTC being deployed to provide training for New Army units rather than its officers being sent on courses. This could also lead to incongruities such as school boys providing training for adult men enlisted in the New Army. The urgent need for officers meant that, even in 1915, contingents lost their officers to the army and its cadets would be accepted on the basis of their membership of an OTC contingent and not necessarily because they were suitable. This and the next chapter discuss the involvement of Public Schools with OTC contingents in the training of their boys to be officers.

Drawing on an Elite

The junior officer corps of the British Army was by early 1916, predominantly, although not entirely made up of public school *alumni*. In the rush to recruit officers, these men were judged to be likely to have the right skills to lead men into battle but the suddenness of the war in 1914 meant that there was no opportunity to carefully identify suitable candidates. The British Army had deliberately been kept small pre-war with the government attaching greater political priority to funding areas such as social welfare. On Kitchener's advice the cabinet agreed in August 1914 to recruit a citizen army, but the pre-war policy of maintaining a small but professional force meant that it was ill-equipped to undertake this rapid expansion, thereby requiring a great deal of improvisation. Basil Williams believed the OTC was 'an admirable nursery for officers on the sudden expansion of the Army' but it did not have sufficient men to supply the need of officers, so commissions were also given to Public School *alumni* 'who, though they had not the O.T.C. training, seemed otherwise to be capable of command.'[2] Once the devolved system of officer recruitment, where battalion COs took responsibility, had ended in December 1914, the Public Schools and their OTC contingents became a key source for junior officers.

There were good reasons for the War Office giving priority to schools which had OTC contingents. Major J. G. Dooner, the officer responsible for the OTC at the War Office, told the December 1914 meeting of the HMC that 'the place for members of the Officers' Training Corps was as an officer and not in the ranks.'[3] It considered OTC cadets as an elite who were suitable to be officers, as they had received a form of technical training which was most likely to produce the most suitable candidates for a commission. While ethos may have been considered important, it played no formal

---

2   Captain Basil Williams, *Raising and Training the New Armies* (London: Constable & Company, 1918), p. 64.
3   HMC, Report of the Headmasters Conference December 1914, p. 60.

part in the criteria used to decide who would make suitable officers. One of the main points of tension between the schools and the army until 1911 was over the curriculum for the Army Entrance Examination. The army believed that a public school education did not equip cadets with enough of the knowledge and skills it required. Part of this gap was addressed with the establishment of the OTC which developed the practical (as opposed to theoretical) skills of boys. Importantly, the pre-war OTC formed part of a continuous and progressive scheme for officers. The Certificate A paper required a strong understanding of *FSR, 1909* and *Infantry Training, 1911*.⁴ The War Office was closely involved in directing the OTC's activities, both nationally and by individual contingent with its aim being to produce a consistently high standard of cadet across all contingents. All arrangements for Field Days required the approval of the War Office and it was closely involved in both their planning and execution.⁵ At a joint Field Day for five schools in November 1911 he exercises were set by Major A. Percival, who was attached to the section of the War Office which oversaw OTC activity. Percival and another officer, Major G. C. Merrick, attached to the same section, were both members of a six strong panel of umpires.⁶ It is clear that the War Office took a close interest in both how the Field Days were conducted as well as developing exercises all OTC contingents undertook. From examining school magazines and Army Council Instructions it is possible to identify clear themes for Field Day activities. For example, from the end of 1912 a major theme was giving cadets the opportunity to develop their leadership skills. Mill Hill's Field Days in November 1912 and February 1913 gave some of its section commanders an opportunity to gain experience in leadership and co-operation.⁷ In both 1913 and 1914 further examples of similar training can be found demonstrating the importance to the War Office of these exercises. In 1913, Rugby and Uppingham held a joint Field Day where the Section Commanders led the exercise, instead of the masters (and OTC officers) taking this role.⁸ At the Tonbridge Field Day in March 1914 the OTC officers stood aside to allow two of the contingent's cadet officers to lead the opposing sides.⁹

The development of leadership skills was not just confined to Section Commanders at Field Days. The instructions for the 1913 OTC Annual Camps placed importance on leadership skills as demonstrated by the instructions for the camps issued by the Army Council, which stated that 'all ranks, and not only Section Commanders and candidates for Certificate A, should be given opportunities of handling small parties of men.'¹⁰ An approach reinforced by the camps including special lectures by

---

4   War Office, *Field Service Regulations (FSR), 1909* and *Infantry Training 1911.*
5   *Regulations for the OTC*, pp. 17-18.
6   *USM*, No. 390, November 1911, pp. 200-203. Both officers were attached to M.T.3 (c).
7   *MHM*, Vol xl., No.4 December 1912, p. 140 and Vol xl., No.5 March 1913, p. 173.
8   *USM*, No. 403, July 1913, p. 171 and *The Meteor*, No. 564. Rugby July 18 1913., p. 73.
9   *The Tonbridgian*, Vol. XXI, No. 16 [No. 447] June 1914, pp. 489-490.
10   *Officers Training Corps. Junior Division: Instructions for the Annual Camps. 1913* (London: HMSO, 1913), p. 23.

regular Army officers which included 'The art of command' and 'Discipline, loyalty and example'.[11] If cadets were to be leaders of men they were to be given as many opportunities as possible to develop their leadership skills. While leadership skills were important there were a wide variety of other skills crucial to being an officer which needed to be developed. A wide range of training objectives were set by the War Office for OTC officers, Section Commanders and the rank and file at the 1913 Annual Camps.

The War Office actively promoted and oversaw, at a high level and by contingent, a scheme to produce potential officers with a view to producing a consistently high standard. Schools followed a uniform approach set by the War Office, no matter what their background was, to training under the direction of the War Office. Of the schools whose Field Days are discussed above, Mill Hill's OTC had only been established in 1911, Rugby was one of the leading providers of officer cadets to the Army while Tonbridge and Uppingham had long established and competent contingents whose Cadet Corps had been established in 1889 and 1892, respectively.[12] Whatever the military traditions of a school, they followed a similar approach. Thus, the use of joint Field Days between schools such as that, described above, in November 1911 were not uncommon. Mill Hill's Field Day in February 1912 was a joint one with at least four other London based school contingents. Schools with different backgrounds were able to work together and learn from each other. At the opposite end of the scale to Mill Hill, Harrow, with its strong military traditions also participated.[13] Joint exercises were not just confined to other schools and could be held with other arms such as the Royal Field Artillery.[14] All training was designed to equip cadets to address contemporary military problems. As illustrated by a question set in the Certificate A paper for November 1912: 'You have used up your supporting squad and have now only twenty men left in your trench. You see fresh troops of the enemy advance across the brook with bayonet fixed, they reach the firing line, and the whole pushes on towards the line of the trenches. What orders do you give?'[15] The OTC was not set up so its members could play at being soldiers, it was established to produce future regular and auxiliary officers.

The officers sent to carry out annual inspections at OTC contingents in 1914 reinforced this in their speeches to the contingents; urging cadets to take up commissions in the Special Reserves and the Territorials.[16] In the rush to arms in 1914, the OTC's approach to training formed the basis of junior officer training, even if its cadets were unable to meet the immediate needs of the army. The War Office's instructions for

---

11 *Junior Division. Instructions for the Annual Camps. 1913*, p. 6.
12 Halstead, *A School in Arms*, p. 49 and Haig-Brown, *The O.T.C. and The Great War*, p. 5.
13 *The Harrovian*, Vol XXVI. No. 1, Saturday 1 March 1913, p. 9.
14 *MHM*, Vol xl., No.5 March 1913, p. 173.
15 Rowland Ryder, *Oliver Leese*, (London: Hamish Hamilton, 1987), p. 9.
16 See for example *The Tonbridgian*, Vol. XXI, No. 17 [No. 448] July 1914, p. 527 and *The Malburian*, Vol. XLIX., No. 738. July 14th 1914, p. 114.

infantry officer training, issued on 20 August 1914 were such that cadets who had served in the OTC were put at an advantage. Notable for their extreme brevity (in total they filled one page of an A5 book and the details of the syllabus less than a quarter of the instructions), they identified five areas of study; two of which, *Infantry Training* and *Field Service Regulations Part I*, already formed part of the syllabus for Certificate A.[17] Peachey was right to observe that those officer cadets who had been enrolled in the OTC had a considerable advantage in officer examinations in 1914, which he as a Boer War veteran resented.[18] The coordinated and extensive pre-war training scheme gave substance to Dooner's view that the place of an OTC cadet was as an officer and not in the ranks.

In the confusion after war was declared, the War Office continued to promote the growth of the OTC. In the period from August to November, the War Office approved the establishment of a further six OTC contingents (three of which were HMC members).[19] That only half of these contingents could be regarded as based at a public school demonstrates that the War Office was not interested in public schools *per se* as a source of officers. It was interested in those schools which met the minimum requirements laid down in the regulations. The regulations set out a minimum requirement of 30 cadets and one commissioned officer per company.[20] They did not extend into the more esoteric criteria of the value of a public school education and the ethos instilled in their boys. The question was: did a school meet the minimum conditions to have a contingent or did it not? Many of the more established public schools did because they had the resources to run a contingent and had done so for a long time but some HMC members had chosen not to have a contingent before the war for a variety of reasons. By December 1914 the War Office had decided that there would be no further expansion of the OTC. New contingents would not be authorised and in addition it would not consent to an increase in the establishment of authorised contingents.[21]

This new approach was, almost certainly, the result of the huge increase in the volume of work the War Office faced as a result of the war.[22] At the outbreak of war many of the senior and junior officers on the War Office General Staff had gone to France with the BEF.[23] The logic of Dooner's explanation for this change demonstrates that significant decisions were being made on the hoof. He explained that the War Office's policy was to concentrate on those cadets who would become officers in

17   TNA, WO293/1/160, Elementary Training of Young Infantry Officers, 20 August 1914 and Appendix XIV. See Instn. 160).
18   See Chapter 4 and LMA, F/PEY 261, Peachey to Steph correspondence, October 1914.
19   Haig-Brown, *The O.T.C. and the Great War*, p. 7.
20   *Regulations for the OTC*, pp. 8.
21   HMC, Report of the Headmasters Conference December 1914, p. 64.
22   Ibid., p. 49.
23   John Gooch, *The Plans of War: The General Staff and British Military Strategy* (London: Routledge and Keegan Paul, 1974), p. 302.

the near future. There was no point, he said, in spending money on boys of 13, 14 and 15 who would be of no use in the current war.[24] However, Kitchener had warned it would take three years to build the New Armies into an effective fighting force and on this basis, those who were 15 years old in 1914 would be needed within three years, and possibly those younger, just to replace casualties. The example of Uppingham demonstrates that this was the case; 104 boys who were aged between 13 and 15 in August 1914 had been granted commissions by the end of the war.[25] A little more thought by the War Office in 1914 would have led to this conclusion but under huge pressure it was incapable of taking long term decisions alongside having to deal with huge increases in costs. Schools which did not have an OTC contingent were also at a substantial financial disadvantage. All funding for their cadet units was given to the local TF Committee and schools received funding from it at the Committee's discretion.[26] Such funding, if received, was considerably lower than that for the OTC. Junior OTC contingents were entitled to a per head grant based on the number of efficient cadets. Gresham's, for the year 1914-15, received a War Office grant of £207.[27] Although Dooner claimed the reason for freezing OTC expansion was to promote the training of those cadets most likely to serve, the real reasons appear to have been a desire to control expenditure and relieve some of the immediate pressures of work at the War Office.

Despite the protests by HMC members who did not have OTC contingents (such as Merchant Taylors' School, Crosby), between 1914 and 1918 the War Office stood by its decision not to authorise any more contingents.[28] Of the 23 HMC members which did not have an OTC contingent, almost all of them had a Cadet Corps by the end of 1915.[29] The 91 HMC members (80% of the membership) which had contingents formed a prominent part of the Junior OTC. It meant that of the 166 contingents, 55% were based at public schools: a ratio which had hardly changed since the establishment of the OTC in 1908. The school corps' foundation had been dominated by the public schools but by 1908 their prominence within the movement was less pronounced.[30] Although public schools remained an important source of officers it was limited to those which had OTC contingents. 20% of HMC members did not fall into this category. The 75 schools outside the Public School (HMC) movement which had OTC contingents were considered to be a better source of potential junior officers. The qualities of the OTC syllabus were of more importance than the general qualities of a public school education in officer recruitment. The majority of public

---

24 HMC, Report of the Headmasters Conference December 1914, p. 64.
25 Based on an analysis of *Uppingham School Roll, 1853-1947*.
26 HMC, Report of the Headmasters Conference January 1919, p. 53.
27 *The Gresham*, Vol. VI. No.6., July 1916, p. 107.
28 HMC, Report of the Headmasters Conference December 1914, p. 57.
29 *The Cadet List being a List of All Cadet Units had received Official Recognition on 31st December 1915* (London: HMSO, 1916), pp. 4-14, 39.
30 Based on analysis of Haig-Brown, *The O.T.C. and The Great War*, pp. 6-7.

schools continued to enjoy a special status in officer recruitment, but only those with OTC contingents.

The belief within the Army that a public school education produced leaders of men who would be well suited to being junior officers had evolved in the years before the war, to one where a set of knowledge was also considered to be important. However, in the initial improvised phase of officer recruitment, a public school education was a strongly persuasive factor for battalion COs who needed to recruit junior officers quickly. Kitchener's decision to recruit the New Army made it possible for Haldane's system of feeding reserves into the Army to be circumvented. At the end of 1914, when the War Office regained control of the recruitment process, OTC membership became more important than having been to the right sort of school. By its nature many those who were commissioned from the OTC were from a social elite but this on its own was not enough. After December 1914, while still needing to recruit many more junior officers, the War Office increasingly sought to recruit those who had already received some of the training junior officers required. Schools where boys would receive preliminary officer training (i.e. with an OTC contingent) were most attractive. The Imperial Services College, Windsor, had been created after the failure of Kipling's USC and was not a member of the HMC. However, with its emphasis on preparing boys for the Army it is no surprise that all 111 of its former OTC cadets who enlisted by March 1915 held commissions. Being the *alumnus* of a public school was not the sole qualification to become an officer. Without doubt those from the higher social classes were more likely to be gazetted, but after December 1914 previous membership of the OTC was an important factor in officer selection. Haig-Brown, writing in 1915, was clear about the importance of the OTC in the early stages of the war:

> What has chiefly to be realized is that the work of the O. T. C. before the war and after its declaration made the forming of the New Armies an absolute possibility and not a chaotic dream. It is possible to train officers and men together—it is indeed the common practice of the Army—but you cannot start a New Army in which nobody knows anything and train it into an officered and efficient force. It was just the start which certain men in this country had received in the O. T. C. that made the enormous increase in our forces feasible.[31]

The OTC helped to bring a little bit of order to the chaotic early response by the British to the declaration of war. It was for the reasons set out by Haig-Brown that the War Office opted to use the OTC as the foundation of a more structured approach. The priority given to OTC cadets from December 1914 marked the end of an *ad hoc* approach to junior officer recruitment. Despite the priority given to the OTC the War Office, overwhelmed by the demands of war, had frozen any future expansion and this

---

31   Haig-Brown, *The O.T.C. and The Great War*, p. 84.

was accompanied by the withdrawal of the pre-war support it had provided. Public Schools with OTC contingents were left to work out how to continue to prepare their boys to be officers without any support.

Withdrawal of Support

The suddenness of the crisis and the decision to create the New Armies meant that resources were required elsewhere more urgently. Almost immediately the Certificate A examination was suspended for the duration.[32] Many of the officers who carried out examinations in peacetime had been despatched to France and those who remained had other priorities. Equipment, such as rifles, was recalled for use in training the New Armies. In addition, a significant number of the men who ran the individual contingents left for active service. By Christmas, many teachers who were officers in the OTC had left to fight in the war. At the same time, many Sergeant-Instructors were recalled to the colours; these men were the bedrock of the contingent. Gordon Hyams described the Sergeant-Major of Charterhouse's OTC contingent, an ex-Guardsman, as the 'sheet anchor' who had taught the school's cadets a great deal.[33] With their close involvement in the detailed training of the cadets they were ideal candidates to carry out similar roles in the New Armies. The uncoordinated suddenness of their withdrawal left schools with significant problems, especially for those smaller schools with little military tradition. The Headmaster of King's School, Worcester reported that he had lost his CO and Sergeant Instructor (as had many schools). Without them, his school would not be able to teach the OTC syllabus. Dooner was sympathetic but the War Office had to make a choice between immediate needs and future needs.[34] However, the adverse consequences for a school with 179 pupils in 1914 with no military tradition and limited resources were far greater than they were for larger schools, such as Harrow, with its strong military background.

The detrimental impact on the contingents was made worse by the general mood within society that men had a duty to serve at the front, if possible. This was a sentiment reflected within the schools themselves. In the early stages of the war governors were more willing to release teachers (the majority of whom were OTC officers) to take commissions. By October 1914 Uppingham had allowed four teachers to depart on service.[35] This willingness to release teachers rapidly dissipated as the schools experienced difficulties securing suitable replacements, and the need to meet the extra responsibilities placed on them by the withdrawal of support for OTC. The War Office had made it clear in September 1914 that teachers with commissions in the OTC

32 TNA WO 293/1/299: Examinations for Certificates A and B in O.T.C., 31 August 1914.
33 IWM 10409, Hyams, Gordon Frank, Oral History.
34 HMC, Report of the Headmasters Conference December 1914, p. 50 and p. 63.
35 Halstead, *A School in Arms*, p. 99.

could be released to other army units only if headmasters decided they could be spared from both from scholastic and OTC work. It was emphasised that the training of the school contingents must not suffer.[36] By late 1914, the HMC was emphasising that the first duty of OTC officers was to stay at home to provide the necessary training for the boys. Further, it pointed out that an excellent way for masters to support the war effort was for them to gain commissions in the OTC so its training obligations could be met.[37]

The Schools are Thrown on Their Own Resources

The War Office was aware of the consequences of withdrawing support for the OTC. At the 1914 HMC meeting, Dooner reiterated the importance of teachers remaining at their schools to both support the OTC and maintain academic standards.[38] Without this he recognised, schools would have great difficulty in running their contingents efficiently and providing potential junior officers for the army. This was particularly important as the War Office's reassumption of control of officer recruitment in December 1914 restored the OTC's place as a key source of officers. At the same time, it was agreed that any application from an OTC cadet required a recommendation from their OTC CO and Headmaster.[39] The effect of this was that boys would not be able to leave until they were 18 if they wanted to apply for a commission. In the Autumn term of 1914, many contingents had been considerably disadvantaged by the sudden departure of senior cadets; many boys had taken commissions with the TF where the minimum age was 17, instead of 18 in the rest of the army. The detrimental effect of losing officers, instructors and senior cadets was reversed as membership of contingents became more stable and the recruitment of more OTC officers commenced. Although the burden of running contingents greatly increased, schools were now better equipped to meet the increased burdens.

Both in their public and private pronouncements schools willingly accepted these increased burdens. In some areas they took on greater responsibility in the face of opposition from the War Office. The ruling that no contingent would be allowed to increase its authorised establishment was widely ignored. The War Office had already attempted to curtail the unofficial expansion of Junior OTC contingents on 14 November (a month before the HMC meeting); stating that this was not permitted without its approval, which would not be forthcoming. It wanted contingents to concentrate on training those cadets 'who may be expected to apply for commissions

---

36 TNA WO 293/1/1189: Employment of Officers of Junior Division O.T.C. in T.F. or other Units, 13 September 1914.
37 HMC, Report of the Committee of the Headmasters Conference for 1914, p. 130.
38 Ibid., p. 64.
39 Ibid., p. 51.

in the near future.'⁴⁰ At the HMC 1914 meeting many headmasters reported they had ignored instructions to reduce the size of their contingents to the authorised establishment. McKenzie of Uppingham advised his fellow headmasters to keep quiet about any expansion. Uppingham, he said, had greatly exceeded its establishment and had been rebuked for doing so.[41] The pressure on the War Office had led it to make this decision, believing it could not support an expanded OTC.

Despite its reservations the War Office did not press the point. At virtually every school almost all of its boys joined the OTC; this was irrespective of whether or not joining the OTC was compulsory. Across all types of public school, the response was equally impressive. At Epsom by December 1914 its OTC contingent had increased by 70 with only four who were eligible not doing so, and that, the school magazine reported, was through no fault of their own.[42] Mill Hill also saw a high level of participation in the OTC. By November 1914 87% of its pupils had enrolled.[43] For a school whose Non-Conformist background made it deeply ambivalent to war this was remarkable; especially when compared to Uppingham's participation rate of 91% (414 out of a school of 450). This participation rate was to be expected of Uppingham, a school which had acquired a good reputation for its efficiency as both a cadet corps and OTC contingent, but not of Mill Hill. There remained within it a strong, if diminished, tradition of pacifism. Some boys such as Basil Kingsley Martin, later editor of the *New Statesman* never joined the OTC. When he left school, he joined the Friends' Ambulance Unit as conscientious objector.[44]

Despite the withdrawal of War Office support, schools rapidly adjusted their syllabus and OTC activity to support the war effort. Although the pre-war level of support had been discontinued the War Office liaised with the HMC's School Corps Committee to provide some guidance. In the Autumn term of 1914, the committee provided brief recommendations on appropriate training. Priority was to be given to special training for those boys who would be ready for commissions in 1915, i.e. those over 17. For these boys a range of areas for instruction were set out which included drill, map-reading, field exercises and musketry. Those under 17 were to form the squads which the over 17s could use to practice with. In addition to more general training, cadets were to participate in route marches and PT to improve their fitness.[45] Deprived of official support schools were forced to fall on their own resources. In the absence of Sergeant Instructors, Cadet Officers and NCOs played a far more promi-

---

40 TNA WO 293/1/159: Enrolment of Cadets in excess of Authorised Establishment, 14 November 1914.
41 HMC, Report of the Headmasters Conference December 1914, p. 53.
42 *The Epsomian*, Vol. XLVI, No. 2 December 1914, p. 1.
43 *MHM*, Vol xlii., No.3 November 1914, p. 101 and MHSA, Minute Book Vol, 12 7 October 1914, p. 330.
44 *1914-1919 The Book of Remembrance and War Record of Mill Hill School* (Reigate: The Surrey Fine Art Press, undated), p. 217.
45 HMC, Report of the Committee of the Headmasters Conference for 1914, p. 131.

nent part in running and leading their contingents. Perhaps unintentionally, Junior OTC contingents now provided far more opportunities for cadets to develop their leadership skills. The *Uppingham School Magazine* set out how it had implemented the School Corps Committee's guidance:

> At the end of October our time for military instruction was increased to three afternoons per week, Swedish Drill being made a part of one of the drills.
>
> Has this innovation proved a success? With more adequate time for instruction the Corps work has been made considerably more varied and interesting; the leaders, especially the Cadet Officers and Platoon Sergeants, have gained a varied elementary experience which cannot fail to be of use to them later on ; and the Rank and File have shown a keenness in all the work, which has been most encouraging to their Instructors.
>
> In September, 120 of our serviceable rifles were requisitioned by the Authorities. We have been handicapped certainly by lack of these, and also by lack of Uniforms But these are minor inconveniences, and we are not alone, by any means, in suffering them. There is much that can be learnt without rifles: — cover, formations in attack, advanced guards, outposts, march discipline, reconnaissance, close order drill, etc., etc. The chief aim, this term, has been to learn the principles of the new Company Organisation, Attack in all its stages, Active Defence, Protection both on the move and when at rest, Elementary Musketry Instruction, and March Discipline.
>
> In addition to the three fixed periods for work, Lectures in attack, defence, protection, reconnaissance and scouting have been given on Tuesday afternoons. Many "half-past-twelve " periods have been utilised for voluntary instruction in signalling, map-reading, etc. ...[46]

Following the outbreak of war, schools varied in their approach to military training. Like Uppingham, many schools made time for more OTC activity by reducing the time spent on the academic timetable and games. Harrow made a number of significant changes which included the OTC CO being relieved of his mathematics teaching commitments so that he could concentrate on military training and lecturing on military topics. The intention of these changes was to prepare every boy to carry out a subaltern's work with the minimum of extra training when they joined the army.[47] Marlborough too made changes to its timetable to minimise the amount of training needed for any of its boys who were commissioned. Parades were held three days a week and over 17s were divided into four classes to cover other aspects of Army work; the classes met four times a week.[48] The withdrawal of War Office support

---

46 *USM,* No. 415 December 1914, p. 298.
47 *The Harrovian*, Vol XXVII. No. 6, Saturday 17 October 1914, pp. 111-112.
48 *The Malburian*, Vol. XLIX., No. 741. 17 October 1914, p. 154.

and a dearth of guidance meant that schools had to use their own initiative in their approach to training. Once commissioned, an officer would have to learn a lot on the job. Public Schools had the advantage that in 1914 they could offer some training before a commission was granted. Not only would a young officer have to learn on the job but also train new recruits. Therefore, as the *Eton College Chronicle* observed in September 1914, on receiving a commission a junior officer was likely to become a teacher as soon as he joined his unit. OTC training, it said, must provide men who could effectively execute orders from their superiors and teach all aspects of military work to recruits.[49] Public schools all strove to achieve these two aims but with no guidance it was impossible to identify the best way to achieve this.

In December 1914 the War Office could be forgiven for a lack of guidance about the best approach to training; by the end of 1915 headmasters were becoming frustrated by the continuing absence of guidance. At the 1915 HMC meeting, this frustration was aired openly in a number of discussions including a motion calling on the War Office to provide a detailed syllabus for senior members of the Junior OTC. W.N. Weech, Headmaster of Sedbergh, complained about the lack of a syllabus for boys aged 17 and over. A consistent approach in training was vital to ensure effective training for potential officers. The guidance from the War Office was too vague and, in some areas, contradictory. A list of subjects which could be taught was of little value. Which subjects should be given the most time? Was it map reading or administration or field engineering? Should signalling be taught and if so, was it Semaphore or Morse or both which should be taught? Of the actual instructions, he complained that some were 'farcical', pointing out that the instruction to include route marching ran contrary to the principles the War Office had laid down for cadet training. Another headmaster pointed out the inefficiencies of a master at each school having to devise a scheme for the Annual Camp. Surely, he argued, the War Office was far better equipped to devise a scheme which was consistent with its requirements for all schools to use.[50] Examples of the inefficiency this created was raised in a later debate. One headmaster reported old boys complaining that after arriving at their training units they often found themselves receiving instruction which had already covered at school. Even worse, on occasions they were attending courses which contradicted what they had already been taught.[51] The War Office was still in a state of disorganisation and had been incapable of designing an integrated training scheme. It would be harsh to describe the Headmasters as armchair generals. Many of them were experienced auxiliaries in their own right. They were well versed in the pre-war OTC training regime; if they were not, they had the expertise of their OTC CO to draw on. All this, together with the letters they received from their old boys, placed them in a good position to make sensible judgements about the inadequacies of OTC training.

---

49 *Eton College Chronicle*, No. 1495. 24 September 1914, p. 619.
50 HMC, Report of the Headmasters Conference December 1915, pp. 11-20.
51 Ibid., pp. 46-55.

With their experience in education and training, they understood the need for clear guidance about what was required. Like the vast majority of British society, they were committed to supporting the war effort as best as they could. They were not arguing with the War Office about the content of the syllabus for gaining a commission. They were not arguing for a more classics-orientated syllabus. What they asked for was for clear guidance about what was required from OTC training. The consequence of the failure to provide this can be seen in the Annual Camps held in 1915.

In 1915 the War Office did not arrange Annual Camps but some schools held their own unofficial camps. This meant schools were left to make their own arrangements and gain what unofficial support they could. As a result, not all schools participated in or held camps; Oundle and Westminster fell into this category. Camps were often arranged at short notice – Dulwich, Merchant Taylor's and St Paul's were only able to complete arrangements for a joint camp 10 days before it was due to start. It had been only at the last minute that Aldershot Command was able to offer a site near Petersfield, with the result there was little time to prepare facilities and plan training exercises.[52] The better connected a school was to the army the easier it found it to make more effective arrangements for a camp. Thanks to two old boys, Lieutenant General W. Pitcairn Campbell, GOC, Southern Command and Major General L. Drummond, GOC Wareham Training District, Eton, found it far easier to arrange a camp with Winchester, Marlborough and Malvern by drawing on these connections with the army. Unlike the camp at Petersfield the schools were able to hold a camp at a site close to Swanage where they benefitted from having Regular Army officers and Sergeant-Instructors to conduct the training.[53] Not even schools with strong connections to the army were guaranteed this level of support. Rugby, a traditional source of officers for the army, held a camp on its own at the nearby Fawsley Hall. Instead of the extensive support enjoyed by the camp at Swanage, the staff work was left entirely to the contingent's officers. It was only able to draw on the support of the contingent's former CO Captain H.H. Hardy, who had been on the War Office Staff since June 1915, for three days of the nine-day camp. As with all school magazine reports, a positive spin was put on the work undertaken but it was made clear that the lack of Regular Army support, which had been enjoyed at the pre-war camps, had led to a considerably inferior outcome.[54] With the exception of the camp at Swanage none of those held in 1915 enjoyed any support from the Regular Army. Schools were forced to seek endorsement of the training activities after the event. In the absence of official guidance, Uppingham sent a complete report of the camp's activities to the War Office for endorsement.[55] Although an endorsement of the activities undertaken was received from the War Office this was of limited benefit. Other schools would have sought

---

52   *The Pauline*, Vol. XXXIII, No. 221, October 1915, pp. 231-232.
53   *Eton College Chronicle*, No. 1542, September 30 1915, pp. 886-887 and No. 1535 July 8 1915 p. 844.
54   *The Meteor*, No. 590. Rugby November 1915., pp. 213-215 and *Record of War Service* p. 142.
55   *USM*, No. 421 October 1915, pp. 217-220.

(and often received) endorsements for their annual camp but endorsing a hodgepodge of different schemes was of limited value. There had been no coordination to ensure the camps met the specific training requirements of the army. The War Office merely reviewed reports of the camps and had no way of assessing the quality of the training. Leaving each school to make its own arrangements made a consistent quality across the OTC even more difficult to achieve. It was far easier for Eton with its strong connections to the army (and the Foot Guards in particular) to obtain a higher quality of training at an annual camp than it was for other schools.

A further block on achieving a uniform approach was that a consistent approach was not taken to providing what little supervision was available. Although all OTC contingents were under the control of the War Office before the war, they were allocated an Army Depot to provide training support. With the outbreak of the war this support was withdrawn, but the Army Depot in which they were located appears to have exercised control over the activities of the contingents. Analysing the Field Day activity there is diversity according to where the school was located. Oundle, Rugby and Uppingham had often held field days together before August 1914 but examining their respective school magazines reveals disparate activities. Oundle and Uppingham held no field days with other schools in 1915. Oundle and Uppingham were 16 miles apart, while Uppingham was only six miles from Oakham with whom it had also conducted many field days before the war. Given these schools were within marching distance of each other it is difficult to understand why they did not undertake joint field days. Rugby, which had held regular joint field days with both Oundle and Uppingham (every Field Day it held in 1913 also included Uppingham), continued to hold joint field days in 1915. Instead in 1915 Rugby held Field Days with two Birmingham schools, King Edward's and the Oratory in July and with Eton and Harrow in November. Unnecessary railway travel was discouraged but despite this, two joint field days which involved railway journeys were held.[56] It is reasonable to assume that those authorising field days considered the journey justified. A Field Day with Eton and Harrow involved considerably more travel than one with Uppingham and Oundle so it appears that different depots were imposing different rules. There is no evidence that joint field days with either Eton or Harrow were repeated in 1916 or 1917 and by November 1916 joint field days with Oakham, Oundle and Uppingham had recommenced.[57] It can be concluded that some schools received more support than others to hold field days. It was not just a problem limited to a small part of the East Midlands. None of the accounts of Tonbridge's Field Days in 1915 mention them being held with other schools. The conclusion that there was a lack of control by the War Office is reinforced when Field Day activity around London is examined. Field

---

56 *The Meteor,* No. 588, Rugby July 1915 p. 163 and No. 592. Rugby December 1915., pp. 236-237.
57 Brian Needham, *Oakham School Officers Training Corps & Junior Training Corps 1910- 1948*, (Oakham: Oakham School, NK), p. 33.

days held by Eton in 1915 also included a Field Day with Bradfield and Wellington College in February.[58] While Harrow held two Field Days, one with Berkhamsted OTC and the other with Westminster School.[59] Joint Field Days were not limited to schools known for their connections with the army. Merchant Taylors' arranged a Field Day in Richmond Park in February 1915 which also involved City of London, Whitgift, Emmanuel, St Paul's, Aldenham and Mill Hill.[60] This activity reflected the pattern of field days which had taken place around London before the war. The benefits of schools working together in training were well understood. Schools had the opportunity of being able to conduct larger and more realistic exercises together, which provided the opportunity for more lessons to be delivered. In one case the depot responsible for an OTC contingent continued its close involvement. Eton maintained an active connection with the Foot Guards, which had been responsible for it before the war. For example, in March 1915 Eton held a Field Day with the Coldstream Guards.[61] The War Office, in effect, withdrew from any oversight of the Junior OTC and left it to its own devices. The different approaches of army depots meant that schools were subject to different regimes solely based on their location. Combined with the lack of training guidance a shambolic and inconsistent approach to training developed within the Junior OTC.

This is the major problem which made training so much less effective than it might have been. Schools also suffered from the withdrawal of equipment such as rifles and the shortage of other equipment such as uniforms. For schools such as Bradford Grammar School, which had only applied for authorisation of its contingent in October 1914, the problems were especially acute.[62] No uniforms arrived until March 1915 and it had to rely on the generosity of the old boys to pay for equipping the contingent. Even after the uniforms arrived it did not have facilities for shooting and the training of the contingent was described was well behind others.[63] Many schools were able to improvise, as the report of December 1914 of Uppingham's OTC activities (quoted above) demonstrates. If the War Office was unable to support all the contingents, its failure to exercise any sort of oversight and quality control for contingents formed in 1914, such as Bradford, is symptomatic of the way it abrogated any effective responsibility for the OTC, retaining responsibility in name only. The evidence of training activity demonstrates that schools were prepared to use their own initiative in developing training for 17 and 18 year olds, but that was totally different to a coordinated training programme. In early 1915, Eton started a term long Proficiency Class, at the

---

58   *Eton College Chronicle*, No. 1519. 25 February 1915, p. 762.
59   *The Harrovian*, Vol XXVIII. No. 2, Saturday April 3rd 1915, pp. 31-32.
60   *MHM*, Vol xlii., No.5 March 1915, p. 154.
61   *Eton College Chronicle*, No. 1523. March 25 1915, pp. 779-780.
62   *Bradford Weekly Telegraph*, 9 October 1914, p. 7.
63   *The Bradfordian: The Bradford Grammar School Magazine*, Vol XX., No. 121., March 1915, pp. 28-30.

end of which the participants took an examination.[64] Uppingham in 1915 placed an emphasis in training in the power of command, which it judged was lacking in the pre-war training. As part of this, 70 senior cadets had undertaken a musketry course with the intention that those who passed would become instructors themselves.[65] Mill Hill in early 1915 started conducting separate theoretical and practical examinations for NCOs and the other members of the OTC.[66] The improvised training was devoted entirely to the training of potential officers. The lack of guidance, and at times obstruction of the training activities of some contingents, severely impeded the effectiveness of this work. As fine as many of the different schools' activities were, they did not collectively represent a coherent training scheme. The War Office in 1915 made positive comments about the OTC producing better qualified candidates for commissions, but it clearly was incapable of articulating why precisely this was the case.[67] It is little wonder headmasters became exasperated with the organisational failures of the War Office and an absence of coherent guidance from it.

A Confusion of Purpose

Combined with the War Office's inability to utilise the OTC effectively, it was often the case that it drifted away from its pre-war purpose of being a feeder organisation for the army. In some cases, schools were over-keen in their desire to support the war effort. The Reverend Arthur Upcott, Headmaster of Christ's Hospital, suggested to the War Office in November 1914, that OTC cadets could be used in the defence of the country in the event of an invasion. This proposal was politely rejected by the War Office which said its wish was for the whole effort of the OTC to be a level of training 'with a view to perfecting themselves for appointment to commissions, and, where possible, assisting in recruiting for the New Army.'[68] This was an isolated case of over-enthusiasm; the minutes of the HMC show that headmasters understood that OTC training should be at the heart of their contribution to the war effort. Despite this, the lack of War Office direction (no attempt at defining 'perfection' was made until 1916) meant there was a confusion of purpose. Some schools, adjacent to training camps, found themselves working closely with the New Armies. Although the War Office had made it clear in August 1914 that school premises were not to be requisitioned by the army (as education was a priority), this did not preclude arrangements for the army to use school facilities.[69] Lancing provided a variety of support to

---

64 *Eton College Chronicle*, No. 1517. 11 February 1915, p. 754, No. 1521. 11 March 1915, p. 770 and No. 1527. 13 May 1915, p. 805.
65 *USM*, No. 417 March 1915, p. 55.
66 *MHM*, Vol xlii., No.6 April 1915, p. 190.
67 See for example, TNA WO 293/3/276: Commissions for Royal Flying Corps, 30 July 1915.
68 TNA WO 374/22052: Major Alfred Cecil Wall Edwards The Welsh Regiment.
69 TNA WO 293/1/151: Certain Schools converted into V.A.D. Hospitals, 19 August 1914.

the 24th Division which was based in nearby Shoreham until June 1915. In the last months of 1914, the school grounds were being used by the Division for rifle exercises and drill.[70] This involvement would go beyond providing facilities; the December 1914 school magazine reported that officers from its contingent had been lecturing officers of the Division.[71] Such support was a consequence of the rapid raising of the New Army. There were very few trained officers and a lack of other facilities and equipment; the Division having no uniforms until March 1915 is one small example.[72] The Royal Fusiliers' training camp had been established at Woodcote Park, near Epsom, in 1914. Like the troops at Shoreham it suffered from a lack of facilities and Epsom College provided its grounds for drill, miniature range for shooting, and gymnasium for lectures, while the swimming bath was used by soldiers during lessons.[73] These activities were peculiar to only a few schools but represent the uncoordinated approach to OTC activity by the War Office. In the early stages of the war such activities are understandable but as 1915 progressed they became less justifiable. Instead of being used as a facility for training future officers, schools were having some of their facilities diverted to other military purposes. At the same time some schools were used as a support for New Army training. Lancing held Field Days in the first half of 1915 with the 13th Middlesex Regiment, 7th Northamptonshire Regiment and 8th The Buffs (East Kent Regiment) which were all based locally.[74] These exercises were typical of the unstructured approach to training. Some schools were allowed to exercise with other schools, some with other units and others were required not to exercise with any other school or unit. Such inconsistencies were manifest in 1914 and 1915.

The support given by officers and cadets to the New Armies suggests the OTC was considered as both a training support and a feeder organisation. Over the 1914 Christmas holidays OTC officers were invited to apply to their local Command if they wished to assist with New Army training.[75] Several masters from different schools (including those of Harrow, Lancing and Uppingham) had their applications accepted. Boys too conducted training for New Army recruits. The *Uppingham School Magazine* reported that all its officers and cadet officers had acted as instructors for New Army units over Christmas.[76] OTC officers were already under greater stress because of the loss of Sergeant-Instructors which placed a greater administrative

---

70　*The Lancing College Magazine*, Vol 7-7. (No. 291) October 1914, p. 92.
71　*The Lancing College Magazine*, Vol 7-8 (No. 292) November 1914, p. 105 and Vol 7-9 (No. 293) December 1914, p. 119.
72　*The Long, Long Trail*, <https://www.longlongtrail.co.uk/Army/order-of-battle-of-divisions/24th-division/> (accessed 16 June 2020).
73　Scadding, *Epsom College*, p. 82.
74　*The Lancing College Magazine*, Vol 8-2. [No. 295], March 1915, p. 16 and Vol 8-3. (No. 296) April 1915 pp. 26-27.
75　TNA WO 293/1/160: O.T.C. Military employment of Officers during Xmas Vacation, 14 November 1914.
76　*USM,* March 1915, p. 55 and USA, Notes on Uppingham School OTC. From the files of R. Sterndale Bennett (1910-1921).

burden on them. Time spent training others left less time for the planning of the contingents' work. Not all schools participated in the provision of training. Senior boys from Sherborne attended a course in company drill and musketry at the Inns of Court OTC. In the School's eyes it was a more effective way of training, and worth repeating.[77] This type of course equipped senior boys with the skills to provide instruction to the rest of their contingent in drill and musketry. The different training activities of Uppingham and Sherborne are representative of the confused approach to the OTC. That both the giving and receiving of training were permitted demonstrates a lack of central coordination. The contingents of Sherborne and Uppingham were of a similar standard. Their participation in totally different training activities shows how any attempt to achieve a common standard across all contingents had been abandoned. It was not until the end of 1915 that the demands on the OTC to support the New Armies' training started to reduce. For the Christmas 1915 holidays it was made clear that those Junior OTC officers assisting with training over the 1915 Christmas holidays must demonstrate an ability as an instructor; there must be a need for them and the state would receive good value for the expenses required. In the past there had been too many inexperienced officers assisting with this work.[78]

Over Christmas 1914 contingents also set about training new officers for their contingents. Before the war this was training which was carried out through the TF (all OTC officers were unattached TF officers) but with the emphasis on training the New Armies this was not possible. OTC contingents at public schools were forced to commence their own training. At Charterhouse its OTC CO provided officer training for several of its own masters as well as masters from Dulwich and Mill Hill. Even a self-help scheme like this was confused in its purpose. Masters from both schools saw this training as a way of gaining a commission in the TF, with a view to military service.[79] Masters also joined their school contingents and served in the ranks; Charterhouse, Mill Hill and Sherborne were some of the schools where this was the case. This improvisation of training led to many anomalies and potential problems. Masters often found themselves under the command of pupils. Gordon Hyams diplomatically touched on one problem. As the Sergeant in command of his house section at Charterhouse he found himself with two masters in it. He recalled that this could present some difficulties but in general he said they were very good.[80] In the early stages of the war, these arrangements might have been more understandable

---

77 *The Shirburnian*, Vol. XXVIII., No. 1. March 1915, p. 12.
78 TNA WO 293/3/72: Attachments of senior Officers of O.T.C. to units of New Armies or T.F. during Xmas Vacation, 24 November 1915.
79 *MHM*, Vol xlii., No.5, February 1915, p. 154, *The Carthusian*, Vol XI, No. 382., February 1915 p. 422 and Bodleian Library Special Collections, Archive of Oxford University OTC: OT 1/1/6 Oxford University School of Instruction Sixth Course (14/06/1915 to 10/07/1915), registration form of 2/Lt GW Beachcroft.
80 IWM, 10409, Hyams, *MHM*, Vol xlii., No.6, March 1915, p. 189 and SSA, Headmaster's Report to the Governors for 1915, p. 11.

but they continued for well over a year. This arrangement along with the OTC continuing to be a provider of training for the New Armies is indicative of the chaotic manner in which training was being provided.

The general tone of ACIs during 1915 indicate that OTC officer training was not a priority. While the army was not interested in employing all OTC officers, it did want to use 'qualified and experienced officers' for training the New Armies over the summer.[81] Some OTC officers who attempted to join courses for young officers were met with the response that they were not intended for them.[82] Solo initiatives to develop their own training schemes also encountered obstacles. Robert Sterndale Bennett attempted to use his strong connections with the Artists' Rifles to spend time at their Loughton Training School during the 1915 summer holidays. Instead his request was declined and as a 'qualified and experienced' officer, he was sent on a 'Musketry (Senior Officers)' Course with the 3/1st London Royal Engineers Field Company Junior Officer School. The trade-off appears to have been that he was also required to act as an Instructor over the summer holidays. In return for one week's instruction, he provided instruction for three weeks. The commendation he received shows his work as an instructor was valued but is further evidence of a disjointed approach. The course was, no doubt, of great value but the time he spent as an instructor might have been better spent developing OTC training.[83] Sterndale Bennett was one of many OTC officers who spent at least part of their summer holidays acting as an instructor to the New Army. Five Stonyhurst OTC officers spent the holidays instructing Third-Line Depots.[84] Meanwhile, officers and NCO cadets from the Sherborne contingent spent part of the holidays training TF units.[85] Lancing also provided masters and boys to support New Army training.[86] Several cadets from Charterhouse served as sergeants with TF battalions.[87] Tonbridge too provided boys to act as instructors at Third-Line TF units. The school magazine put a positive spin on this novel arrangement speaking of the benefits of them learning from their experience.[88] There is no doubt that the training of the New Army was deficient but using OTC officers and cadets as instructors was a case of robbing Peter to pay Paul. Novel this approach may have been but any benefit to the officers and cadets was a by-product and made a limited contribution to the OTC's role as a feeder organisation for the junior officer corps.

However, this did not mean that no training was provided to the OTC. Uppingham, as well as providing all its officers for New Army training, was also able to send

---

81   TNA WO 293/2: Officers of the O.T.C. desirous of obtaining Military Employment during Summer Vacation, 22 May 1915.
82   TNA WO 293/3/260: Classes of Instruction for Young Officers, 28 July 1915.
83   USA, Notes on Uppingham School OTC.
84   *The Stonyhurst Magazine*, Vol XIII. (Part2) No. 202, October 1915, p. 1365.
85   *The Shirburnian*, Vol. XXVIII., No. 5. October 1915, p. 185.
86   *The Lancing College Magazine*, Vol 8-7. [No. 300], October 1915, pp. 104-105.
87   *The Carthusian*, Vol. XI. No. 388., October 1915, p. 526.
88   *The Tonbridgian*, Vol XXII. No. 5 [No. 455.], November 1915, pp. 201-202.

four masters and four boys on courses in musketry, signalling and instruction.[89] One boy from The Leys attended the same instruction course at Cambridge as the party from Uppingham.[90] Lancing sent an officer on a musketry course in the summer of 1915.[91] This was not a sign of a more structured approach by the War Office. Many of the contingents did not benefit from training courses. It appears that only those whose COs were dynamic and well connected were able to arrange training for their contingents. Sterndale Bennett at Uppingham and Haig Brown at Lancing were both leading figures in the OTC and both had strong connections with the army. The pre-war CO at the The Leys had become CO of the Cambridge University School of Instruction for Officers. That schools were able to arrange training for their officers and cadets, on the basis of the strength of their connections, but this was not conducive to raising the quality of training throughout the OTC.

The quality of training within the OTC was also adversely affected by the loss of its officers to the army. Although the official position remained that OTC officers should stay with their contingents, competent officers often left to join the New Armies. Often this was a result of having worked closely with the army. Captain E.N. Hale left to join-up after acting as an instructor with Sterndale Bennett at the same Young Officer school. Instead of returning to Uppingham for the 1915 winter term he remained at the officer school as an officer, before accepting a commission in the Black Watch.[92] Hale was not the only OTC officer to leave for the New Armies after being attached to them as an instructor. Haig Brown, the CO of Lancing OTC, was recommended for the command of a New Army battalion by the CO of the infantry brigade he had been attached to in the summer of 1915.[93] Ultimately, he was not selected but this was only a temporary reprieve. By early 1916, he had been appointed CO of 23rd Middlesex Battalion. The absence of conscription and effective manpower planning made it easy for OTC officers with ability to be poached by the army. The departure to the war of comparatively old masters such as Hale, aged 45 and Widdowson of Christ's Hospital, aged 46, illustrates how short the army was of junior officers.[94] None of this was likely to help OTC contingents in their role of providing effective training for potential officers. Using the OTC to provide training for the New Armies inhibited its pre-war role as a feeder organisation providing potential officers. It was a short-term approach which impeded it in its stated role.

---

89   *USM*, No. 421 October 1915, p. 221.
90   *The Leys Fortnightly*, Vol XL. No. 699., Oct. 1 1915, p. 11.
91   *The Lancing College Magazine*, Vol 8-8. [No. 301], November 1915, p. 120.
92   *USM*, March 1915, p. 55, USA, Notes on Uppingham School OTC and *Record of War Service 1919-1918 Officers Training Corps (Junior Division) Public School Officers and Other Members of the Staffs*, (London: privately published, 1919), p. 178.
93   *The Lancing College Magazine*, Vol 8-8. [No. 301], November 1915, p. 120.
94   *The Blue*, Vol XLIII No.1 October 1915, p. 2 and *Alumni Cantabrigieneses* Part II Volume VI, p. 458.

Conclusion

The problems for public schools during 1914-15 were well summarised by Sterndale Bennett:

> In the first 2 years, lack of Officers, lack of a Sergt-Instructor and lack of official support, threw the Contingent on its own resources. The whole of the Training and administration duties fell on the Officers and Senior Cadets, who were already working on a full School timetable. Under these conditions over 300 recruits were trained, complete headquarters established with an efficient system of Interior Economy on military lines, and 2 successful CAMPS were organised in the summers of 1915 and 1916. Voluntary was strained to its highest point and was not confined to term-time, Officer and cadets making use of, and increasing their military knowledge as attached Instructors and on courses during vacations.[95]

In August 1914 the War Office withdrew all the pre-war support it had given to the OTC. The primary effect of this was there was no longer a mechanism to ensure the consistency of training within each contingent. Each contingent was left to draw on its own resources and initiative to provide suitable training. Inevitably, the approach varied by school and those with stronger military connections were able to carry out more effective training. Schools were often impeded in their training by restrictions imposed by their local army depots. The lack of detailed guidance increasingly became a source of deep frustration to the public schools. They were keen to support the war effort as best as they could and their argument with the War Office was not about a syllabus for potential officers, as it had been before the war. What was asked for was detailed technical guidance about what was to be covered in preparing boys to be officers Schools support for providing this training was demonstrated by their willingness to take time from games to ensure it could be provided effectively. It represented a realisation that the playing of games by public schoolboys was helpful but not sufficient in preparing them to be junior officers. Their efforts to provide proper training were also hampered by a confusion of what the purpose of the OTC was. Often it was looked upon as a resource for training the New Armies rather than part of a progressive scheme for officer training. This was further hampered by the loss of OTC officers to the army, who had come to its attention when they were assisting in training the New Armies.

The War Office was overstretched and grappling with the problems of training the New Armies in 1914 and 1915. It had identified the Junior OTC was an important source of candidates to be junior officers but, overwhelmed by the pressures on it, had withdrawn all the support it had provided before the war. The change in CIGS

---

95 USA, Notes on Uppingham School OTC.

in late 1915 coincided with a change of approach by the War Office. From the end of 1915 Junior OTC cadets were no longer able to apply directly for a commission in the infantry. Commissions would only be given to men who had been through the ranks or served in the Artists' or Inns of Court OTC. This was possible because a large reserve of officers had been built up and there was a lull in demand for them.[96] The introduction of conscription in January 1916 gave the War Office far more control over the recruitment of officers and the allocation of manpower. With these new powers and a temporarily adequate supply of junior officer reserves the War Office was no longer inclined to unquestioningly accept OTC cadets as being suitable junior officer material. From 1916 it started to offer more guidance of what it required of the OTC and gradually restored its support to a level which was similar to that offered before the war.

---

96   HMC, Report of the Committee of the Headmasters Conference for 1915, p. 147.

6

Setting and Raising the Standard: The OTC 1916-1919

Desperate for junior officers and with no effective officer recruitment infrastructure, in 1914 and 1915 the War Office had relied on the OTC as a primary source of candidates. Yet it withdrew all practical support from it. The OTC between 1914 and 1915 was no longer part of an integrated training scheme. It was treated as a resource which would produce cadets almost ready to be officers and could be used in other *ad hoc* tasks such as training the New Armies. From 1916 the OTC was returned to its role as a feeder organisation for the provision of officer cadets and its participation in *ad hoc* tasks ended. The change in leadership at the War Office led to a more integrated approach towards the OTC where it resumed its role as a feeder organisation, although the pre-war scheme was only replicated in form. The OTC syllabus was significantly reduced from that which pertained before the war. It concentrated on providing cadets with basic leadership and practical skills which would make them eligible to join an OCB. Those OTC cadets judged to be suitable officer material were sent to OCBs where they had to successfully pass the course before being awarded a commission. From the end of 1915 until November 1918, the War Office took an increasingly interventionist approach in an effort to raise the quality of cadets and ensure that whatever contingent they came from they met a universal standard. 1916 marked the start of a new approach to officer recruitment. As part of this, in 1916 the War Office offered an increasing level of guidance on the nature of training to be provided by Junior OTC contingents. In 1917 this level of support increased to one where the War Office became far more proactive and prescriptive in its approach. This chapter discusses the implications of this for Public School OTC contingents.

Setting the Standard

The change in approach by the War Office followed a reorganisation which included the Director of Staff Duties being given responsibility for the OTC.[1] This was part of the changes implemented by the new CIGS, Sir William Robertson, which aimed to make its General Staff more effective and influential. By establishing the same organisational structure as that of the BEF's Staff it enabled a more coordinated and effective approach.[2] Robertson's two predecessors in 1914 and 1915 had proved to be ineffectual in the face of Kitchener's attempt to run the War Office single-handed.[3] When Robertson took up his position on 23 December 1915 he found the General Staff to be in a far worse state of confusion than he had feared.[4] Almost immediately, changes were accompanied by a more proactive approach to Public Schools and their OTC contingents. As well as providing more detailed guidance on training the War Office set out to manage the supply of OTC cadets more efficiently.

In late December 1915 it started to consider and plan for future requirements. The advent of a more coordinated and effective approach and the introduction of conscription meant the War Office no longer needed to unquestioningly accept OTC cadets as being suitable junior officer material.[5] Ahead of the introduction of conscription, in December 1915 it requested a list of Junior OTC cadets who would be reaching 18-and-a-half in age in the near future.[6] The haphazard approach to officer recruitment in 1914 and 1915 was replaced by one where it attempted to establish the number of potential recruits it could expect from a key source. In February 1916 it sought a better understanding of the supply of potential officers, when it asked all Junior OTC COs to forward a list of any cadets, they did not consider suitable for a commission.[7] Since December 1914 applications for commissions from Junior OTC cadets had had to be signed by their headmaster and OTC CO. Many boys deemed unsuitable had found it easy to circumvent this system. This new approach made it easier to weed out unsuitable applicants. The measure made the imposition of a minimum standard easier to enforce but was a long way from the pre-war approach a of seeking a consistent and high quality in all OTC cadets.

In a move towards achieving a consistent quality for OTC cadets the War Office set out, in more detail, what training was required from the schools. This was a

---

1 War Office: Directorate of Military Training, later Directorate of Army Training: Papers <https://discovery.nationalarchives.gov.uk/details/r/C14437> (accessed 25 June 2020).
2 Field-Marshal Sir William Robertson Bart., *From Private to Field-Marshal* (London: Constable, 1921), p. 249.
3 John Spencer, 'Sir William Robertson as CIGS', in Spencer Jones (ed), *At All Costs: The British Army on the Western Front 1916* (Warwick: Helion, 2018), p. 69.
4 Ibid., p. 53.
5 HMC, Report of the Committee of the Headmasters Conference for 1915, p. 147.
6 TNA WO 293/3/259: War Office Instructions, Return of Cadets, OTC who have attained the age of 18 1/2 years., 23 December 1915.
7 *The Lancing College Magazine*, Vol 9-1. [No. 303], February 1916, p. 5.

change of approach which had not been expected by the HMC. In December 1915, the Headmaster of Tonbridge, on behalf of the Corps Sub-Committee, had failed to persuade the War Office to provide a Junior OTC syllabus. Instead, the HMC decided to draft its own syllabus, working as closely as possible with the War Office to achieve this.[8] However, in February 1916, under new leadership, the War Office changed its approach and issued guidance Training was to be based on the syllabus for Certificate A with the relevant sections of *Notes from the front* added to the existing reading list.[9] Although there would be no examinations it represented a move towards the pre-war approach. At the heart of the Certificate A syllabus was the approach set out in the *FSR 1909* and *Infantry Training 1911*. This set out the doctrine of the British Army and its significance is set out in its opening paragraph:

> The principles given in this manual have been evolved by experience as generally applicable to the leading of troops. They are to be regarded by all ranks as authoritative, for their violation in the past, has often been followed by mishap, if not by disaster. They should be thoroughly impressed on the mind of every commander that, whenever he has to come to a decision in the field, he instinctively gives them their full weight.[10]

This was important as it set out how the army operated and at a more detailed level included the thought processes to be employed by officers and how responsibility was to be devolved within the army.[11] The OTC syllabus concentrated on the parts of the *FSR* which would give cadets the ability to act as a subaltern and lead an infantry company. As the *FSR* continued to be the doctrine of the British Army throughout the Great War it was logical that Certificate A should underpin the approach to training by the OTC.

This new guidance marked a reintegration of the OTC into the officer training scheme. It was a switch which formed part of a wider set of changes to officer training made by the War Office. In February 1916 it had also established OCBs to address the failings in junior officer training. These inadequacies were many and included a failure to provide cadets with an appropriate understanding of tactical knowledge and training.[12] Before 1916 New Army training was too short, lacked

---

8 HMC, Report of the Headmasters' Conference December 1915, p. 72.
9 Army Council Instructions WO 293/4/269, Junior Division Officers Training Corps, 2 February 1916.
10 *Field Service Regulations Part I Operations 1909 (Reprinted, with Amendments, 1912)* (London: HMSO, 1912), p. 13.
11 Strictly speaking *FSR* is the closest the army came to having a doctrine. It set an ethos which allowed the army to take a flexible approach. For a fuller discussion, see Andy Simpson, *Directing Operations: British Corps Command on the Western Front 1914-1918* (Stroud: Spellmount, 2006), pp. xvi-xvii.
12 Gary Sheffield, *The Chief: Douglas Haig and the British Army* (London: Aurum, 2011), p. 147. Quote from Haig to Lady Haig correspondence, 14 Oct 1915.

central co-ordination and the quality of training varied significantly.[13] In 1915 cadets spent one month with Senior OTC units (such as the Inns of Court) and a further month at a Young Officers' Company.[14] The reports by headmasters, that old boys complained they had to repeat training they had already received or even worse be told the opposite to what they learnt in the OTC, demonstrates just one consequence of these inadequacies.[15] A lack of useful guidance meant Junior OTC training was inefficient in the way it prepared cadets and led to problems such as this. OCBs were set up to address these shortcomings and became part of a 'methodical and progressive system of training for officers.'[16] The introduction of OCBs was a significant change as instead of junior officers receiving training after being commissioned, cadets would instead only receive a commission after they had successfully completed their training.[17] The creation of OCBs established fixed paths for men to be awarded a commission. They were to be open to suitably qualified candidates who had served in the ranks, from other parts of the Empire, and OTC cadets aged at least 18-and-a-half. Commissions in virtually all branches of the army (the only exception was for doctors and the clergy) would only be awarded to those candidates who had successfully passed through the four-month long course with an OCB.[18] This was a move away from the pre-war preference for recruiting junior officers from public schools. Many commissions were subsequently awarded on the basis of the man showing an aptitude for leadership while fighting at the front.[19] Public School OTCs however, were recognised as providing a foundation for training at OCBs. From 1916, public school boys had to meet a series of technical requirements before they gained a commission. They had to be an OTC cadet, they had to be considered suitable for a commission (by avoiding being placed on the list of unsuitable candidates), and they were required to pass their course at an OCB. While in many ways the public school ethos was considered to be a valuable quality in an officer it was not sufficient. The technical requirements to enter an OCB were of greater importance. Public school OTC contingents had greater clarity about what was required of them (even if the training requirements still lacked precision) and this was welcomed by the schools. For Lancing, the introduction of OCBs gave a specific purpose to

---

13 Williams, *Raising and Training the New Armies*, pp. 96-97.
14 G. D. Sheffield, *Leadership in the Trenches: Officer-Man Relations, Morale and Discipline in the British Army in the Era of the First World War* (Basingstoke: Palgrave Macmillan, 2000), pp. 53-54.
15 See Chapter 5.
16 Williams, *Raising and Training the New Armies*, p. 97.
17 Charles Fair, 'From OTC to OCB: The Professionalisation of the Selection and Training of Junior Temporary Officers During the Great War' in Spencer Jones (ed.) *The Darkest Year: The British Army on the Western Front 1917* (Warwick: Helion, 2022), p. 86.
18 TNA WO 293/4/357: Army Council Instructions, Temporary Commissions in the Regular Army; Commissions in the Special reserve of Officers and in the Territorial Force, 14 February 1916.
19 Sheffield, *Leadership in the Trenches*, p. 101.

the OTC, which had been lacking since the start of the war.[20] Harrow echoed this sentiment, arguing the introduction of OCBs demonstrated the importance of gaining as much military training as possible before joining one.[21] Cadets from the public schools needed to be able to hold their own against experienced soldiers who had already served at the front.

From February to August 1916 the War Office took a series of steps to strengthen the training activity of the Junior OTC. It marked a move towards the integrated pre-war approach, in style if not detail. Conscription, which had been introduced in January 1916, enabled the War Office to regulate more closely when boys commenced training with an OCB. From April 1916 boys who were recommended by their OTC CO as suitable to hold a commission were able to stay at school and train with their contingents until they were 19 (as opposed to all other men who were called up at 18).[22] Boys considered to be officer material remained at school and received more relevant training, instead of a basic training in the ranks. By June 1916, steps were taken to raise the quality of cadets being sent to the OCBs; as schools were placed under an obligation to only recommend OTC cadets 'who are considered in every respect suitable for admission to an officer cadet unit.'[23] More specific guidance about the contents of OTC training was offered to ensure the limited available time was used effectively. From August 1916 all boys who were over 18 and staying on at school until they could join an OCB were required to undertake a minimum of 10 hours' training per week. To ensure all boys received the same training before they joined an OCB, it set out how the ten hours should be allocated. Three hours were to be spent on drill, two and a half hours on tactical schemes, one and a half hours on physical training, two hours on musketry and one hour on map reading. The training on these topics was to be based on the Certificate A syllabus.[24] However, undertaking this training was not the equivalent of passing the pre-war Certificate A. The pre-war syllabus had specified a far wider scope of study and training than the four subjects the contingents were now told to concentrate on. For example, an understanding of how to gather intelligence at the front was no longer required of the OTC cadet. Some of the Certificate A topics were transferred to the OCB training but even for this large sections of *FSR* were removed from the syllabus.[25] The aim of the course was to develop the practical

---

20   *The Lancing College Magazine*, Vol 9-2. (No. 304), March 1916, p. 16.
21   *The Harrovian*, Vol. XXIX. No. 1, Saturday, February 26th 1916, p. 10.
22   TNA WO 293/4/863: Army Council Instructions, Military Service Act, 1916. Cadets of the Officers Training Corps belonging to Group 1 or Class I, 23 April 1916.
23   TNA WO 293/4/1142: Army Council Instructions, Military Service Acts, 1916. Cadets of the Officers Training Corps, 6 June 1916.
24   TNA WO 293/6/1676: Army Council Instructions, Training of Cadets of the Officers Training Corps, 30 August 1916.
25   University of Cambridge Library, OP.2100.8.5, "B" Company No.2 Officer Cadet Battalion: Summary of lectures, private study and practical work for the 4 months' course, exclusive of drill, bayonet fighting and physical training.

skills needed to be a junior officer. Basil Williams, an education officer in the RFA, summarised what the core of what OCB training aimed to achieve:

> For all cadets the points on which especial stress is laid are: leadership, cultivation of initiative and self-confidence, a high standard of drill and discipline, care of arms and smartness of turn-out, close co-operation with other arms and a knowledge of the use of the map, of the King's Regulations and of Military Law.[26]

An analysis of the detailed OCB syllabus shows that the training required of OTC cadets was designed to prepare them for the OCB course by giving them a grounding in drill, map reading, musketry and tactics.[27] The personal qualities required in junior officers were often associated with public school boys but not guaranteed, as the case of Maurice Ellinger showed.[28] The guidance set out clear technical requirements of which leadership skills (which were believed to flow from public school ethos), was only one part. The schools now had greater clarity as to what was required of them. It stood in stark contrast to the War Office's approach in 1915.

Its resources remained stretched but the creation of an integrated training scheme for officers enabled it to build on the initiatives of individual schools. Unable to conduct examinations it encouraged schools to conduct their own unofficial examinations. As the syllabus had been reduced, they were not the equivalent of success in Certificate A but evidence of success in an unofficial examination should be included in a cadet's application.[29] In the absence of enough officers to conduct examinations this was a sensible approach. Many schools, including Eton, had already started to conduct their own examinations in early 1915.[30] While there was no inspection system, schools appear to have been submitting reports and receiving feedback as to whether their examinations were an appropriate test for the specified training.[31] Evidence included in applications provided details of oral and written tests passed and the subjects they had been instructed in. Humphrey Ward's unofficial Certificate A (from Shrewsbury School OTC) recorded he had passed tests in drill, command in the field, musketry and tactics (on the Certificate A syllabus) as well as listing seven subjects he had received instruction in. In addition, the certificate provided details of Ward's experience of leadership in the OTC (one and a half years) while on the application form his

---

26 Williams, *Raising and Training the New Armies*, p. 100.
27 University of Cambridge Library, No.2 Officer Cadet Battalion: Summary of lectures, private study and practical work.
28 See Chapter 4.
29 TNA WO 293/4/269: Army Council Instructions, Junior Division Officers Training Corps, 2 February 1916.
30 *Eton College Chronicle*, No. 1521. 11 March 1915, p. 770.
31 *USM*, No. 426 June 1916, p. 96.

CO attested to his strong leadership skills.[32] These were all skills and qualities which demonstrated the suitability of a boy to join an OCB. Recommendations from OTC COs about the suitability of a candidate were not readily given. Sterndale Bennett at Uppingham remarked on Alan Hett's application that he had no marked ability as a leader.[33] Hett was given a commission in the RFC, as a pilot, where leadership skills were less important. While not perfect the system of public schools self-policing the quality of candidates served as an important filter for cadets applying for a temporary commission.

The training received by boys such as Ward and Hett was primarily based on *Infantry Training 1911*. The sections of *Infantry Training 1911*, specified in the Certificate A syllabus, set out the key elements of much of the training the OTC was expected to provide from the beginning of 1916. These sections covered company and section drill and what was to be covered in tactical training. Table Three sets out the topics specified for tactical training:

Table 3 *Infantry Training 1911* – **Section IV Training**[34]

General Principles
Fire
Ground, Inter-communication and orders
Infantry in Attack
The Company in the Firing Line
Infantry in Defence
The Active Defence
The Passive Defence
The Delaying Action by Means of Manoeuvre
The Encounter Battle
Retirements
Fighting in Close Country
Infantry in Mountain Warfare
Machine Guns in Battle

School Field Days were devoted to practising the principles of open warfare. In November 1916, for example, Eton, Marlborough, Wellington, Imperial Service College and Bradfield took part in an exercise designed to practice infantry in attack, active defence and retirements.[35] It may seem surprising that OTC contingents were practising open warfare when the army was involved in trench warfare on the Western

---

32 TNA WO 339/99018 Lieutenant Humphrey Plowden Ward Royal Field Artillery.
33 TNA WO 339/60216: Lieutenant Alan Stanley Hett Royal Flying Corps.
34 War Office, *Infantry Training 1911* (London, HMSO, 1911).
35 *Eton College Chronicle,* No. 1590. 16 November 1916, pp. 118-119.

Front. However, *Infantry Training 1911* was the standard for all infantry training throughout the war. Whilst it is solid on fundamental drills and key principles, it lacked the specifics relating to trench warfare that were necessary by 1916. It was thus supplemented (but not replaced) by the SS series (for example, *SS 143* on platoon organisation and tactics) as well as some of the training included in the OCB syllabus. OTC training was designed to train cadets in the principles of the way the British Army fought. Training at OCBs introduced cadets to the requirements of the current war by covering subjects such as trench warfare.[36] It's also important to note that OTC contingents provided lectures on the detailed duties and work a Junior Officer would be expected to carry out. Sterndale Bennett listed 60 topics (see Table Four) on which lectures were given, to the Uppingham OTC, during the war. This is not a definitive list for all schools but is representative of the lectures offered at all schools (who would also have received advice about this from the HMC Corps Sub-Committee).

Table 4 Uppingham School – Subjects for Lectures[37]

1. History of the Corps	31. Fire Action
2. Drill	32. Fire Discipline and Control
3. Discipline	33. Care of Arms
4. Morale	34. Correspondence
5. Marching and Marching Discipline	35. Etiquette
6. A Day's Life at Camp	36. Command, Leadership
7. Use of Cover and Ground	37. Obstacles
8. Formations, reasons for	38. Tactical Features
9. The Attack	39. Visual Training and I.D.
10. The Defence	40. Range Duties
11. Physical training	41. Spies
12. Advanced Guards	42. Observation
13. Flank and Rear Guards	43. Orderly Room
14. Guard Duties	44. Rank in Navy
15. Organisation of Battalion	45. Foreign Maps
16. Night Work	46. Patrols (Infantry)
17. Scouting	47. Duties of Section Commander
18. Reports and Messages	48. History of the O.T.C.
19. Orders and Appreciations	49. Explosives
20. Reconnaissance	50. Guns
21. Map Reading	51. Tactics of Lewis Gun

36 University of Cambridge Library, "B" Company No.2 Officer Cadet Battalion: Summary of lectures.
37 Extracted from USA, Notes on Uppingham School OTC.

22. Sketching	52. Aeroplane Photography
23. Anti-Gas Measures	53. The Intelligence Officer
24. Ammunition Supply	54. Snipers
25. Characteristics of Troops	55. The importance of Method
26. Sanitation	56. Writing of Precis
27. First Aid	57. Initiative
28. Entrenchments	58. Estimation of Time, Distances and Numbers
29. Communication	59. Development of Soldierly Spirit
30. Observers and Runners and Connecting Files	60. Marching Songs

Many of these subjects can be found in the OCB syllabus and demonstrates how by 1916 OTC training had been integrated into the training scheme for New Army officers. The lecturers to the contingents were a mixture of OTC officers and outside speakers who had relevant knowledge. At Uppingham first aid courses were conducted by local doctors.[38] Old boys and masters returning from the front on leave or because of wounds were popular sources for speakers. As one Headmaster observed these speakers provided welcome variety in OTC activity and minimised the risk of monotony.[39] Speakers with direct experience of the war were able to give boys a better understanding of what was involved. The background of some of the speakers also gave glamour to what otherwise might have been dry subjects. In October 1917 Captain A. J. Evans, an Old Wykehamist of the RFC, lectured at the school on flying and artillery work.[40] Evans was an attractive speaker, as he had recently escaped from a German prisoner of war camp at the fifth attempt, even if his subject was far from glamorous.

The training provided by the contingents had a different emphasis to that provided by them pre-war. Firstly, it was not as ambitious as the pre-war curriculum; its aim was to place boys on an equivalent status at an OCB to those cadets who had joined from the ranks. Without a basic understanding of subjects such as drill and musketry OTC cadets would be at a severe disadvantage. Secondly, OCB cadets now received instruction in subjects they would have received in the OTC before the war. Finally, the nature of the OCB examinations was different to the Certificate A (and B) examinations taken before the war. To an extent, they combined both sets the papers but a comparison of OCB papers with those for Certificates A and B reveals papers which were more geared to the circumstances of the Western Front and to producing officers with the necessary practical skills. While subjects such as military law and the open war principles of *FSR 1909* continued to be examined in two papers, the third one concentrated on trench warfare (which was not dealt with in *FSR 1909* or

---

38   *USM*, No. 433 March 1917, p. 38.
39   WCA, Report of the Head Master for the School Year ending August 1916, p. 3.
40   *The Wykehamist*, No. 568. October 1917, p. 183.

Infantry Training 1911). In addition, the OCB questions were more practically based, numerous and individually earned less marks.[41] In an integrated training scheme it meant that the OTC syllabus became more limited than it was pre-war and focussed on developing practical skills.

A more focussed approach to OTC training by the War Office was matched by more a structured training for the contingents' officers. Many of these men had joined contingents since 1914 and were in need of training to equip them to teach the revised syllabus. Durham's OTC, which had been authorised in late 1914, was run by officers who had received little training. Cecil Gee, who was a member of the contingent from 1914 to 1916, recalled that the work of the contingent was limited to drill and route marches, in contrast to the more varied training provided by schools such as Harrow and Uppingham.[42] At the same time as guidance on training was given in February 1916, training courses were made available to all OTC officers. For example, seven courses in Instruction at Chelsea were offered.[43] Not only did the courses provide officers with the requisite skills but ensured that drill was taught consistently throughout the OTC as preparation for joining an OCB. Other courses included 'Physical and Bayonet Training'.[44] For the remainder of the war OTC officers were regularly offered the opportunity to participate in relevant courses.

Training to take account of developments in warfare since August 1914 were also provided for more experienced OTC officers. In March 1916, a 19-day course of instruction was announced for OTC officers who were experienced in infantry drill and met a Certificate A standard.[45] Clearly, demand for the course was high, as a repeat of it was run in August and September 1916 but this still does not appear to have met demand.[46] The closer specification of the required OTC training meant that it was possible for contingents to arrange their own training with War Office approval. It agreed to Sterndale Bennett arranging a 22-day-long 'Special O.T.C. Course' at Gidea Park, with the Artists' Rifles OCB over the summer of 1916. After consulting with the COs of 56 contingents he agreed a syllabus which covered open fighting, musketry, trench warfare and reconnaissance, all subjects which OTC

---

41   *Report of the Examination for Certificates "A" and "B." held in March 1912 for Cadets of the Junior and Senior Division, Officers Training Corps, with copies of the examination papers* (London: HMSO, 1912) and NAM, 1990-09-7, Papers of Second Lieutenant Theodore Farquhar Twist.
42   IWM 13717, Gee, Charles Hilton Roderick (Oral History).
43   TNA WO 293/4/438: Army Council Instructions, Initial courses of instruction for officers of the Officer Training Corps, 25 February 1916.
44   TNA WO 293/4/443: Army Council Instructions, Attendance at Instructional Courses at Headquarters, Gymnasium Aldershot, of Officers and N.C.Os. of Officers Training Corps, 26 February 1916.
45   TNA WO 293/4/509: Army Council Instructions, Course of Instruction at Chelsea (17th April to 6th May) for officers of the Junior Division, O.T.C., 6 March 1916.
46   TNA WO 293/5/1415: Army Council Instructions, Course of Instruction at Chelsea (21st August to 9th September) for officers of the Junior Division, O.T.C., 16 July 1916.

cadets would need to have a knowledge of. The length of the course made it possible to cover these subjects in a great detail. Topics covered in the open fighting section included: outposts and defensive positions; combined attack and defence; and tactical schemes. Even Sterndale Bennett, an experienced OTC officer, and Volunteer, who had received 56 days of training with the OTC between 1910 and 1913 needed to be brought up to date on the latest military thinking and ensure OTC recruits to the OCBs had the required training. From 1916 to 1918 he spent a total of 68 days on training courses.[47] It demonstrated a strong commitment to ensuring the OTCs were an effective part of the revised progressive training scheme. Even where War office support remained limited, the revised syllabus reduced the problems faced in 1915.

The War Office again announced it was unable to run Annual Camps in 1916 but encouraged schools to run their own unofficial camps.[48] The guidance on what activities time was to be devoted to, and that it was to be based on the Certificate A syllabus, made the training more effective. Uppingham's OTC held a camp on its own where its programme of activities focused on training, based on the Certificate A syllabus, in tactics, drill and physical training.[49] A picture of cadets at the camp shows that the work was physically demanding. The lack of official support meant that some schools were better provided for than others. Some schools with strong military connections were able to hold camps with support equivalent to that provided pre-war. Bradfield, Charterhouse, Clifton, Eton, Imperial Services College, Malvern, Marlborough, Westminster and Winchester held a joint summer camp at Tidworth Pennings, an army garrison. The camp included various demonstrations by the army and the participating contingents took part in an exercise with the 2nd Reserve Cavalry Brigade.[50] Less well-connected schools which combined for annual camps did not enjoy the same level of support; 600 cadets from Eastbourne, Dover, Felsted, St Edmund's Canterbury, Tonbridge and Whitgift attended a camp at Penshurst Park, on land provided by Lord de Lisle. Without official support, the schools prepared for and ran the camp entirely on their own. Training consisted of exercises already undertaken by the individual contingents, but on a larger scale.[51] These exercises are likely to have been based on the official guidance and gave the schools concerned a valuable opportunity to learn from each other and practise the required skills. Despite the inconsistent level of support schools were able to work to a common training scheme with the aim of preparing cadets for OCBs.

OTC training by 1916 was focussed on the practical aspects of becoming an officer and developing the relevant skills was the key emphasis. At Uppingham, in a return to

---

47 USA, Notes on Uppingham School OTC.
48 Army Council Instructions WO 293/4/269, Junior Division Officers Training Corps, 2 February 1916.
49 USM, No. 429 October 1916, pp. 203-205.
50 *Eton College Chronicle*, No. 1579. July 27 1916, p. 58 and No. 1582 September 28 1916, p. 75.
51 *The Tonbridgian*, Vol. XXII, No. 12 [No. 462] December 1916, pp. 563-565.

the pre-war approach of teaching all boys to be leaders, nearly all cadets were trained in the skills of taking a parade. Boys' instruction skills were developed through a system of 'mutual instruction' where much training was provided by boys to other boys. The result, Sterndale Bennett observed, was that it was realised that the importance of the playing of games in developing leadership skills was not as valuable as had been believed before the war. Boys who had been 'dark horses' because of their lack of athletic ability were often found during parades to be 'remarkably fitted for leadership.'[52] It can be assumed that many other public schools made similar discoveries. This should not have come as a surprise. As the war progressed OCBs trained many men from other backgrounds who made excellent junior officers. All OCB cadets received training in the leadership skills which previously had given public schools an advantage in officer recruitment. The practical training public school boys received in the OTC became of greater importance in their preparation to be a junior officer and the qualities gained through public school ethos less so.

Despite the improved support, the contingents often found themselves stretched. Equipment and facilities withdrawn by the War Office in August 1914 were not restored in 1916, forcing schools to continue to fall on their own resources to fill the gaps in their OTC work. The approaches to addressing this varied from school to school. Some schools were able to recruit wounded officers to replace teachers who had left to join the army. Sherborne recruited Percy Broke Freeman who had been invalided out of the army, as a Second Lieutenant, after an appendix operation. His background was ideal having been educated at Bradfield and Cambridge and then taught at Radley before enlisting. Despite his operation he was able to make a significant contribution to the work of the OTC.[53] In many cases these arrangements were temporary and relied on connections the schools had. Captain. H.R. Bowlby, a son of the Lancing Headmaster, was invalided out of the Rifle Brigade in April 1916 and by the start of 1917 was assisting the school's OTC contingent.[54] The withdrawal Sergeant-Instructors placed considerable burdens on those running the OTC. Mill Hill was typical in not being able to appoint a Sergeant Instructor until early 1917.[55] In their absence, OTC officers found themselves having to take on responsibility for the administration and organisation of their contingents, in addition to their teaching duties. Sherborne also without a Sergeant Instructor until 1917 decided to move a teacher, G.M. Carey, from teaching French to teaching physical training in 1916.[56] As well as academic teaching being adversely affected, a lack of support made it difficult for schools to meet some of the training requirements the War Office had laid

---

52   USA, Notes on Uppingham School OTC.
53   SSA, Percy Broke Freeman (1887-1960).
54   *The Lancing College Magazine*, The Great War (1914-1918) Forum Bowlby, Henry <https://www.greatwarforum.org/topic/66238-bowlby-henry/> (accessed 22 July 2020).
55   *MHM*, Vol xliv., No.5 March 1917, p. 150.
56   SSA, Headmaster's Report to the Governors for 1916, p. 8 and Headmaster's Report to the Governors for 1917, p. 10.

down. Under its guidance for training cadets over 18, two hours per week was to be devoted to musketry. At the start of the war many schools had had all their .303 rifles taken by the War Office. It was only in 1917 that schools were issued with replacements at the rate of 25 per platoon of the authorised establishment.[57] In the meantime, schools had to improvise as best they could with the use of mini-ranges, where rifles not required by the army were used. Many of the more established schools had ranges for .303s but not mini-ranges and had to take urgent action to develop facilities. Winchester, an army school, had to build one which was not opened until December 1915.[58] Uppingham, whose OTC was also well established, was not able to open a mini-range until June 1916.[59] Unintentionally, there was a levelling up of the facilities different schools enjoyed. Mill Hill, with its ambivalent approach to the army, already had an established rifle club with a mini-range by the outbreak of war. Bradford Grammar School, whose contingent was only authorised in the early stages of war, and lacked any real facilities for OTC work, by March 1916 had built a mini-range in the school playground.[60] Despite other improvements the work of the school of contingents often varied in quality.

1916 saw a substantial change in the role of public school OTCs as a source of junior officer candidates. Public schools were no longer the primary source of junior officers, although they remained a significant one. The OCBs introduced in early 1916 drew cadets not only from the Junior OTC contingents but also from the ranks and the Empire. Once again OTCs became part of a progressive officer training scheme but one which differed from the pre-war approach. The syllabus was scaled down and training focussed on giving boys similar basic skills and abilities to those men joining OCBs straight from the army. Unlike 1914 and 1915 where public schoolboys received officer training once they had been awarded a commission, from 1916 a commission was only earnt once they had successfully passed through an OCB. To prepare boys for the OCBs the War Office set out clear guidance as to what training boys should be given and laid down a clear requirement that only boys who were suitable candidates, both in terms of the training they had received and their leadership ability, should be recommended. The improved guidance made it easier for schools to manage activities where there continued to be a lack of support, such as field days, but schools continued to struggle with the lack of support and facilities enjoyed before the war. In December 1916, the HMC's representatives raised their concerns with the War Office and were offered vague assurances that if possible wounded officers would be provided

---

57 Army Council Instructions WO 293/6/161, Issue of Rifles to contingents of the Officers Training Corps, 26 January 1916.
58 WCA, Report of the Head Master for the School Year ending August 1915, p. 6 and *The Wykehamist*, No. 548, December 1915, pp. 473-474.
59 *USM*, No. 426 June 1916, p. 96.
60 *The Bradfordian: The Bradford Grammar School Magazine*, Vol XXI., No. 124., March 1916, p. 28.

to support OTC contingents.⁶¹ In 1917 the War Office rapidly turned this vague assurance into specific action. Its emphasis changed, from one offering guidance on the required approach to training, to one where it became increasingly pro-active in providing guidance for OTC training and sought to achieve and raise a common high standard within all OTC contingents.

Raising the Standard

The advent of Lloyd George's government saw, from 1917, an approach based on the idea of National Efficiency to direct the country's efforts more effectively towards winning the war. It is no surprise that the War Office appointed officers to be responsible for the Junior OTC who had suitable experience and skills, but who were unable to serve at the front. Lieutenant Colonel F.E. Whitton was appointed to this role from 1 March 1917 and was well qualified to provide effective support for the OTC. After being severely wounded in October 1914 he had spent the 1916 Autumn term teaching at Harrow, while on half-pay.⁶² Although, never formally on the OTC establishment while at Harrow, it is highly likely that he had a close involvement with the OTC. Bowlby, who taught at Lancing (see above), was never formally attached to its contingent but worked with the OTC.⁶³ It would be surprising if there was not a similar arrangement for Whitton at Harrow. His professional background as an experienced pre-war Staff Officer was such that it would have been his natural inclination to take a close interest in the school's OTC and this made him well suited to overseeing its work he oversaw the first steps towards building a far closer engagement with the public schools.

In the event, his responsibilities for the OTC only lasted for seven months and ended with the return of Lieutenant Colonel Maxwell Earle to the War Office in October 1917.⁶⁴ As well qualified as Whitton was (he was deployed to other responsibilities), Earle was even better qualified. He had overseen officer recruitment at the War Office, from 1910 to 1914, had been a frequent visitor to the public schools and had greatly improved what had been a fraught relationship between them and the army. He was held in high esteem by the HMC, especially by those members most concerned with military matters. Despite Whitton's qualifications, when Earle returned (which would not have been anticipated in March 1917 as he was interned

---

61   HMC, Report of the Headmasters' Conference December 1916, pp. 62-63.
62   *The Harrovian*, Vol XXIX. No. 6, Saturday October 21st 1916, p. 76, *The War Office List. 1917* (London: HMSO, 1917) p. 75 and DNW, The Michael McGoona Collection to the Leinster Regiment <https://www.dnw.co.uk/auction-archive/special-collections/lot.php?specialcollection_id=408&specialcollectionpart_id=439&lot_uid=56960> (accessed 28 July 2020).
63   *The Lancing College Magazine*, Vol 10-1. [No. 312], February 1917, pp. 7, 12.
64   NAM, Earle and *The War Office List. 1918* (London: HMSO, 1918) p. 84.

in Switzerland after a spell in a POW camp), giving him responsibility for the OTC took best advantage of his skills and experience. He was a critical friend to the schools; not afraid to criticise inadequacies in officers recruited from public schools, while making considerable efforts to ensure the Junior OTC received the support it needed, and regularly visiting contingents.[65] This approach contributed to a closer engagement between the War Office and the Public Schools. After his arrival, there was a further escalation in both support for and quality control of the OTC.

The greater level of clarity in training requirements was accompanied by a recognition by the public schools that it was both their obligation, and in their interest, only to recommend suitable boys for a commission. The HMC recognised that if unsuitable boys were recommended this was likely to lead to a loss of confidence by the army in the schools which had sent them, and in the role of the OTC in the progressive training scheme. Schools which had an OTC contingent did not enjoy a special privilege for their boys, but a responsibility only to recommend suitable cadets.[66] In the absence of Certificate A examinations, it was important to maintain the quality of OTC cadets progressing to OCBs. March 1917 saw further steps to develop the role of the Junior OTC in providing cadets for the OCBs. The War Office sought to more closely manage the supply of officer cadets from the Junior OTC. It reaffirmed that only boys considered suitable for a commission should be recommended for admission to an OCB on the condition they carried out 10 hours of training a week. Those deemed unsuitable would be called up as soon as they were 18. The War Office also sought to better understand the number of cadets available from the Junior OTC. All contingents were now required to provide a monthly return to the War Office listing all those cadets over 18 with details of their service in the OTC and whether or not they were suitable to join an OCB.[67] To ensure a consistent quality of OCB cadets from the OTC the guidance that Certificate A should form the basis of training was now converted to a requirement.[68] This imitated the pre-war practice but was not the equivalent of it. Before August 1914, success in Certificate A offered cadets an advantage when entering the Regular Army or exemptions from SR and TF training which provided part qualification. However, as previously noted, from 1916 the prescribed training covered only part of the pre-war syllabus. Certificate A training during the war was designed to give the basic skills so that cadets had a level of competence to those joining an OCB directly from the ranks. To ensure a common standard for boys

---

65 See for example, HMC, Report of the Headmasters' Conference December 1917, pp. 116-117 and HMC, Report of the Committee of the Headmasters' Conference for September 1917 to December 1918, p. 27.
66 HMC, Report of the Committee of the Headmasters' Conference for 1916, p. 22.
67 TNA WO 293/6/409: Army Council Instructions, Applications for admissions to an Officer Cadet Unit from cadets of the Senior and Junior Divisions, Officers Training Corps, 7 March 1917.
68 Army Council Instructions WO 293/6/488, Training of Cadets of the Junior Division, O.T.C., 21 March 1917.

arriving at an OCB, the nature of the required training was more closely defined. For example, until late 1916 no method for teaching drill had been set out but after this was set down contingents were required to follow a prescribed method. Cadets arrived at OCBs with the same basic training in drill and at a similar standard to other entrants. For some schools, such as Harrow, this was a significant change of practice, but there was a far clearer understanding of what was required of the Junior OTC.[69]

Although what was to be covered in the ten hours per week of training was clearly set out, schools were free to decide how this would be achieved. Even during the war headmasters asserted their right to run their schools as they saw fit. In 1916 they had resisted an attempt to impose a requirement of 15 hours training per week. However, even 10 hours per week of training meant schools needed to have flexibility in how this was done to meet their different priorities and educational approaches. At Marlborough, with close ties to the army, little change in its OTC activities was required from that established in 1914, of four classes a week in military matters.[70] Winchester, which like Marlborough had close ties to the army, preferred to take its pre-war stance that only the minimum required to gain a commission should be done. All of its boys over 18 were required to spend some time outside normal school hours on training but their commitment to work with OTC was reduced.[71] Mill Hill, with its non-militaristic background, also chose to require boys to spend time outside normal school hours undertaking the required 10 hours training per week but unlike other schools this was extended to all boys over 17 (and not 18 as required by the Army Council).[72] Like Marlborough, Oundle's approach went beyond the minimum requirements. Known for its emphasis on engineering and science, it took a more integrated approach. By April 1916, in addition to OTC training for nearly every boy in the school, military theory was integrated into the school's wider curriculum. For example, science lessons included subjects such as the theory of range finding and the trajectory of projectiles.[73] By 1917 it had recognised that training could impose too much of a burden on boys and it introduced a Cadet Sixth for all boys over 18 so that all military work was done in school hours.[74] Other schools chose to follow Oundle by integrating training with other educational activity. In 1916 Uppingham had established a Cadet Class for boys over 18 where a minimum of ten hours of military work was undertaken, in addition to normal school work.[75] However, by March 1917 training had been integrated into normal school activities with the formation of a Special Class for over 18s where six of the 10 required hours a week were spent

---

69 *The Harrovian*, Vol XXIX. No. 6, Saturday October 21st 1916, p. 86.
70 *The Malburian,*, Vol. XLIX., No. 741. October 17th 1914, p. 154.
71 WCA, Report of the Head Master for the School Year ending August 1917, p. 4.
72 *MHM*, Vol xliv, No.5 March 1917, p. 151.
73 *The Laxtonian,*, Vol. IX, No. 1. April 1916, p. 12.
74 *The Laxtonian*, Vol. IX, No. 6. December 1917, p. 1.
75 *USM*, No. 429 October 1916, p. 207.

in school.⁷⁶ Many headmasters had to make similar compromises to ensure that the over-18 boys were not overburdened by the competing demands of military training and academic work.

From 1917, the recognition that the training requirements needed to be realistic was accompanied by steps to reduce the burden on OTC officers. Stricter training requirements were accompanied by more support from the army and as a result the responsibility for planning and implementing training schemes no longer fell on the schools. The provision of support was devolved by the War Office to individual Army Commands. The consequence of this was that the support a school received varied according to which area it was in. Different commands had different priorities, approaches and resources and this meant there was not a one size fits all approach to supporting the OTC contingents. In 1917 the War Office announced that it would sanction and support annual camps, but they could only be held with the permission of the Army Command in which it was planned to hold them.⁷⁷ As a result, not all the schools were given permission to hold annual camps. Eton, Marlborough, Radley, Beaumont, Imperial Service College, Harrow, Charterhouse, Malvern, Westminster and Bradfield were able to hold a camp at Tidworth Pennings, located in Southern Command.⁷⁸ Uppingham, which on the other hand was under Northern Command and had held its own camps in 1915 and 1916, was not able to participate in one.⁷⁹ However, the amount of training undertaken during term time made the holding of an annual camp less important. At the heart of its approach lay the War Office's belief that membership of an OTC was an essential part of preparation for an OCB and not the general benefits of a public school education, despite the HMC's protests to the contrary.⁸⁰ The priority given to the OTC by the War Office was not new (that had been its position since December 1914); what was different was that the OTC was no longer left to its own devices.

During 1917 the War Office developed this approach in stages; seeking to monitor standards at individual contingents while devolving responsibility for achieving them. It started to develop an inspection regime for the contingents. The first step in this direction was to relieve OTC COs of their responsibility to certify whether candidates for the regular army had attained a Certificate A standard and thus earn a 400-mark exemption for the Army Entrance Examination. This arrangement had caused headmasters considerable concern in 1916 as they were expected to certify their boys had reached a standard which merited the exemption.⁸¹ To them it was tantamount to marking their own homework and represented a conflict of interest. Instead, the War Office restored the pre-war system of sending inspecting officers on a day long visit,

---

76 *USM*, No. 433 March 1917, p. 377.
77 TNA WO293/6/940: Annual Camps. Junior Division Officers Training Corps, 14 June 1917.
78 *Eton College Chronicle*, No. 1623. 27 September 1917, pp. 275-276.
79 *USM*, No. 441 May 1918, p. 93.
80 HMC, Report of the Headmasters' Conference December 1916, p. 59.
81 HMC, Report of the Headmasters' Conference December 1916, pp. 58-63.

to carry out examinations to assess whether candidates had a Certificate A standard of knowledge of drill, field training, musketry and tactics.[82] As with the New Army throughout the conflict, officer training in the Regular Army concentrated on developing the practical skills of cadets.[83] It meant that the required standards were enforced centrally and there was a lower risk of an inconsistent approach to the awarding of the 400-mark exemption.[84] It also gave the War Office an opportunity to monitor more closely the standard of training at individual contingents ensure that basic requirements were the same for OCB candidates as they were for regular army candidates. To assess whether the required standards had been met candidates were required to command members of their contingents in a number of exercises. This also had the benefit of enabling the inspecting officer of seeing the wider contingent at work. Not only did the War Office receive a report on the regular army candidates, but also a report on the contingent's work, of which the school received a copy.[85] Through this system of examinations the War Office was once again able to monitor the work of individual contingents and provide feedback on the strengths and weaknesses of their work. However, this did not replicate all parts of the pre-war approach to supporting the work of contingents. From the middle of 1917 another element of the pre-war approach was introduced with a system of inspections by designated officers. This was aimed at improving the quality of the training in the contingents.[86] The initiative enjoyed backing at the highest levels of the War Office. Lieutenant-General F. J. Davies, the Military Secretary at the War Office, attended one of the inspections of training activities at Marlborough during the 1917 summer term. His interest, as the senior officer responsible for promotions in the army demonstrates that by 1917 the War Office was attaching a great deal of importance to the OTC as an established source of officers. Addressing the contingent, he emphasised the importance of the OTC as a source of officers and praised the quality of the candidates for commissions it was producing.[87] Rather than leaving the Junior OTC to its own devices, as it had in 1914 and 1915, the War Office had set in place a system which aimed to effectively exploit it as a source of junior officers.

By October 1917, inspections often at short notice, were taking place at all Junior OTC contingents. The short notice given of them meant that contingents had little time to prepare and the inspecting officers were able to gain a better understanding of

82 *The Stonyhurst Magazine,* Vol XIII. (Part2) No. 210, February 1917, p. 165.
83 Ian Beckett, Timothy Bowman and Mark Connelly, *The British Army and the First World War* (Paperback edition, Cambridge: Cambridge University Press, 2017), pp. 55-56.
84 Army Council Instructions WO 293/5/26, Army Entrance Examination. Dates. Age Limits. Award of marks for efficiency in the Officers Training Corps, November 1916. Age limits, 11 August 1916.
85 *The Harrovian,* Vol XXX,. No. 5, Saturday July 28th 1917, p. 69.
86 *The Harrovian,* Vol XXX,. No. 7, Saturday November 17th 1917, p. 109.
87 *The Malburian,* Vol. LII., No. 776. July 12th 1917, p. 96 and *The Malburian,* Vol. LII., No. 777. July 30th 1917, p. 124.

training activity, as opposed to being treated to a polished performance which might have hidden shortcomings in the work of the contingents.[88] Typically, the inspecting officer was from a nearby training battalion; Major W. S. W. Parker Jervis OC of the King's Royal Rifle Corps (KRRC), a training battalion based at Sheerness, was assigned to oversee the work of Epsom's OTC.[89] Unusually, he was also responsible for the OTC inspection at St John's Leatherhead.[90] However, most inspecting officers were assigned to only one contingent to ensure they could effectively develop a uniformly high standard at all Junior OTCs.[91] There were three main purposes of the inspections: to assess the progress of individual contingents in training cadets in the specified activities (drill, tactical schemes, physical training, musketry and map reading); identify what improvements could be made, and recommend training for a contingent's officers to address deficiencies which had been identified. The system aimed to address deficiencies speedily and the follow up was often rapid. Following the inspection at Stonyhurst in October 1917 the inspecting officer arranged for an officer from the contingent to attend a two week 'Physical Training and Bayonet Fighting' course.[92] Schools were often provided with other support from their Army Commands which varied according to their circumstances. For example, schools which were more isolated from other schools and army training camps, had wounded officers posted to them. At Uppingham an officer, Captain A. R. A. Dickins, South Staffordshire Regiment, was seconded to it at the start of the 1917 Summer Term.[93] Bradford Grammar School had an officer on light duty posted to it shortly after an inspection took place. No information is available about his duties but one of his successors, in addition to offering general support, provided instruction in tactics and map reading (two subjects which formed part of the OTC syllabus).[94] Uppingham and Bradford both fell under Northern Command, but other commands took a similar approach, where necessary. Eastern Command also provided support for some OTC contingents in its area. Both Oundle and The Leys had junior officers attached to them.[95] However, other schools in Eastern Command were not offered wounded officers to assist with training. Schools close to London, such as Aldenham, Berkhamsted, Harrow and Mill Hill fell under the same command but did not have wounded officers attached to them. All were close to the Inns of Court OCB at Berkhamsted and could participate in exercises with it and enjoy other support which prepared cadets for OCB training.

---

88 *The Stonyhurst Magazine*, Vol XIV, No. 214, December 1917, p. 168.
89 *The Epsomian*, Vol. XLIX, No. 1 Christmas 1917, p. 11
90 *The Johnian*, Vol. XXXII., No. 6, December 1917, p. 78.
91 *The Epsomian*, Vol. XLIX, No. 1 Christmas 1917, p. 11.
92 *The Stonyhurst Magazine*, Vol XIV, No. 214, December 1917, p. 168.
93 *USM*, No. 435 July 1917, p. 100.
94 *The Bradfordian: The Bradford Grammar School Magazine*, Vol XXI., No. 129., November 1917, p. 30 and Vol XXII., No. 132., November 1918, p. 18.
95 *The Laxtonian*, Vol. IX. No.7., April 1918, p. 207 and *The Leys Fortnightly*, Vol. XLII. No. 744, May 17 1918, p. 238

For these schools there were often other factors which made it unnecessary to have wounded officers attached to them. Mill Hill enjoyed a close relationship with the Middlesex Regiment whose barracks were just over a mile away. Harrow enjoyed close ties with the Army and was able to draw on these for training support and joint exercises. The result of this devolution of support to the Army Commands was that the most appropriate assistance was given to each school to ensure that, as far as possible, cadets sent to OCBs by all contingents were of a common high standard.

By 1918 the War Office was prepared to authorise and pay for the expansion in the authorised establishment of Junior OTC contingents.[96] The worsening manpower crisis made it essential that every source of junior officers was expanded to its maximum potential. This was coupled with further efforts to improve the quality of training of contingents. Over the Christmas holidays of 1917 many Junior OTC COs took up the offer of an attachment to observe the training activities of OCBs, gain a better understanding of them and exchange ideas.[97] These visits continued in subsequent holidays to enable OTC COs to widen their understanding of training requirements. In the summer of 1918, the COs at Uppingham and Sedbergh were attached to the RAF No. 1 Cadet Wing.[98] It is clear that both the RAF and the OTC COs benefitted from the visit. Sterndale Bennett's five-page report to the Cadet Wing's CO offered ideas on where the unit's training might be improved and how joining the RAF might be made more attractive for public school boys.[99] A further development in the drive to improve training within the OTC came in the summer of 1918 when all masters from schools with OTC contingents and who had served for at least six months abroad, were permitted to return to their schools if they wished.[100] Teachers who had military experience would be more useful in preparing boys for training in an OCB. This may appear to be late in the day but the war was expected to continue into 1919. It demonstrated the War Office's desire to raise the quality of training at schools as well as support the wider educational efficiency of the schools.[101] Schools, many of whom found it difficult to recruit good quality replacement teachers, benefitted from experienced officers training their contingents and a general improvement in training standards.

---

96 *Brighton College Magazine*, Vol. 6. No. 2, pp. 78-79.
97 For example, see *The Lancing College Magazine*, Vol 10-9. [No. 319], December 1917, p. 115 and Vol 11-1. (No. 320), February 1918, p. 6.
98 *Roosters and Fledglings: No. 1 Cadet Wing News and Notes*, Vol 1 No. 5, September 1918, p. 255.
99 USA, Notes on Uppingham School OTC.
100 SSA, Headmaster's Report to the Governors for 1918, p. 4.
101 HMC, Report of the Committee of the Headmasters Conference for September 1917 to December 1918, p. 49.

Conclusion

From 1916 onwards the General Staff at the War Office adopted an increasingly proactive and supportive approach towards the Junior OTC contingents. This support was not specifically aimed at the Public Schools which made up 55 percent of the total number of contingents. 20 percent of Public Schools did not have OTC contingents and the War Office was steadfast in its refusal to approve new contingents after the end of 1914, although existing contingents were allowed to increase their authorised establishments. The authorities were not interested in Public Schools *per se* as a source of junior officers but in those which had contingents. Training in the OTCs was developed with the aim of achieving a consistently high quality of cadets for the OCBs. From 1916 the OTC syllabus was a slimmed down version of its pre-war syllabus. The emphasis was no longer on developing a whole range of skills required to be a junior officer but in giving cadets the basic training to put them at the same level as men joining the OCBs from the ranks. Public schoolboys were not guaranteed a place in an OCB and a subsequent commission. To gain one they had to attain a Certificate A in topics such as drill and tactics and demonstrate leadership skills. Schools only nominated cadets for an OCB who had met all these requirements. An ability at games was not necessarily an indication of suitability for a commission; as Sterndale Bennett observed, the training undertaken showed that those who were not good at games often demonstrated themselves to be better leaders than games players. Support from the War Office evolved in the final three years of the war. In 1916 the emphasis was on providing better guidance although there were not enough resources available to monitor and control the quality of the training. In 1917 and 1918 the War Office developed a programme to monitor the work of the contingents and equip them to attain a higher standard of basic training. By the end of 1917, the War Office was aiming for a universally high standard of training in the school's contingents. The army was not solely interested in the qualities of a Public School education but also in the practical skills developed by Junior OTC contingents (45% of whom were at schools which were not members of the HMC). This did not mean that the contribution of individual schools was necessarily identical or very similar. The contribution of each public school to the war effort was also dictated by its individual circumstances and educational approach. How and why this contribution varied is discussed in the next chapter.

7

Status, Class, Curriculum and Connections: Public Schoolboys and Military Service

Debate about the contribution of public school old boys to the military effort has centred on the ethos of the schools, the playing of games and the leadership qualities which flowed from this. An approach which, it is argued, made them attractive officer material for the army. Public schoolboys were an important source of officers but the reasons for this went beyond the playing of games. As Sterndale Bennett had discovered, a lack of ability at games was not an obstacle to being an effective leader of men.[1] Of equal importance is the training public schoolboys received with their Junior OTC contingents. This training aimed to produce men with the basic skills required for junior officers. After 1916, the OTC syllabus was reduced so that instead of being prepared to a level where they could immediately receive commissions as subalterns in the TF, boys received enough training to qualify them to join an OCB. In an OCB they would continue to receive training and upon successfully completing the course, be granted a commission. Although all public schoolboys who joined an OTC contingent received the same basic training, there were other important factors which meant there was a great deal of variation between individual schools in the contributions they made to the military effort. Beyond public school ethos and the playing of games, the differing contributions of schools also needs to be understood in terms of status, class, curriculum and connections.

There are two main ways in which the contributions of each school to the military effort varied. Firstly, the percentage of their old boys who became officers and the relative seniority of their old boys within the military differed by school. Secondly, schools differed in the skills their old boys provided to the military effort. This difference manifested itself through the proportion from each school which served in the different arms. For example, Epsom's old boys had a particularly strong representation in the RAMC and the Navy's medical service. This chapter examines why these differences arose and how the schools contributed to officer training within the army,

1   See Chapter 6.

as opposed to within the Junior OTC. It addresses why the varying contributions of each school can be explained by status, class, curriculum and connections.

Pigeon-holing schools into particular categories, however, is unhelpful. It can over elevate the importance of a group of schools at the expense of a more nuanced explanation of individual contributions. The nine original public school investigated by the Cavendish Commission, enjoyed an elevated status.[2] However, their contributions varied and in any case by 1914 the public school movement had undergone a substantial expansion (the HMC had 114 members) and there were many schools (such as Uppingham and Oundle) whose status had significantly grown. As previously discussed, John Honey classified each school in a five-stage ranking of I to IV for those he identified as the leading schools and no classification for the remainder (NC). Within this group there were other sub-sets such as the 10 schools which the pre-war army primarily drew on for its officers corps.[3] Schools could often fall into more than one category or sub-set. Charterhouse, Eton, Harrow, Rugby and Winchester were both Cavendish schools and members of the group of 10 schools from which the army had traditionally drawn most of its officers. Membership of one or more of these groups is just one factor which explains the differing contributions of individual schools.

At many of these schools their boys were drawn from the upper and upper middle-class schools but this was not always the case. At Christ's Hospital where many parents were not required to pay fees (and those for the rest of the parents were subsidised), many of the boys had lower middle-class background. Other schools such as Oakham and Bradford Grammar School had a substantial proportion of boys with scholarships from their local education authority. However, examining the figures for different schools demonstrates that there is no clear correlation between class and, for example, the proportion of old boys who became officers. The education boys received at public school was also an important factor. In considering the curriculum, it is not only a question of what schools taught in the classroom and whether, for example, the emphasis was on the classics or science. Consideration also needs to be given to be to aspects such as the military training they received. The educational approach of schools varied and, in some cases, was far from the militaristic approach which the public school movement has been accused of. In addition to the accusation of militarism, it is alleged that the old boys' network of the schools meant that those with the best connections benefitted most and that their roles in the military were not always based on merit. However, this was not always the case and there is evidence that patronage and connections were an important way to override hierarchy within the army. Patronage, it has been argued, was used to override the concept of 'Buggins'

---

2   Eton, Charterhouse, Harrow, Merchant Taylors', Rugby, Shrewsbury, St Paul's Westminster and Winchester.
3   Charterhouse, Cheltenham, Clifton, Eton, Haileybury, Harrow, Marlborough, Rugby, Wellington College and Winchester.

turn and identify men who were able to provide the skills the army needed as it rapidly grew and had to address many new problems.[4] Connections were important but not always the primary factor in explaining a man's involvement. When connections were a significant factor, it was not always because of the boy's superior social background. The involvement of old boys in the military effort is explained by an often complex mixture of factors relating to status, class, curriculum and connections.

Public Schoolboys and the Officers Corps

In Chapter Four the role of public schoolboys in building the New Army in 1914 and 1915 was discussed. The need to build the New Army rapidly and provide a junior officer corps for it meant that a great deal of improvisation was required. There were not enough former OTC cadets to fill the expanded junior officer corps so a public school education was often accepted as evidence of suitability for a commission. However, this was the consequence of a necessarily improvised approach where suitable candidates were drawn from a variety of sources. The nature of this improvised approach is demonstrated by the case of Grimsby Municipal College where all its former OTC cadets who had enlisted by 1915 had been awarded commissions.[5]

The introduction of OCBs in February 1916 marked the final stage of a move to a more structured system for officer recruitment. OCBs drew both on the Junior OTC and the ranks for its recruits. By this time, the supply of public school educated men was insufficient to meet the demand for junior officers, while also by the start of 1916 there was an increasing supply of men, without a public school background, who had demonstrated leadership skills while serving in the ranks.[6] This is confirmed by analysis which suggests by 1918 in the region of 5 percent of entrants to OCBs were from a public school OTC.[7] This does not mean that the commitment of public schoolboys faded away after the euphoria of the initial rush to arms. Analysis of the entrants of a sample of public schools from 1909 onwards (i.e., boys who would have gone straight into the wartime army after leaving school) shows that they made up between 25 to 30 percent of those who served from the schools examined in detail. In other words, the youngest played a significant part in the military effort. This section will address the overall contribution of different public schools to the military effort and also examine whether the public school OTCs remained an effective source of potential officers.

---

4   Aimée Fox, 'The Secret of Efficiency? Social relations and Patronage in the British Army in the Era of the First World War' *English Historical Review* (11 December 2020), pp. 1527-1557.
5   See Chapter 4.
6   Sheffield, *Leadership in the Trenches*, p. 56.
7   I am grateful to Charles Fair for this information.

Table 5 Analysis of % of Old Boys with Commissions by School

School	HMC Member	'Honey' HMC Classification (I to IV)	OTC	Major & Above	Junior Officers	Total % of Officers	% of OTC Cadets with Commissions in March 1915
Bloxham	N	NA	Y	12.1%	51.0%	63.1%	37.5%
Bradford GS	Y	NC	Y	2.4%	34.9%	37.3%	0.0%
Charterhouse	Y	I	Y	26.5%	69.0%	95.4%	88.5%
Christ's Hospital	Y	NC	Y	7.5%	58.2%	65.7%	NK
Colfes	N	NA	N	2.3%	38.0%	40.3%	NA
Eastbourne	Y	II	Y	11.7%	69.2%	80.9%	34.9%
Epsom	Y	III	Y	21.0%	66.5%	87.5%	60.0%
Handsworth GS	N	NA	Y	1.5%	43.2%	44.7%	100.0%
Lancing	Y	II	Y	11.1%	68.0%	79.1%	83.1%
Mill Hill	Y	NC	Y	8.4%	68.8%	77.2%	16.3%
Oakham	Y	NC	Y	12.2%	58.8%	71.0%	86.7%
Oundle	Y	IV	Y	5.6%	74.2%	79.8%	75.0%
Sherborne	Y	I	Y	22.5%	64.7%	87.2%	NK
Shrewsbury	Y	III	Y	18.4%	68.9%	87.3%	77.3%
St George's, Harpenden	N	NA	N	0.0%	55.7%	55.7%	NA
Stonyhurst	Y	NC	Y	12.9%	62.5%	75.4%	78.7%
Tonbridge	Y	I	Y	15.6%	68.3%	83.9%	65.6%
Uppingham	Y	I	Y	17.1%	72.1%	89.2%	78.9%
Wakefield GS	Y	NC	N	3.6%	37.9%	41.5%	NA
Winchester	Y	I	Y	26.3%	65.7%	92.0%	87.5%

Key:
NA = Not applicable
NC = No classification
NK = Not known

To understand the contribution of public schools it is important to compare it with some schools which were not part of the public school movement. Table Five provides analysis for a range of different schools. The schools include several HMC members (and by definition a public school) of varying status ranging from Winchester to Wakefield Grammar School. Also included is Bloxham which was not part of the HMC but had an OTC (authorised in 1910) and whose boys were from upper middle-class families.⁸ In addition, two schools which drew on the lower middle-class families have been included. One, Handsworth Grammar School, had an OTC contingent (established in 1907 as a Cadet Corps) while the other, Colfes Grammar School did not.⁹ Analysing their contribution provides additional insight into the contribution of the public schools. On the face of it the Colfes and Handsworth figures are similar, and better than those for Bradford Grammar School, which was a member of the HMC, but analysis illustrates the difference between them and most public schools.

There was a need to recruit officers from outside the public schools. The casualty rates for junior officers made it impossible for public schools to fill the gap.[10] Colfes and Handsworth both drew on the lower middle-classes. Their boys were the sons of clerks, shopkeepers, middlemen, small merchants and industrialists. At both schools many boys left before they were 18, usually at 15.[11] When the figures for their boys who joined each school in 1909 and subsequent years are analysed more closely, there is a different profile for their old boys who became officers. At Colfes only 18 percent of this cohort was granted commissions, while at Handsworth the equivalent figure was 38 percent. The Handsworth figures demonstrate that OTC (and the associated) training was considered to be an advantage in applications for commissions via the OCBs, although it was not a guarantee of a commission. In the case of Colfes, the figures show that older men who had demonstrated leadership skills at the front while serving in the ranks were also a valuable source of junior officers. In both case the two schools had a higher proportion of second lieutenants than many public schools,.[12] Their old boys were being used to man the lowest level of the officer corps, whereas the old boys of public schools were far more likely to progress within the officer corps.

Further support for the idea public schools were a preferred source of officers comes from an analysis of the intake of a sample of schools from 1909 onwards. The percentage of their boys who had become officers ranged between 70 percent and 90 percent and in the region of a further 10 percent were, at the end of the war, waiting to progress from an OCB into the officer corps. Of those who were not awarded a commission, some may have simply not sought one but many were not recommended by their OTC CO or rejected by the army. Not even those boys from schools with a close connection to the army were guaranteed a commission. Richard Leir, who was

---

8   Paul Methven, 'Children ardent for some desperate glory' Public Schools and First World War volunteering' (MPhil thesis, Cardiff, 2013), p. 19 and Haig-Brown, *The O.T.C. and The Great War*, p. 7.
9   Haig-Brown, *The O.T.C. and The Great War*, p. 6.
10 I am grateful to Charles Fair for sharing his research on this.
11 Records of Handsworth School <https://discovery.nationalarchives.gov.uk/details/r/553530a9-09a2-474f-96ae-405d570bc551> (accessed 12 February 2021) and Andrew Whittaker email correspondence, 13 December 2019.
12 *Colfes Grammar School Lewisham and The Great War 1914-1919 with Rolls of Honour and of Service* (Privately published: 1920) and *Handsworth Grammar School (Bridge Trust) Records of Service 1914-1918* (Privately published: n.d.).

educated at Clifton, after enlisting with a Public Schools Battalion went to Sandhurst. However, in May 1915 he returned to his unit after it was concluded he was unsuitable officer material. When his battalion was disbanded in April 1916, Leir like many of its men were transferred to OCBs. However, by August 1916, it had once again been concluded he was not suitable for a commission.[13] Even before 1916, the army was not prepared to unquestioningly accept the product of a public school for a commission. Although OTC COs were honest about the potential of their cadets to be officers, their judgement was limited to what they saw in school. Not all of them were ready to graduate from an OCB at the end of their course. John Clarke was recommended by the CO of Shrewsbury OTC but at the end of his OCB course it was proposed he received further training before being commissioned.[14]

Although OCBs were an important method of entry into the officer corps for public school boys the majority did not enter via this route. By February 1916, when the OCBs were introduced, 72 percent of Old Uppinghamians had already enlisted, many as officers.[15] Analysis of figures for other schools suggests that their equivalent ratios were similar. Recruitment in in 1914 and 1915 was, as Chapter Four demonstrated, a haphazard affair. The need to recruit quickly meant that short cuts needed to be taken. As with Grimsby Technical College all Handsworth's enlisting OTC cadets were given commissions in the period up to March 1915. For those in charge of recruiting battalions from their local area it was an easy way to find officers who had a connection with the men they led. However, this was a short-term measure and over the course of the war it is the case that public school old boys were most likely to become officers. Eastbourne, identified by Simon Robbins as being within the top 40 schools providing the leaders of the BEF, had a surprisingly low proportion of its OTC cadets gaining commissions by March 1915 (34.9 percent) but by the end of the war 83 percent of its post-1909 intake (many of whom would have joined the OTC) had become officers.[16] Although most public schools had a high percentage of their *alumni* become officers, those who contributed senior officers was a more exclusive group. Charterhouse and Winchester, with long standing connections to the army had, as expected, a higher proportion of their old boys become senior officers. Long-standing connections were not the only factor in the percentage of old boys who became senior officers. Curriculum combined with connections to a relatively small part of the armed forces was also an important factor. Epsom, which was not

---

13 TNA WO 339/63675: Officer Cadet Richard Thomas Marriott Leir Officer Cadet Battalion and *The Long Long Trail, Royal Fusiliers (City of London Regiment)* <https://www.longlongtrail.co.uk/army/regiments-and-corps/the-british-infantry-regiments-of-1914-1918/royal-fusiliers-city-of-london-regiment/> (accessed 12 February 2021).
14 TNA WO 1139/137032: Officer Cadet John Holden Kempe Clarke, Officer Cadet Battalion.
15 Halstead, *A School in Arms*, p. 79.
16 Simon Robbins, 'British Generalship in the First World War, 1914-1918' (PhD thesis, London 2001), p. 510.

a significant contributor to the BEF leadership, had a surprisingly high proportion of senior officers (21 percent) when compared to other schools. Robbins does not include it in his list whereas just over 17 percent of Uppingham (20th in the list) old boys became senior officers while the comparable figure for Winchester, which ranked sixth, is 26.3 percent. This apparent anomaly can be explained by the curriculum and background of Epsom. Its curriculum and the medical background of its foundation meant that it was a significant source of doctors for the military. The army did not stick to a precise formula in recruiting and promoting its officers. While a public school education was an advantage there were still disparities between schools which superficially appeared to be similar.

While status, class, curriculum and connections are the main factors which explained the varying contributions of different schools the way these factors interact varied in different schools. Christ's Hospital, Bradford Grammar School and Wakefield Grammar School all offered education to many from the lower middle-classes, whose parents would not otherwise be able to afford it. Many of the boys at these three schools left at 15 (as was also the case for Colfes and Handsworth) and when the war came and did not have backgrounds which made them immediately attractive to the army as officer material. However, the proportion of old boys from Christ's Hospital who became officers (66 percent) is substantially higher than that for Bradford (37 percent) and Wakefield (41 percent). Part of this difference can be put down to curriculum, Christ's Hospital had had a Cadet Corps since 1904.[17] Neither Bradford or Wakefield had a Cadet Corps or OTC contingent before the war and their headmasters were also ambivalent about the idea of military training for schoolboys, until war was declared. As the games ethos was not prevalent at Christ's Hospital it demonstrates the premium that the army placed on any officer training schoolboys had received in the OTC. The importance of officer training is reinforced when the contribution of Bradford to the officer corps is examined, after it established an OTC contingent in October 1914. Virtually all its OTC cadets who left the school went on to an OCB. For example, the 50 cadets who left at the end of the 1917 summer term all joined an OCB.[18] Some schools were probably favoured because of their status and standing with the military but the armed forces were prepared to throw a wide net in their effort to recruit junior officers, which included drawing on those who had received some officer training.

The cases of Epsom, Mill Hill and Oundle are further examples of how the army put this into practice. All three schools were ascribed a relatively low status by Honey but closer examination of their contribution reveals a more nuanced story. At Mill Hill and Oundle nearly four out of five of their old boys became officers but in both cases the percentage of senior officers was comparatively small when compared to Epsom.

---

17 Haig-Brown, *The O.T.C. and The Great War*, p. 6.
18 *The Bradfordian: The Bradford Grammar School Magazine*, Vol XXI., No. 129., November 1917, p. 29.

Compared to the 21 percent for Epsom the figure for Mill Hill was 8.4 percent and for Oundle 5.6 percent. On the face of it, they are substantially inferior contributions. In the case of Mill Hill this can be explained by its Non-Conformist background, which discouraged service in the peacetime army. This was reflected in the low percentage of its old boys who became officers in the early stages of the war. By December 1914, 31.2 percent of the old boys serving had commissions, while 72.6 percent of the Epsomians serving were officers. For Oundle a comparative figure is not available but by March 1915, 75 percent of its former OTC cadets had been awarded a commission (Mill Hills's figure was 16.3 percent) which implies a far higher comparative figure than Mill Hill. Oundle had a pre-war record of sending boys to the military colleges and yet the percentage of old boys who became senior officers is lower than Mill Hill.

How can the differences between the three schools be explained when they all drew on upper middle-class parents? In the case of Epsom, the comparatively high proportion of senior officers can be explained be explained by a mix of status, curriculum and connections. The improved medical care in the Great War was the result of the British Army learning from its mistakes in the Boer War and in the years before 1914 committing itself to better medical care for its men during conflict.[19] The results of which can be seen in the grizzly statistic that the war from 1914 to 1918 was the first time more men died of wounds than of disease. Although the infrastructure of medical care was in place, the demands of war meant the RAMC needed to be rapidly expanded; between 1914 and 1918 its regular and territorial arms expanded in total from 18,738 to 144,396 men. For officers (i.e., predominantly the medical professionals) the equivalent figures were 2,407 and 13,305.[20] In other words, the number of professionals deployed in the army increased by a factor of five and a half times. Epsom, with its medical connections and science-based curriculum, had already been a strong source of military medical officers before the war, with its old boys joining the medical services of the British Army, Indian Army and Royal Navy.[21] The wartime expansion of the wartime medical services meant that they needed more senior officers; those already in the military were strong candidates to be senior officers. Epsom was understandably favoured in this process. In addition, old boys who were prominent in medicine were obvious candidates to rise to senior positions within the medical services. Frank Coleman, a prominent dentist before the war, served as a Lieutenant Colonel in the RAMC during the war.[22]

---

19   For a fuller discussion of this, see Andrew Duncan, 'Resistance and Reform: Transformation in the British Army Medical Services 1854-1914,' in Michael LoCicero, Ross Mahoney and Stuart Mitchell (eds.) *A Military Transformed? Adaption and Innovation in the British Military 1792-1+45* (Solihull: Helion, 2014), pp. 36-50.
20   *Statistics of the Military Effort of the British Empire During the Great War*, p. 185.
21   See ECA, Index of Old Epsomian Biographies between 1890 and 1914 Doctors: GPs, Consultants and the Most Eminent.
22   ECA, Index of Old Epsomian Biographies.

Mill Hill and Oundle did not have the same strong connections to one profession in the way that Epsom did. However, like Epsom, they offered a science-based curriculum as an alternative to a classics-based one, which was attractive to many parents with backgrounds in the professions or business who sent their sons to these schools to prepare them for a career in similar backgrounds. Alexander Todd was educated at Mill Hill, the son of a wine merchant, he worked in the business before the war.[23] Maurice Basden, also educated at Mill Hill, was the son of a Nottingham solicitor and articled to the London office of his father's Firm.[24] William Livens was educated at Oundle and when war broke was training to be a civil engineer. His father was Chief Engineer at Ruston and Hornby and vice-president of the Institute of Mechanical Engineers.[25] Percy Burrell, also of Oundle, the son of a businessman was managing director of the family firm at the start of the war.[26] These examples are not untypical of these schools and their education and backgrounds meant these men were good officer material. This was a background which in the case of the younger old boys was supplemented by service in both schools' OTC contingents. Thus, although a low percentage of Mill Hill old boys became officers in 1914 it is no surprise that by the end of war 77 percent of the old boys who had served during the war were officers. However, as nearly all of them had virtually no military background before the war most of them were not able to advance beyond junior officer rank. For Oundle the low percentage of junior officers were the related to different aspects of its status. Oundle, under Sanderson, had become highly respected by the outbreak of war and had undergone rapid growth. In just over 20 years the school had tripled in size. The result was that the age profile of the old boys who served was more skewed towards younger men than other more established schools. At Oundle 39 percent of those who served joined the school from 1909 onwards, whereas at the more established Shrewsbury the equivalent figure was 25 percent. With a considerably lower age profile it was less likely that Oundle's old boys would advance beyond captain.

However, the background of men was a strong factor in their becoming officers. St Georges, Harpenden which was only founded in 1907, drew on the professional and business classes and although it had no OTC (from 1914 it had a Cadet Corps) still saw just under 56 percent of its old boys gain commissions. Bloxham, which was not an HMC school but had an OTC saw 63 percent of its old boys become officers.

23　RFU, *Remembering Alexander Findlater Todd* <https://www.englandrugby.com/news/article/remembering-alexander-findlater-todd> (accessed 19 February 2021).
24　*Small Town Hucknall 1914-1918* <https://www.facebook.com/117600881609310/posts/second-lieutenant-maurice-duncan-basden-16th-battalion-queens-westminster-rifles/1005077326194990/> (accessed 19 February 2021).
25　Oundle School Archives, William Howard Livens (Laxton 1908) and Spink, Auction: 18002 - Orders, Decorations and Medals, Lot: 486 <https://www.spink.com/lot/18002000486> (accessed 19 February 2021).
26　*Oundle Memorials of the Great War MCMXIV-MCMXIX* (Oundle: Privately published, 1920), p. 32.

Taking Bloxham's figures together with those for Colfes and Handsworth, it demonstrates a flexible approach by the army to the recruitment of its junior officer corps as the war progressed. A bias towards the schools which had traditionally provided officers was no longer possible, so the army spread its net through the wider public school movement while not excluding suitable candidates from other schools. Schools such as Mill Hill not only had boys from an 'attractive' social background but also many with some basic officer training through the OTC. Public school boys who were found to be unsuitable were not given commissions as the war progressed, but in general the schools remained an important source of junior officers.

Military Effort, Curriculum and Connections

So far, the contribution of public schools to the military effort and in particular to the officer corps has been discussed in general terms. However, the contribution of different schools cannot only be understood in terms of the proportion of old boys who became senior and junior officers. The military required a variety of different skills and part of its success in the Great War can be attributed to an ability to marry civilian expertise to the needs of the army more successfully than the Germans.[27] The increasingly sophisticated military effort required a wider range of skills because of the change in the proportions of men serving in the different arms and in the ratio of combatant to non-combatant. At the start of the war the percentage of combatants was just over 83 percent but by the war's end had declined to just under 65 percent. The proportion which made up the infantry within combatant soldiers declined from 64.6 percent to 49.2 percent in the same period, while the proportion of men in the Royal Garrison Artillery (RGA) increased from 1 percent to just over 6 percent.[28] This was a consequence of the growth of the army and the way it fought the war. The growth in the artillery reflected its increasing importance in the tactics and strategy of the British Army as the war progressed. The increased proportion of non-combatants was a consequence of a more sophisticated fighting machine which needed increasing support in areas such as logistics, labour and medicine. The increasing sophistication of its activities and the substantial growth in its size meant the army had a need for a wider range of skills than it had within its pre-war ranks.

However, the process of matching the skills public school boys (and all those who enlisted) with the requirements of the army was a haphazard affair in 1914 and 1915. In the rush to arms men were allowed to serve in the infantry when their skills would be better used elsewhere. Inevitably, it led to vital skills being wasted on the front line. It was not just a problem in the way limited to the deployment of the skills of public

---

27   Jonathan Boff, *Haig's Enemy: Crown Prince Ruprecht and Germany's War on the Western Front* (Oxford: Oxford University Press, 2018), p. 4.
28   Beckett, et al, *The British Army and the First World War*, pp. 137-138.

schoolboys. Volunteering at the start of the war meant that the munitions industry was badly affected by skilled workers joining the New Armies. There are numerous examples of talent being wasted because of the inability in the early stages of the war to allocate men to where they were best deployed. Erasmus Darwin, educated at Marlborough, had studied Mathematics and Mechanical Engineering at Cambridge and subsequently worked in industry. On the outbreak of war, he immediately joined up and received a commission in the Yorkshire Regiment but was killed in April 1915.[29] His skills would have been better deployed not in the infantry but elsewhere such as in the artillery or engineers. However, by the second half of 1915 the first moves to deploy men in roles that best suited their skills were starting to take place. The shell shortage of 1915 forced the government to act and restrict the ability of munitions workers to volunteer. Steps were also taken to return men to Britain whose skills industry badly needed. Lionel Holliday, who had been educated at Uppingham, was recalled from the front with the West Riding Regiment as his knowledge of picric acid was needed for munitions production.[30] Even when men were already serving in arms of the armed forces where their scientific skills were of value, they were being redeployed to more suitable duties. Reginald Platts had been educated at Oundle and then worked in the family firm which was involved the production of pharmaceuticals. At the start of the war, he enlisted with the RGA which was a natural place for a man with his scientific skills but was recalled in August 1915 to work, in the even more appropriate role, on the production of painkillers. Although he avoided the dangers of the front line he was killed in May 1918 in an explosion at his laboratory.[31]

The early problems with deploying public schoolboys cannot exclusively be placed on public school ethos and the militarism which claimed to be a consequence of it. The rush to arms was not unique to public school boys. The failure to plan for a citizen army meant that there no effective mechanism for manpower planning and allocation when the New Armies were established. Headmasters recognised this early on and raised concerns about the implications. The 1915 HMC conference unanimously passed a motion expressing concern about the deployment of students with scientific and mathematical ability to the infantry. Concern was expressed that boys who would have pursued careers in the artillery or engineers had joined infantry battalions instead and subsequently lost their lives. The Registrar of the Faculty of Medicine at Oxford had written to the Chairman of the HMC warning that the practice of boys deferring a career in medicine by signing up would lead to a serious shortage of doctors, both in the armed forces and civilian life. An observation supported by the Headmaster of Epsom who reported that many of his old boys had joined up before completing their medical training.[32] These problems were a consequence of the hasty mobilisation of the

---

29 Robert J Harding, *The Savile Club 1914-1918 War Memorial* (London: privately published, 2018), pp. 52-54.
30 Halstead, *A School in Arms*, pp. 105-106.
31 Pendrill, *And We Were Young*, pp. 274-275.
32 HMC, Report of the Headmasters' Conference December 1915, pp. 73-77.

New Armies, it meant that square pegs regularly ended up in round holes. The regular army was better prepared to recruit its officers from the most appropriate existing and new sources. The figures for the period from 29 December 1914 to 29 October 1915 show it drawing not only on the schools it traditionally favoured but also from schools which were not prominent in the pre-war intake. Before the war, Cavendish schools such as Eton and Harrow were prominent amongst those providing Sandhurst cadets while schools such as Cheltenham, Clifton and Wellington well known as army schools, many of whose parents had army connections, continued to be prominent in the Woolwich intake.[33] In the first 10 months of 1915, schools, such as Oundle and Tonbridge, which had army classes played a more prominent place in the entrants to both Sandhurst and Woolwich. At both of these schools, which were also known for the strength of their science curricula, a significant proportion of those entering one of the military colleges went to Woolwich.[34] The army, with an established structure, was able to adjust its recruitment practices to adjust to the changed circumstances than the hastily assembled New Armies, devoid at the start of the most basic facilities, including uniforms.

Despite this dysfunctionality within the New Armies in the early stages of the war, examining the rolls of service of a sample of schools shows that the nature of each school's curriculum had a strong influence on the arms which their old boys served in throughout the war. The unusually high percentage of senior officers for Epsom can be explained by its strong medical connections and science-based curriculum. The RAMC was deploying five and a half times more doctors by the end of the war and the requirements of the medical branches and the air force and navy were also substantial. It is no surprise that the percentage of old boys who were involved in the medical branches of the armed forces dwarfs equivalent figures for other schools. Of its old boys who served about 35 percent were attached to the medical services. No other school in the sample had more than 7 percent of its old boys attached to the medical services and in these cases a greater proportion of them served as orderlies or in another ancillary role.[35] The school's strong connections to the medical profession and its science-based curriculum were highly influential in where the skills of its old boys were employed. When its contribution to the other arms where a science-based education was an advantage (the air force, artillery and engineers) are analysed over 50 percent of Old Epsomians spent at least part of their service in one of these arms of the services. No other school, of those examined in detail, achieved such a high proportion of old boys in the services where an aptitude for science was an advantage.

---

33 Duncan, 'The Military Education of Junior Officers', pp. 222-224.
34 H F W Deane and Bulkeley Evans (eds.), *The Public Schools Yearbook: The Official Book of Reference of the Headmasters' Conference* (London: Year Book Press, 1916), pp. 419-425.
35 The sample consists of Bradford Grammar School, Christ's Hospital, Epsom, Lancing, Mill Hill, Oundle, Shrewsbury, Sherborne, Stonyhurst, Tonbridge, Uppingham and Winchester.

Epsom was unusually high in its provision of science-based skills to the military, but excluding the medical services, four other schools in the sample studied stand out for their contribution to the air force, artillery, and engineers. At Oundle 31.1 percent of its old boys spent at least part of their service in one of these arms. At the other three schools, Tonbridge, Mill Hill and Uppingham, the proportion serving was, respectively 30 percent, 29.1 percent and 26.6 percent. The figures for Oundle reflect the opportunity to concentrate on science and engineering within its curriculum. The war record of the Old Oundelian, Livens (see above), is an example of the application of these skills. With his father he designed the gas projector, named after him, used by the army during the war, and was responsible for other wartime inventions including the British flamethrower.[36] Tonbridge also had a science-based curriculum and an army class which taught the technical knowledge required to enter Woolwich. This combination of a science-based curriculum and an army class meant that the old boys had skills which were attractive to those branches of the military where scientific knowledge was an advantage. The Tonbridge old boy, William Sholto Douglas, enlisted with the RFA in August 1914, as it was the service he believed his education made him best qualified for.[37] Subsequently, he transferred to the RFC. At Uppingham, a broadly-based curriculum was designed to bring the best out of every boy. By 1914, the classics were kept to the bare minimum for those who had no real aptitude for them and the school had a strong reputation for both science and music. These two subjects complement each other more than is often appreciated. In particular, musicians often have a strong aptitude for mathematics. As a result, the influences of the curriculum could at times be ones which were not immediately obvious. The officer file for the composer and Charterhouse Old Boy, Ralph Vaughan Williams, provides an excellent example of this. Vaughan Williams had joined up in December 1914 and served as a private in the London Field Ambulance until August 1917 when he was admitted to an artillery OCB. In the light of the increasing demand for officers, his musical background appears to have made him a suitable candidate. However, possession of the required technical skills, directly or indirectly, and a public school background did not mean that Vaughan Williams conformed with what was expected of an officer. While his officer file describes him as 'a most reliable and energetic officer' it was held against him that he was untidy.[38] Although he did not conform with the army's expectations of an officer, he was clearly a capable officer. However, the army was open-minded enough to recognise that it needed to look more widely for suitable candidates for commissions. Thus, Mill Hill, despite its distinct ambivalence towards the military before the war, became an important source of men for the science-based branches of the armed forces.

36 *Spink, Auction: 18002 – Orders, Decorations and Medals, Lot: 486* <https://www.spink.com/lot/18002000486> (accessed 19 February 2021).
37 Lord Douglas of Kirtleside, *Year of Combat* (London: The Quality Book Club, 1963), p. 43.
38 TNA WO 1139/137032,: 2/Lieutenant Ralph Vaughan Williams, Royal Garrison Artillery.

As the war progressed, the army placed a greater emphasis on the skills and aptitude of men. As previously noted, boys joining directly from schools were expected to have successfully completed OTC training. However, recruitment of officers also considered the background of men in deciding where they should be attached. The records of Bradford Grammar School illustrate this. For reasons already examined, compared to nearly every other HMC member a relatively low percentage (37.3 percent) of its old boys became officers. However, its *Sixth Form Mathematical Roll of Honour* demonstrates the importance of mathematics and science to the army. It lists 25 old boys who served, 13 of these men served in the artillery, air force or engineers, 12 as officers. A further six ended the war with commissions in other branches of the armed forces, in total 72 percent of this cohort ended the war with commissions.[39] Philip Slicer, had been awarded an open mathematical scholarship to Brasenose College, Oxford but on leaving school he joined an artillery OCB and progressed to a commission in the RGA. This was typical of the Mathematical Sixth Form he was part of, consisting of nine boys, eight of them were offered scholarships at Oxbridge of whom five served in the RGA and one in the RFA. The nickname for the RGA of the 'slide rule gunners' demonstrates the importance of mathematics to ensure accurate firing.[40] The army placed a high value on the importance of mathematics and expected the schools to maintain a high standard in its teaching.[41]

Although a background in science was clearly an important factor in where men served, official guidance often emphasised other qualities as being more important. In 1916 the War Office rebuked headmasters for nominating boys with leadership ability for the RFC when there was a great need for leaders in the artillery and infantry. Boys most suitable for the RFC were likely to be those with sporting ability and 'plenty of nerve.'[42] A study in *The Lancet* of 28 September 1918 reinforced this idea with its observation that those in an outside occupation, with sporting ability and in particular accomplished horse-riders (especially those who followed the hunt), made the best pilots. The authors argued that those without mechanical ability also made better pilots as they were prepared to test their machines to the limit without realising how close they were coming to breaking up under the strain.[43] The evidence available now demonstrates that science and mathematics were of great importance in officer selection for the RFC. Officer files frequently make reference to the mechanical ability of candidates. In the sample studied Oundle, with its strong emphasis on science and engineering, had the highest percentage of old boys in the air force. Mill Hill,

---

39 Bradford Grammar School Archives, Roll of Honour, Sixth Mathematical.
40 *Philip Sydney Slicer* <https://www.bradfordgrammar.com/wp-content/uploads/2018/09/1918-September-30-Slicer-194.pdf> (accessed 1 March 2021).
41 HMC, Minutes of the Committee of the Headmasters Conference, 16 May 1917, p. 49.
42 HMC, Report of the Headmasters' Conference December 1916, p. 60.
43 T S Ripon and E G Manuel, 'Report on the Essential Characteristics of Successful and Unsuccessful with Special Reference to Temperament', *The Lancet* (28 September 1918) pp. 411-415.

Tonbridge and Uppingham's contribution to the air force was above average when compared to other schools in the sample. Obituaries of old boys killed while flying often made reference to their scientific or mathematical background. Lieutenant H. R. Hele-Shaw of Marlborough won an Applied Mathematics scholarship to Clare College, Cambridge and was awarded a commission in the RFC.[44] The army's insistence on having first call on boys with leadership ability forced the RFC to look beyond the leading army schools for its officers, as until the second half of 1918 pilots had to be officers.[45] The result was that the air force was forced to look outside the leading army schools and it was natural that they would look to boys from schools where they had received a mathematics and science based education. This is not to say the ethos of a public school was of no importance but a scientific background was an important factor in some branches of the armed forces.

While the ethos of individual schools was a factor in producing officers to lead men into battle it influenced their contributions in other ways. At Stonyhurst just over 3.5 percent of its old boys were attached to the armed forces as chaplains. This might be explained by the need to cater for the spiritual needs of Roman Catholics in the expanded armed forces. However, at Downside, another prominent Roman Catholic public school, the proportion of its old boys who became chaplains was just under 2 percent. At its nearest Anglican equivalent, the Anglo-Catholic Lancing, the figure was just over 1.25 percent (which was high compared with many other schools). So how can the prominent contribution of Stonyhurst to the chaplaincy be explained? Stonyhurst was a Jesuit school and this had three main consequences. The organisational structure meant that there was far more capacity for those in the Society of Jesus to be directed into particular work. This was not the case for the Benedictines at Downside. Jesuits also had a strong tradition of apostolic work with small groups, whereas the work of the Benedictines was based on a more enclosed approach to its religious practice. The work of the Jesuits in the wider community thus drew them into working as chaplains during the war. Finally, Stonyhurst acted as a training centre for members of its order which meant many Jesuit chaplains would have had a connection with the school.[46] Bloxham provides a useful comparison to illustrate the importance of a school's ethos and culture as an influence on the military service of old boys. Like Lancing it was a member of the Woodard Group, although not the HMC in 1914, its religious approach was also High Church. Between the 1870s and 1920s Bloxham had a run of very influential and extremely High Church chaplains. Like Stonyhurst, over 3.5 percent of its old boys served as chaplains.[47] The High Church too placed a strong emphasis on apostolic work. Serving as chaplains during wartime was a natural

---

44   *The Marlburian*, Vol. LII., No. 777. July 30th 1917, p. 114 and Henry Rathbone Hele-Shaw, <http://archive.marlboroughcollege.org/Filename.ashx?systemFileName=%2fDOCS%2fHele-Shaw_HR.pdf&origFilename=,> (accessed 1 March 2021).
45   TNA AIR/1/120/15/14/80: Officer Cadets for Officers Cadet Technical Corps.
46   I am grateful to Rev. Nigel Cave for advice on this matter.
47   Email, Simon Batten, Bloxham School Archivist, 19 December 2020.

extension of this work. The Archbishop of Canterbury encouraged priests to stay in their parishes but especially for High Church chaplains it was their duty as Christians to provide pastoral care to the men at the front.[48] At Lancing the influence of chaplains had been curtailed as a result of them encroaching on the normal responsibilities of a headmaster. At Bloxham, this does not appear to have happened and the chaplains retained enough influence to be able to successfully promote the priesthood as a vocation. However, there could be other factors which influenced the decision to serve as a chaplain in the armed forces. A boy's wider background could also be a strong influence. Sherborne, an Anglican school but with no strong religious connections, saw a far higher percentage (1.74 percent) of its old boys become chaplains than most other schools, including Lancing. The explanation for this lies in parental influence. Of its 20 old boys who served as chaplains 11 of them were the sons of Anglican clergymen.[49] For both Sherborne and Stonyhurst, a combination of background and connections as well as ethos explains their involvement in the wartime chaplaincy.

Throughout the public school movement there were connections which were an influence (although not a dominating one) in where their old boys served in the armed forces. These connections should not always be seen as a malign form of patronage. A nation in arms meant that those seeking to expand the armed forces needed to take a pragmatic approach. Alongside the bureaucracy of recruitment, a system of networks developed where officers in particular were transferred into work where their skills were best applied.[50] The 10 schools with strong connections to the army, such as Eton and Cheltenham, were more likely to provide staff officers.[51] To undergo training to become a staff officer it was necessary for officers to have had experience of staff work or, in exceptional circumstances, to have been recommended. Such recommendations only carried weight if they came from a senior officer.[52] The old boys from the leading army schools with their connections to the regular army were more likely to have the appropriate experience or be already known to senior officers looking for men to recommend. However, the advantages of having the right connections did not always correlate to social privilege and affluence. Many of the pupils and old boys (Old Blues) of Christ's Hospital did not come from an affluent or upper middle-class background and yet the importance of connections can be seen in the way its old boys were deployed during the war. The percentage of them who served for at least

---

48 Edward Madigan, *Faith under Fire: Anglican Army Chaplains and the Great War* (Basingstoke: Palgrave MacMillan, 2011), p. 44.
49 Email, Patrick Ferguson, Sherborne School, 22 January 2021.
50 Fox, 'The Secret of Efficiency?', p. 1542.
51 Paul Harris, *The Men who Planned the War: A Study of the Staff of the British Army on the Western Front, 1914-1918* (Farnham: Ashgate, 2015), p. 217.
52 Army Council Instructions TNA WO 293/4/46, The Selection and Training of Officers for Administrative Staff Appointments, 7 January 1916 and TNA WO 293/7/1379: Army Council Instructions, Selection and Training of Officers for Temporary Staff Appointments, 7 September 1917.

part of the war in the navy (10.7 percent) is significantly higher than that for any other school in the sample examined. Typically, at other schools in the region of 3.5 percent of their old boys served in the navy. At Winchester, with its strong connections to the army, the equivalent figure was just over 1.25 percent. The navy had never drawn its officers in any great numbers from the public schools. The usual route to becoming an officer started at Osbourne between the ages of 11 and 13, from where boys progressed to Dartmouth prior to a commission. However, even this educational path required parents to pay fees so was an unlikely option for the families of boys educated at Christ's Hospital. Despite that, the school had connections that led to many Old Blues serving with the navy. The main route into the navy as an officer, which did not require the payment of fees, was through the Paymaster Branch, where boys joined between 16 and 19 and underwent a short course. For boys whose parents were not well off this was an attractive route, especially as many of them left at 15. In the years before the war a significant number of senior paymasters in the navy were Old Blues. When war broke out, the expansion of the armed forces meant that there was an increased requirement for paymasters. That many of the Old Blues who served in the Royal Navy were Paymasters suggests that an informal system of recruitment which had existed before the war (with Old Blues recruiting Old Blues) was accelerated between 1914 and 1918.[53] There were other aspects of the educational background of these men which also made them suitable candidates. The school's Royal Mathematical School had been established to prepare boys for careers as navigators. Apart from the existing strong connections with the navy, those recruiting Old Blues could be confident, they had a basic mathematical training which gave them an aptitude to be paymasters. The connections of a school with a particular branch of the armed forces were often a logical area to be exploited when specialist roles needed to be filled.

Building Connections

The use of connections and networks was a pragmatic approach to the recruitment of suitable men, it helped the armed forces fit skills to work that needed to be carried out. Douglas Haig, as Commander-in-Chief (C-in-C) of the BEF, was keen to appoint officers on merit rather than seniority. He recognised the importance of the appointment of civilian experts as demonstrated by the appointment of civilians such as Eric Geddes as Major General to run the Western Front transport system. Haig was firmly of the view that the increased complexity of the army's organisation made it essential that men were appointed to roles which matched their pre-war experience.[54] It was a

---

53   Email, Bill Richards, Christ's Hospital Museum, 7 February 2020.
54   Fox, 'The Secret of Efficiency?', pp. 1538-1540.

practical way to address skill shortages and organisations continue to be run in this way.[55]

There are many examples of logical and successful appointments being made on the basis of connections. A good network was invaluable in locating suitable candidates for specialist positions which needed to be filled. The appointment of instructors to OCBs is a good example of where public school connections played an important role. H. H. Hardy played a significant role in the recruitment of instructors for the OCBs. He had been a pupil and then a teacher at Rugby before the war and since 1913 been CO of the school's OTC contingent.[56] He went to the front in October 1914 and from June 1915 until April 1918 he was attached to the staff of the War Office.[57] Although there is little in the archives about what his duties were, other evidence suggests he was involved in training from the time he joined the War Office. By 1917 he was attached to SD3 which was responsible for OCBs including the recruitment of instructors.[58] Other evidence strongly suggests he was involved in officer training from 1915. He participated in part of the Rugby OTC Annual Camp in August 1915 and by the end of 1916 he was playing a leading role in the recruitment of OCB instructors. With regular army officers in short supply he sought alternatives. The qualities he looked for in instructors were appropriate military qualities and more importantly an ability to train cadets. For him, OTC officers fitted this category very well, although he did not wish to call on teachers still at school.[59]

However, OTC officers, wounded on service, were an important source of OCB instructors for him. Many of these men had also been educated at public schools. Hardy as an OTC CO was able to use both his direct and indirect connections to recruit OTC officers who had been wounded. Major R.P. Shea, CO of Uppingham's OTC until the outbreak of war, was severely wounded at the end of March 1917 and after a period of recuperation became an instructor at No. 24 OCB in September 1917. His skills as a teacher and leader of men were well employed in this role and by March 1918 was Chief Instructor.[60] Shea was well known to Hardy from the joint Field Days Uppingham, and Rugby had held before the war. Through his wider connections within the Junior OTC, he was able to identify and recruit other OTC officers as instructors. Organisations such as the OTC Club (for OTC officers) would have helped him to get in touch with these men. Major C.H. Pigg, who had both been a pupil and teacher at Cheltenham, after being gassed in 1915 was introduced to Hardy and as a result became an OTC instructor in 1917.[61] At least 39 teachers held a role

---

55 Sheffield, *The Chief*, p. 24.
56 George Higginbotham, *Rugby School Register Volume IV From January 1892 to September 1921* (Rugby: George Over, 1929) p. 69.
57 *Record of War Service*, p. 142.
58 War Office, *War Office List* (London: HMO, 1917), p. 73.
59 HMC, Report of the Headmasters' Conference December 1917, p. 104.
60 *Record of War Service*, p. 174.
61 *Floreat Cheltonia*, Issue Number 12, January 2019, p. 55.

as an instructor at some point during the war according to the *Record of War Service*, which recorded the war service of teachers at schools with OTC contingents. The records in it were gathered by requests for information, are not official figures. Pigg's service as an instructor is not recorded in the book and it can be concluded that it is not a complete record of service for public school teachers. It is not known what percentage the 39 OTC officers represent of the total number of OCB instructors, but Hardy's preference for teachers as instructors indicates they were sought after in this role.

Hardy also used a network of contacts to find other men who would make suitable instructors Men such as the Reverend Frederick Matheson acted as part of this network. He was an academic at Keble College, Oxford, an officer in the University's OTC and attached to the No.4 OCB at Oxford, during the war, and looked out for former students who would make suitable instructors.[62] Captain Neil Weir, educated at Wellington College, had been wounded and could hardly walk when he received a visit in late 1916 at his Oxford hospital from his former tutor, Matheson, who suggested to Weir that he become an instructor. Weir was attracted to the idea but felt he lacked the experience to do the job. Despite that Matheson passed his name on to Hardy who, after interviewing Weir, told him that he would be appointed to an OCB once he had been passed by a medical board. Matheson's involvement did not end there. After Weir's medical board he was invited by the CO of No.4 OCB (and the CO of Oxford University's OTC) to join the battalion to familiarise himself with the workings of an OCB until a posting came through. Within days he was transferred to the company Matheson was CO of. There, he said, he was able to develop skills as an instructor and in February 1917 he was posted to the newly established No. 21 OCB.[63] Weir's account offers an insight into how these networks operated. As an ex-public schoolboy and OTC cadet with substantial combat experience he was a strong candidate to be an instructor. An ability to instruct was one of the skills required of a junior officer. Placing him under Matheson gave him an opportunity to develop these skills under the guidance of an officer who knew him well. Living in the Senior Common Room with other instructors gave him more opportunities to learn from them while they had the opportunity to assess him. As a result, Matheson was able to draw on this to report to Hardy as to whether Weir would make a suitable instructor. Hardy was able to monitor Weir's progress through Matheson and offer him the posting to No. 21 OCB.[64] It is clear networks and patronage paid an important part in the appointment of OCB instructors. This was far from a malign factor in these appointments. Hardy could appoint instructors with more confidence that they had the requisite skills. Appointing men who had no teaching experience was more

---

62   E S Craig and W M Gibson, *Oxford University Roll of Service* (Oxford: Clarendon Press, 1920), p. 575.
63   Saul David (ed.), *Mud and Bodies: The War Diaries and Letters of Captain N.A.C. Weir, 1914-1920* (London: Frontline Books, 2013), pp. 94-95.
64   Ibid., p. 95.

problematic. Rather than going through a formal recruitment process, he sought suitable candidates through his network using it to assess their suitability. It was typical of the pragmatic approach the British Army took to filling the more specialist roles.

Conclusion

Status, class, curriculum and connections were important factors in explaining the involvement of public schools in the Great War and ethos was not the sole factor in explaining this involvement. Public schools before and during the Great War were not homogenous in their nature. Their origins varied as did the way they had developed. While class was a factor in the route to becoming an officer, the reasons for the contribution of schools to the war effort is far more nuanced than an explanation solely based on the advantages of privilege. Curriculum was also an important factor in explaining it. Schools such as Oundle and Tonbridge switched from an emphasis on the classics to one where science became far more important. Their emphasis on science is reflected in the high proportion, when compared to other schools, of their old boys who served in the sections of the armed forces where a scientific background was an advantage, as was the case for Epsom and Uppingham. However, as the case of Epsom demonstrates, the status and history of a school were also factors to be considered. With its strong connection to the medical profession and a long history of its old boys becoming doctors it contributed to the RAMC and other medical services far more than other schools. Epsom's medical background meant that it played a prominent part in the senior ranks of the medical branches. Schools such as Charterhouse and Winchester, with their strong connections to the army, also made a strong contribution to senior leadership of the army. The war effort of the leading army schools varied in other ways. Having produced more regular army officers before the war, they were always likely to provide more staff officers, where greater military experience was called for. It could be argued that their connections and those of Epsom to the medical profession gave their old boys an unfair advantage. However, the need to utilise skills in an increasingly sophisticated fighting force made it inevitable that those given the task of looking for specialist skills would look where they knew suitable candidates could be found. This did not necessarily benefit those who came from better off backgrounds. The Old Blues of Christ's Hospital, whose background was less affluent than many other schools, provided an unusually large number of paymasters to the navy. This was the result of its old boys already serving in this role and knowing that the school was likely to have produced men with skills which would help fill an expanded requirement for paymasters. In many cases patronage and connections were employed as a pragmatic response to the need to fill a multitude of diverse roles. This is not to say that patronage was never used in an unfair manner, but it cannot be dismissed as an exclusively negative factor. The increasing demand for officers meant that the army had to widen its net in the recruitment of officers. Nonetheless, the public schools with OTCs remained a favoured source for officers although those who had shown leadership qualities on the front line became an increasingly important source. Public schools played a more important part than other schools in the provision of officers but on the home front their contribution had far more common with other schools. This is the focus of the next chapter.

8

Home Front

The previous three chapters have considered the role of public schools in preparing boys to be junior officers and leaders of men, and the contributions of their old boys to the armed forces. In studies of public schools during the war, little consideration has been given to their role on the home front. At the start of the war they saw their contribution in terms of supporting the military effort. This is no surprise as the country as a whole was unprepared for war in 1914 and the military requirements were perceived to be the most urgent. Inevitably, the nature of the support required for the war effort evolved. Especially from 1917, when the government centralised the direction of the war effort, all schools, whether private, public or state, were called on to make a greater contribution to the home front, especially as the manpower shortage became more critical. The contribution of public schools needs to be understood within the wider context of that made by other schools and society in general. The headmasters were keen for their schools to make a practical contribution in whatever way they could. Much of the work done was mundane and lacked romance. What was required was appropriate skills and not boys imbued with romantic ideas about becoming military heroes.

Support for the Military Effort

During the war the differences between the contributions of different types of school narrowed but even state schools were not treated as unfavourably at the start of the war, when compared to public and private schools, as the figures suggest. State schools were far more likely to be taken over by the military authorities, in the first three months of the war 705 elementary schools were requisitioned. In addition, 33 secondary schools and 15 Technical Schools were taken over by the authorities as billets and training facilities.[1] In contrast, the military hardly

---

1   Barry Blades, *Roll of Honour Schooling & the Great War 1914-1919* (Barnsley: Pen & Sword, 2015), p. 41.

made any demands from public schools for the use of their facilities. Two schools, Winchester and Christ's Hospital, close to the south coast where troop embarkation was concentrated, had their premises taken over.[2] By the start of the term at Winchester, the military was only using the school's sanatorium.[3] Christ's Hospital found itself requisitioned as a POW Camp on 6 August 1914.[4] The early requisitions were often made with little thought and in a spirit of overenthusiasm. One of the more notorious examples of this was the requisition of a milkman's horse in the middle of his round.[5] Little thought appears to have been given to the importance of the Christ's Hospital OTC as a source of junior officers for an army which was hastily expanding. A protest by the Headmaster led to the removal of the prisoners so that the school and OTC training could start on time.[6] In the early days of the war the experience of the school was typical of the requisitions being made over enthusiastically. This imbalance in the requisitioning of state schools and public schools was not just because the latter were treated more favourably. Most public schools were in parts of the country where there was no substantial military presence at any stage of the war and therefore less likely to be requisitioned. As Winchester and Christ's Hospital demonstrate those closer to substantial military activity were in greater danger of having their facilities requisitioned. St Albans School, a member of the HMC, had a significant part of its facilities taken over by the miliary, including its sports grounds for training and library which was converted into a military prison.[7] 'St Albans became a major military centre requiring accommodation and training facilities for 7,000 men who arrived soon after the declaration of war, St Albans School and nine other local schools were requisitioned at the start of the war.[8] The location of schools was more important than their status. At Sutton-on-Sea on the Lincolnshire coast, where there was a constant fear of invasion, the military took over the Council School at least four times during the war.[9] Most of the military demand on schools was short-lived: by November 1914, the War Office started to curtail the use of school buildings for military purposes.[10] The end of the initial phase in the rapid growth in the New Armies meant there was less need for training facilities in the UK and the use of school facilities declined. By the spring of 1915 the army was returning St Albans

2   *The Wykehamist*, No. 534. October 1914, pp. 339-340.
3   WCA, Report of the Head Master for the year 1914, p. 3.
4   *The Blue*, Vol XLII No.1 October 1914, p. 11.
5   Jonathan Mein, Anne Wares & Sue Mann (eds.), *St Albans Life on the Home Front 1914-1918* (Hatfield: Hertfordshire Publications, 2016), p. 27.
6   CHA, Report on the Boys School, p. 6.
7   *The Albaninan*, Vol IX No.8 December 1914, pp. 230-231.
8   Blades, *Roll of Honour*, p. 42.
9   Tony Baker, *Sutton-on-Sea Remembers – A tribute to those whose names are on the village war memorial* (Brinkhill: Corner House Books, 2006), p. 16.
10 TNA WO 293/1/274: War Office Instructions, Schools used as Auxiliary Hospitals, 24 November 1915.

School's facilities to it,[11] leaving behind a new mini range for its OTC to conduct its shooting practice.[12]

Pre-war games had played an important part of life of public schools but on the outbreak of war military training was given priority. Wellington College in September 1914 chose to play no games, instead devoting the time to OTC training.[13] Military training was not carried out exclusively by public schools. Many schools established Cadet Corps which aimed to give boys basic soldiering (as opposed to leadership) skills. In Hertfordshire Watford Grammar School and Queen Elizabeth Grammar School, Barnet, were just two schools to establish these units in 1915.[14] This was no passing whim. The expansion of Cadet Corps in secondary schools continued throughout the war. Military training extended to Elementary Schools and moved away from sports and games towards military drill.[15] Public schools with an OTC contingent were considered to be a good source for officer cadets, but their commitment to providing military training was not unique. Nearly every school was committed to supporting the military effort and public schools cannot be seen as having a greater commitment to military training. The values of public school ethos did not set them apart. What did set them apart was their ability to prepare boys to be officers.

School Life

A similar theme can be seen in the way the war was presented to pupils. It was not just public schools which were promoting the war effort to their children. While Epsom College held events with visiting speakers about the war effort the neighbouring, council run, Pound Lane School was holding similar events.[16] Similar comparisons can be made throughout the country. Perhaps unsurprisingly, many of the speakers took an approach which was bellicose and anti-German and the editors of school magazines were in sympathy with them. Dr Smith, formerly a Professor in Nuremberg, spoke to Harrow Boys in March 1915. The mildest of his accusations was that Germans were not capable of fair play and chivalry and the most extreme was that they were monsters.[17] Allan Adair, who attended the lecture recalled treating this talk and others with a certain amount of scepticism. For him, there were limits to the patriotism of boys. They were willing to raise funds for

---

11   *The Albaninan*, Vol IX, No. 9 April 1915, p. 273.
12   *The Albaninan*, Vol IX, No. 10 August 1915, p. 304.
13   G.A. Long, 'Wellington College in 1914', *Stand To!*, No. 79 April 2007, pp. 45-48.
14   J D Sainsbury, *Hertfordshire's Army Cadets* (Welwyn: Hart Books 2010), p. 287.
15   David Parker, *Hertfordshire Children in War and Peace, 1914-1939* (Hatfield, Hertfordshire Publications, 2007), p. 86.
16   Pound Lane School – World War I, Epsom & Ewell History Explorer <https://eehe.org.uk/?p=33387> (accessed 24 May 2021)
17   *The Harrovian*, Vol. XXVIII., No. 2. April 3rd, 1915, p. 26.

a YMCA hut but less willing to respond to appeals to work for the organisation during their school holidays.[18]

A natural suspicion of authority meant boys were capable of questioning what they were told. In any event, an examination of school magazines shows that they were not being fed a diet of stories which were militaristic and took a romantic view of war based on chivalry and fair play. It comes as no surprise that the magazines' initial approach was predominantly to romanticise the conflict, often describing battles in a positive and understated manner. The December 1914 edition of Oundle's *The Laxtonian* described the Battle of the Aisne as 'quite exciting' although it is clear the writer was under heavy bombardment.[19] The tone soon changed and by December 1915 the majority of letters in *The Laxtonian* from old boys recounted the realities of war and did not attempt to glorify events. There was no attempt to hide the fact that much of war was unromantic. One account centred on the writer's homesickness and the monotony of trench life which was 'a dreary succession of days and weeks of muddy and apparently aimless digging, without excitement, hope or interest.'[20] Descriptions of military action reflected the brutality of war. One described an action at Second Ypres in early May 1915. It recorded the effects of a gas attack, recounting the ferocity of a bombardment ('shells fell around us like hailstones') and the 'murderous rifle and machine-gun fire.' The consequences of this action were made clear. Of the 14 officers and 590 men involved, 11 officers and 300 men were killed or wounded.[21] Readers were left in no doubt that there was no romance in war. Oundle's approach was typical, those of more traditional public schools contained similar accounts. *The Marlburian* included articles which ranged from descriptions of both the brutal and the mundane with a sprinkling of the irreverent. The March 1917 edition included an account which parodied training at an artillery OCB. The same edition included a brutal but realistic report recorded one night's work for a trench party with descriptions of the dead lying on the ground and a hand sticking out of the earth as the men marched to the front line.[22] Like *The Laxtonian*, Marlborough's magazine had accounts of the mundane nature of life at the front when there was no offensive action.[23] Accounts of life at school also often played down the idea of young men being prepared for battle. The *Mill Hill Magazine* described the air raids as 'the nocturnal visits of brother Bosche' and remarked they had become excuses for not having done prep.[24] It struck a similar tone when it reported on a German aircraft which passed overhead while

---

18 Oliver Lindsay (ed.), *A Guard's General: The Memoirs of Major General Allan Adair* (London: Hamish Hamilton, 1986), pp. 8-9.
19 *The Laxtonian*, Vol. VIII., No. 9. December 1914, p. 389.
20 *The Laxtonian*, Vol. VIII., No. 13. December 1915, pp. 498-504.
21 Ibid., pp. 509-511.
22 *The Marlburian*, Vol. LII., No. 773. 30 March 1917, pp. 45-46 and 47-48.
23 *The Marlburian*, Vol. LII., No. 776. 12 July 1917, pp. 96-97.
24 *Mill Hill Magazine*, Vol. XLV., No. 3. November 1917, p. 60.

the OTC was practising for its annual inspection. 'Notes and Jottings', which cast a sceptical eye over school affairs, observed that it suspected that the aircraft had not attacked because of the coolness of the corps but for less romantic reasons. It was more likely that the pilot's 'cultured brain was so shocked at the sight of our miserable attempt to perform a wheel in close column, that he was forced to avert his eyes, and so missed his aim.'[25] This account together with the description of artillery OCB training in *Marlburian* had more of the feel of *Dad's Army* than young warriors being prepared for military action.

Apart from talking and writing about the war the schools set about making an immediate and practical contribution to the war effort. There were many problems, including supporting Belgian refugees. The response of schools was uncoordinated and each one did what it thought was best Some schools such as Eton and Sherborne offered places to Belgian boys.[26] Others set out to provide practical support for refugee families. Winchester provided one of the college's houses for 17 refugees and financial support through a weekly collection amongst the boys. Some places at the school were offered but with stipulations. Winchester also provided free places to two 16-year-old Belgian boys, but they did not participate in all aspects of school life.[27] Harrow also made stipulations about the background of those they took in, and required refugees to speak English and Latin.[28] This approach was typical of the national response to the war which was often improvised and fractured.

Support for refugees was inevitably limited because public schools had to deal with more mundane but urgent problems. All schools had to address an increase in costs and decline in funding. By September 1914, Epsom was receiving letters from its suppliers asking for rises in contracted prices because they were suffering from increased costs.[29] It also had to deal with several supporters withdrawing their financial support for scholarships.[30] These problems were common to many schools in 1914 which also suffered from a loss of fees as boys left earlier than expected to take up commissions as well as difficult financial conditions which forced some parents to withdraw their sons. Nowell Smith at Sherborne reported to the governing body that in the first year of the war the most common enquiry he received was about the possibility of a reduction in fees. In the early stage many other schools suffered a decline in school numbers but it was a situation repeated throughout the public school movement. Winchester and Epsom were typical in suffering from the loss of boys at an earlier age but fears that numbers would decline as the war proceeded proved to

---

25 Ibid., No. 2. July 1917, pp. 51-52.
26 Blades, *Roll of Honour*, p. 53.
27 WCA, Reports of the Head Master for the year 1914, pp. 3-4 and for the School Year ending July 1915, p. 3.
28 Blades, *Roll of Honour*, p. 53.
29 ECA, Meeting of the Finance Committee 30 September 1914, p. 2.
30 ECA, Report of The Council 25 June 1915, p. 1.

be unfounded.[31] Indeed, the situation was rapidly reversed and school numbers rose throughout the war. By 1916, the number of boys at Sherborne was at its highest since 1888.[32] This state of affairs was repeated throughout the public school movement. The initial fears of parents about the financial consequences of the war proved to be ill-founded. Public schools remained attractive as a place there made it more likely their son would get a commission. From 1916, with the introduction of conscription, the War Office allowed young men to stay with their public school OTC contingents until they were 18 and a half (six months longer than anyone else). Boys who met the required standards were admitted directly to an OCB, without having to serve in the ranks and joining up at 18. It was attractive option for parents which allowed their sons to continue their education while receiving some training to prepare them for the junior officer corps and the status of a gentleman.

Other problems caused by manpower shortages and rising costs persisted throughout the war. Initially, schools considered it their patriotic duty to allow masters and other employees to serve, but as the effects of this on school life became obvious, from the end of 1914 there was a change to a more pragmatic approach. In the absence of centralised direction each school varied in its approach to releasing staff. Winchester followed the guidance of Lord Kitchener that those masters essential for the running of the school or the OTC should stay put.[33] Nowell Smith at Sherborne felt that he could not stop masters who wished to go to war 'solely out of a sense of duty,' and not 'a spirit of adventure.'[34] The desire to support the war effort had to be balanced against the welfare of the school. Pragmaticism rather than martial spirit was the governing factor in deciding whether to release teachers. Low quality replacements for teachers who had been released had caused disciplinary problems and forced the Trustees at Uppingham, in June 1915, to stop releasing any more for military service.[35] The consequences for schools with a higher proportion of younger and unmarried teachers were serious. The December 1915 HMC annual meeting heard that one school had lost seven out 12 of its staff and another had lost 12 out of 27 masters. Both were struggling to find replacements, let alone competent ones, which was having a severe adverse effect on the quality of the education they provided.[36] The introduction of conscription compounded these problems. By December 1917, Berkhamsted had lost 12 of its 30 pre-war staff and experienced great difficulty in finding replacements.[37] The shortage of teachers meant good teachers were at a premium and the salaries

---

31 ECA, Headmaster's Report to the Governing, Body October1915, p. 8, SSA, Headmaster's Report to the Governing, Body October1915, p. 8, and WCA, Report of the Head Master for the School Year ending July 1915, p. 3.
32 SSA, Headmaster's Report to the Governing, Body October1916, p. 5.
33 WCA, Report of the Head Master for the year 1914, p. 2.
34 SSA, Headmaster's Report to the Governors for 1915, p. 5.
35 USA, Minutes of the Trustees, 8 June 1915 and Matthews, *By God's Grace*, p. 140.
36 HMC, Report of the Headmasters Conference December 1915, pp. 55-56.
37 HMC, Report of the Headmasters' Conference December 1917, p. 106.

offered increased. Epsom, a school with considerable financial problems, was forced to offer improved salaries in 1917 for the first time since 1914, for fear of losing teachers to other schools.[38] By 1917, several headmasters were deeply concerned about the conscription of more of their teachers. Set against this was a recognition that their schools enjoyed a privileged status which allowed their boys to stay longer. As one headmaster who sat on a military tribunal pointed out, it was difficult to argue that young men should be allowed to stay and teach, when 40-year-old fathers with seven children were being conscripted.[39] Schools took a pragmatic approach and understood they had to accept a further loss of teachers. It did not preclude some headmasters from challenging this from time to time. The Headmaster of Uppingham, Owen, despite claiming to support the release of teachers to the armed force backed a 39-year-old teacher in his appeal against being called up.[40]

The decision not to challenge conscription was based on a belief amongst headmasters that their schools could not be seen to be enjoying special privileges. This also drove discussions at the end of 1915 about how to achieve more simplicity in public school life. The Headmaster of Christ's Hospital, a school known for its support for the less privileged, suggested that his school, where boys did much of the work done by servants in other schools, might be a good example of how economy could be achieved. There was no enthusiasm for this idea from other headmasters. The suggestion was that boys and their parents were not used to this approach and therefore it would be difficult to implement.[41] Christ's Hospital provided education for children whose parents could not afford the full fees, all parents were subsidised by the school's endowments and many paid no fees at all. This made it easier for the school to require its pupils to do the work of servants. It was an option less easy to implement at schools where most parents paid the full fees. Nonetheless, the schools had to identify possible economies and the 1915 HMC meeting decided to establish a War Economy Sub-Committee to investigate this. After consulting with HMC members it issued a report with a series of suggestions including reduced uniform requirements, a greater use of second-hand books and a change in the dates of terms to reduce fuel consumption, but its biggest focus was on games. Not only did it suggest a reduction in expenditure on clothing which demonstrated athletic distinction but also lowering the amount spent on athletic facilities, such as cricket pitches.[42] This was a further diminution in the importance given to games which it has been argued helped make public schoolboys suitable to be junior officers. As will be shown, the importance of games declined as the need to make a greater practical contribution to the war effort grew.

38 ECA, Meeting of the School Committee 21 March 1917, pp. 2-3.
39 Ibid., pp. 105-109.
40 USA, Minutes of the Trustees, 12 June 1917.
41 HMC, Report of the Headmasters Conference December 1915, pp. 20-33.
42 HMC, Report of the Committee of the Headmasters Conference for 1916, pp. 34-36.

The economies made by the schools were also designed to reduce inevitable rises in the fees charged to parents and lower the risks of losing boys. Efforts to reduce costs could lead to actions which appeared to be militaristic. At the Perse the school uniform was replaced by the cadet uniform for its OTC while the rest of school was required to wear the uniform of the school's scout pack instead of its uniform.[43] The main reason for this was not a militaristic expression of support for the war but the financial circumstances of its pupils, many of whom had county (council) scholarships and came from a modest background.[44] Making it a requirement to wear OTC or scout uniform, instead of the pre-war school uniform, reduced the amount parents needed to spend on school clothing.

Life at the public schools had to adjust to circumstances of war including the threat of air raids. As already noted, Mill Hill was one school directly threatened by them. Westminster School issued instructions on the action to be taken in the event of an air raid.[45] Epsom was one of several schools to consider taking out insurance against air raids.[46] It was not just schools in locations in or close to London which were affected. In more rural locations, schools were often threatened by air raids because of their closeness to strategic targets. Oundle, close to Corby ironstone works and the strategically important Harringworth viaduct, often had Zeppelins pass over it and during a raid on 1 October 1916 bombs were dropped near the school.[47] Uppingham, with Zeppelins passing over on their way to nearby industrial towns in the Midlands, was also affected. Public schools did not suffer any loss of life or damage as a result of air raids. Nonetheless, at best the raids were inconvenient and at worst frightening but despite this a stoical approach was taken. On one occasion as Zeppelins passed over Uppingham, a Housemaster is said to have commenced his evening prayers with 'Darken our lightness, we beseech Thee.'[48] Although probably an apocryphal tale, it demonstrates that a phlegmatic and humorous approach to the inconveniences of war was common amongst public schools. Schools and their boys adapted to war by adopting an approach which was pragmatic rather than unquestioningly brave. William Hayman (at Sherborne from 1917 to 1921) recalled rushing back to his house during the blackout to get back before lock up and colliding with somebody and knocking them over. From the torrent of abuse which followed he realised it was his Housemaster. 'Deeming discretion the better part of valour,' he crept away reassuring himself that his Housemaster would not wish to know one of his boys had

---

43 Patenden, 'Old Perseans and the Great War', p. 633.
44 Ibid., p. 631.
45 *The Elizabethan*, Vol. XVI., No. 13. November 1917, p. 211.
46 ECA, Meeting of Epsom College Council 12 January 1916, p. 10.
47 Pendrill, *And We Were Young*, p. 129 and 'The Menace of the Zeppelin', *Collyweston Historical & Preservation Society* <https://www.collywestonhistoricalsociety.org.uk/the-mennace-of-the-zeppelin> (accessed 9 July 2021).
48 John P. Graham, *Forty Years of Uppingham Memories and Sketches* (London: Macmillan, 1932), pp. 132-136.

discovered previously unknown parts of his vocabulary.[49] Boys approached the war not in a militaristic way but by responding to the circumstances they found themselves in with a sense of humour and a sense of reality. They learnt from parents and old boys, both from meeting them and accounts in school magazines, what fighting the Germans was like and wished to play their part in a cause they believed was right and necessary. Hayman's view was that war was unavoidable and young men needed to be prepared for it.[50] The training required to prepare public schoolboys to serve in the armed forces meant that games had to take second place. The reduction in 'athletic drapery' was a visible representation of the switch to a practical approach to the war. When *The Shirburnian* of April 1915 observed that 'games have ceased to wield their former sway' and 'is now a sort of military depot, and no longer a home of athletics', it reflected the approach of virtually every public school.[51] Throughout the war the discussions of the HMC revolved topics such as the importance of providing effective military training via the OTC to develop boys as junior officers, rather than of the importance of games in developing leadership skills.

A further constraint on the playing of games was the need to address the problems caused by food shortages. These had two consequences: firstly, time and other resources had to be taken from games so boys could work on cultivating vegetables, and secondly the shortages meant boys had less energy to play games, especially toward the end of the war. These shortages meant that life at public school became even more austere than it was before the war. The ability of schools to manage food shortages varied for a host of reasons. Oundle's educational approach made it better equipped to produce food than many other schools, this is discussed below. Sherborne, based in a rural location, was able to provide food which was 'adequate but poor in quality.'[52] The ability of schools to manage food shortages was influenced not only by factors such as their location and curriculum but also by the competence of individuals to manage them. Rex Herdman, at Winchester from 1916 to 1921, recalled that his Housemaster did not have a wife to oversee the catering and believed consequently that food in his house was in such short supply that boys felt hungry most of the time. The situation was particularly bad in the 1917 summer term when the potato crop failed, and the substitutes were often inedible. Some culinary innovations in his house verged on the poisonous. On one occasion, boiled rhubarb leaves were served as a vegetable. This item only made one appearance on the menu, after it was reported in the press others had died as a result of eating them. Boys from another house went to the shops to buy bread, which was never rationed, but which the Housemaster had failed to supply.[53] The ability of boys to supplement their diet by buying hot meals, cakes and confectionery at the two school shops became

---

49   SSA, Hayman.
50   Ibid.
51   *The Shirburnian*, Vol XXVIII., No. 2. April 1915, pp. 41-42.
52   SSA, Hayman.
53   Gregory, *The Last Great War*, p. 215 and WCA, Rex Herdman, During after the First World War, 1916-1921.

increasingly restricted and by 1918, only hot meals were available and they had become very expensive. Winchester's patriotic intention in withdrawing unneeded luxuries went unappreciated by its boys. Some flouted the prohibition on buying sweets and food in the town and even turned to the black market. Herdman described how, in a cloak and dagger exercise, he would visit a shop which was out of bounds and purchase slab cake on the black market. This was not the only illicit practice Wykehamists engaged in; some boys even resorted to poaching.[54] Apart from the decline in discipline the food shortages had an adverse effect on the energy levels of boys. As a result, many schools reduced the amount of games played. Sherborne in 1917, reduced the number and duration of rugby matches.[55] By 1918, a survey by the HMC revealed that just under half of its members had reduced the amount of school work and games.[56] The approach to food of shortages was overseen by the HMC in close cooperation and based on a regular exchange of information with the Ministry of Food about the effects of rationing, especially on the energy levels of boys. Shortages persisted although over time supplies became more predictable.[57] The response of headmasters was in contrast to their approach before the war. They no longer treated government instructions as an imposition on their right to run their schools as they saw fit. The instruction from the Ministry of Food, later in 1918, to stop schoolwork and drill before breakfast met with no complaints.[58]

Food shortages were faced by the whole nation and public schools suffered no more than other parts of the population;[59] Headmasters recognised their schools needed to take practical steps to address the shortages. Public school ethos and the playing of games was not a sufficient response. What was required was a practical response by the schools. From early 1917 the government imposed more central direction of the war and asked schools to grow more of their own food. Oundle ploughed up lawns to grow potatoes, with the boys providing the labour.[60] Most schools were quick to respond. The governors of Winchester allocated an old sports ground outside the town for the cultivation of potatoes.[61] Herdman recorded that boys were placed on a rota to carry out hoeing and weeding.[62] Extra parades and training to prepare boys for commissions had already reduced the amount of time devoted to games and the addition of potato growing meant that there was a further reduction in the time available for games. Some schools had to employ playing fields for the growing of vegetables.

---

54 WCA, Herdman.
55 Patrick Francis, *Vivat Shirburnia: Sherborne School and the Great War 1914-1918* (London: Impress, 2014), p. 181.
56 HMC, Report of the Committee of the Headmasters Conference for September 1917 to December 1918, p 41.
57 ECA, Report of the School Committee for Lent Term 1918, 20 March 1918.
58 HMC, Report of the Committee of the Headmasters Conference for September 1917 to December 1918, p. 43.
59 Gregory, *The Last Great War*, pp. 214-215.
60 *The Laxtonian*, Vol. IX., No. 4. April 1917, p. 104.
61 *The Wykehamist*, No. 560. February 1917, p. 97.
62 WCA, Herdman.

At Sherborne playing fields were ploughed and the amount of rugby played reduced.[63] Virtually every school limited itself to the cultivation of vegetables. Government policy was to increase the amount of arable farming. Only Oundle, which had its own farm and a large experimental area for teaching practical farming and horticulture, went beyond this. Its reputation led the Department of Agriculture to engage it to carry out experimental work on crop production. The school was also able to turn the production of potatoes and other vegetables into a profitable activity. The crops were also used to feed the school's pigs, which supplied a ton of home-grown bacon for the school in 1917.[64] This was a significant contribution, with meat in short supply, but one other schools struggled to emulate. All schools made sure that within their limitations they provided practical support for the war effort at the expense of activities such as games.

Farming for the Nation

At the start of the war the public schools saw themselves as having a duty to support the war effort through preparing their boys to be junior officers. Few schools would have anticipated that their boys, especially the older ones, would be used to support the agricultural sector. Much of the work was unskilled and arduous but something fit young men were suited to. After 1916 many of the farm workers who had elected not to join up found themselves conscripted. This led to a shortage of labour, especially at harvest time and from 1916, at the request of the government, schools offered their boys to local farmers to provide replacements. This support was substantial. Marlborough provided 116 boys to assist with hay making, with the wages earned by the boys donated to the local military hospital.[65] Not all schools had their offers accepted. Local market gardeners declined Epsom's offer of assistance as the specialist and skilled nature of the of the work made the school's boys unsuitable.[66] The work was not just confined to helping with the harvest. Harrow's boys were asked to volunteer for wood felling camps organised by the Cavendish Association. Wood felling was hard work and in seeking volunteers the school made it clear living conditions would be uncomfortable with an expectation that boys must volunteer for at least a month.[67] Stamina and strength and not a martial spirit were the key requirements. Herdman recalled hay making was hard work and involved a six hour shift as well as

---

63   Francis, *Vivat Shirburnia*, p. 181.
64   Palmer, The Life of F W Sanderson, pp. 231-233.
65   *The Marlburian*, Vol. LI., No. 763. July 12th 1916, p. 95.
66   ECA, Epsom College and the First World War and conversation with Alan Spedding (Epsom College), 23 May 2019.
67   *The Harrovian*, Vol. XXIX., No. 5. July 29th, 1916, p. 62. The Cavendish Association was established in 1912 to encourage those who had been to university and public school to engage in national and social service. In 1921 it merged with Toc H. The Cavendish Association <https://www.saxonlodge.net/histories/cavendish_association.php> (accessed 30 July 2021).

an eight mile bike journey to and from the farm. After finishing at 8 p.m., he would return to his boarding house to a tea which consisted of leftovers, before collapsing into bed exhausted.[68] The provision of agricultural support was not unique to public schools. As the war progressed, all children became a source of cheap labour and by 1917 all schools were a source of labour for food production.

The centralisation of the direction of the war effort by Lloyd George's government meant public schools, along with other schools, were called on to play a part in this and to complement the military front.[69] From 1917, not only were they expected to produce food for themselves but also encouraged to support the agricultural sector. The Ministry of National Service was given the task of recruiting men and women into work of national importance, including food production. The deployment of school children was part of a wider effort to achieve an increase in arable production. By December 1916, at least a quarter of all farm labourers had left the farms and to achieve increased production labour had to be found elsewhere.[70] Some skilled labour was needed to prepare land for arable production but unskilled labour was the main requirement for gathering in the harvest and, in the summer of 1917, public schoolboys were one of many groups which attended camps to carry out this work which the unfortunately named Major Belcher of the Ministry of Food reported to the HMC had been a success. At one camp, 100 boys over three weeks harvested enough potatoes to feed a brigade for three months. Despite the wet conditions, he said, most schoolboy parties had been very productive.[71] In total, over 4,000 boys had worked on the camps in 1917.[72] While the work of the boys may have been appreciated it was not the overwhelming success Belcher claimed it to be. Many headmasters were dissatisfied and believed a great deal more was possible and complained that the camps had been poorly organised by the Cavendish Association and the National Service Department which had led to an inefficient employment of the boys.[73] 40 boys from The Leys who had stayed at Henley after their Annual OTC Camp to assist with the harvest had found themselves unused by the local farmers.[74] Dulwich arrived at their harvest camp to find that the authorities had made no effort to find them work. It was left to a master to organise the working day which consisted of weeding and cutting timber.[75] Several headmasters anticipated these problems and made their own

68 WCA, Herdman.
69 Rosie Kennedy, *The Children's War: Britain, 1914-1918* (Basingstoke: Palgrave Macmillan, 2014), p. 155.
70 Mary Fraser, 'Policing the Plough' *History Today,* 70: 5 (May 2020), pp. 42-49.
71 HMC, Report of the Headmasters' Conference December 1917, p. 43.
72 HMC, Report of the Committee of the Headmasters Conference for September 1917 to December 1918, p. 28.
73 Ibid., pp. 48-49.
74 *The Leys Fortnightly,* Vol. XLII., No. 733. Oct. 5, 1917, pp. 14-16.
75 *Dulwich College: The Fallen of the Great War, Life at Dulwich College 1914-1919* <https://dulwichcollege1914-18.co.uk/essay/life-at-dulwich-college-1914-1919/> (accessed 7 March 2022).

arrangements. Sherborne sent parties out to three local farms while Uppingham with the assistance of an old boy, Canon Hardwicke Rawnsley a vicar in the Lake District, held a camp in Cumbria.[76]

The performance of the 1917 Harvest Camps was far from satisfactory in the eyes of headmasters. Instead of falling out with the authorities, as they had with the army before the war over the entrance requirements for the military colleges the headmasters worked to ensure the manual labour they provided was used as effectively as possible. They continued to offer *ad hoc* support such as that of nine boys from Clifton who carried out tree felling work during the 1917 Christmas holidays.[77] There was little call for *ad hoc* contributions and the focus was on optimising support for the 1918 camps by working with the Ministry of National Service. After discussing the 1917 Harvest Camps, the HMC appointed a sub-committee to work with those in charge of the 1917 camps and examine what lessons could be learnt. There were several problems to be addressed, one of the more urgent ones was whether Harvest Camps should be given priority over the summer OTC camps. If both activities took place, it would place a considerable burden on boys with five weeks of the summer holidays taken up with extra activities. The War Office was prepared to compromise, despite believing OTC camps were valuable, and allow Harvest Camps priority over the OTC Camps. The Ministry of National Service and the County Agricultural Sub-Committees had forecast a far higher demand for agricultural labour in the summer of 1918 than in 1917. There was a vigorous debate in the HMC Committee with opinion evenly divided between those which solely wished to hold an OTC Camp, those which wished only to hold a Harvest Camp and those that were in favour of holding an OTC Camp as long as a Harvest Camp was also held.[78] This was not an ideological debate between supporters and opponents of military training. Both sides of the argument were led by the headmasters of schools which before the war had been the main providers of junior officers. Those in favour were led by the Headmaster of Eton, whose school had not supported the Harvest Camps in 1917. The Headmaster of Rugby led the opposition to the OTC Camps; in contrast to Eton his school had provided a large number of boys for the Harvest Camps. Officials argued that holding an OTC camp would reduce the number of boys who would attend a Harvest Camp. The option of supporting both activities also presented problems as boys could lose five weeks out of an eight week holiday, if they attended both camps. The committee was dominated by some of the leading public schools and within the wider HMC movement there was no strong feeling that OTC camps must be held. Eventually, it was agreed with the Ministry of National Service that the headmasters would extend

---

76 HMC, Report of the Headmasters' Conference December 1917, *pp.* 48-49 and TNA, NATS/1/653: Harvest Camps Schoolboy Labour Reports of Cavendish Association.
77 TNA NATS 1/652: Employment of schoolboy labour: Public Schools report; Navy and Army Canteen Board.
78 NATS 1/658: Commandant conference. The following two paragraphs are drawn from these records.

the summer holidays by one week while the Ministry of National Service agreed that OTC camps as well as Harvest Camps could be held. The prevailing mood amongst headmasters was not to protect the status of their schools as a source of junior officers but to take the course of action which served the country best.

It was not until June 1918 that the Government formally requested volunteers for the Harvest Camps. Public schoolboys were asked to volunteer because they were physically capable of carrying out the work and not because public school ethos made them more suitable than other boys. Only boys over 16 would be automatically accepted for the camps, but boys over 15 were also allowed to volunteer if their headmasters certified that they were strong enough to carry out the arduous work of gathering in the harvest. The War Office stipulation that at least the same number of boys from each school must attend a Harvest camp as the OTC Camp provided a clear message that the gathering of the harvest had priority over military training. By the summer of 1918 influenza was spreading through the UK and it was decided to cancel the OTC Camps. However, the Harvest Camps were still held. It apperas it was decided that it was necessary to concentrate the effort of boys and cancel the OTC camps. The implication was that it was better to use boys on the harvest than prepare them to be junior officers, of which there was also a shortage. By cancelling the OTC Camps any conflict between them was removed and priority could be given to the Harvest Camps. Boys from public schools were used in gathering the harvest because they were part of a wider group with the necessary attributes for the work. The call for volunteers was not solely made to the public schools. Boys over 16 at all secondary schools were invited to attend and many of them took up the invitation. Schools with pupils from a wide variety of backgrounds took part, such as Greengate Street Secondary School, Oldham, and Bablake School, Coventry, alongside public schools such as Malvern and Dulwich. An estimated shortfall of 17,000 agricultural labourers meant that the appeal for volunteers was not just directed at secondary schools. Groups of young men who had left school at 14 but were too young to be conscripted also took part. Among those groups gathering the harvest were young men from organisations such as the Boy Scouts Association and clerks from the City, who spent part of their holidays on this work. There was no special calling for public schools. They were part of a wider centrally directed effort to support food production. The physical fitness of their boys, and not public school ethos, made them suitable for this work. Public schools willingly contributed to this work and the majority understood it had to take priority over military training. Virtually every HMC member sent more boys to the Harvest Camps in 1918 than they did in 1917. Uppingham, which sent 150 boys in 1918 compared with 50 in 1917, was typical of this increased commitment.[79]

79 Halstead, *A School in Arms*, p. 102.

Producing the Goods

The efforts to support agricultural production demonstrates an approach which went beyond one based on romantic idealism. Many schools were able to go beyond this in providing practical support for the war effort. The nature of their support varied and was influenced by their curriculum and the facilities they had. Schools with a technical emphasis, such as Oundle, were able to produce components needed for the war effort while army schools, such as Eton, Harrow and Marlborough chose to concentrate on using their facilities and connections to prepare their boys to be junior officers.[80] Those schools which supplied components often used the profits to develop their workshop facilities.

Oundle's educational approach encouraged boys to develop problem solving skills which would be useful in business and industry. It was an easy step to adapt this 'learning by doing' approach so that supporting the war effort was integrated into the curriculum. As noted in Chapter Six, practical problems of fighting the war became part of its curriculum.[81] Almost from the beginning, its extensive facilities, which included a school farm, laboratories and workshops made it well equipped to supporting the war effort in ways which went beyond the provision of military training and agricultural labour. The farm's contribution has already been discussed but the contribution of the light engineering workshops was also significant. Not only were they well equipped but had six members of staff to oversee their work. Sanderson's strong business instincts were a distinct advantage, compared to other schools, and he actively marketed the services of the workshops, drawing up contracts for the orders received.[82] One result of this proactive approach was that in January 1915 the school received its first orders from the Munitions Board. A further consequence of the Headmaster's strong commercial acumen was that he was able to use the profits to purchase more equipment which enabled more orders to be fulfilled and strengthened the technical education provided by the school.[83] The whole life of the school was geared towards supporting the war effort. As well as lessons having a strong bias towards the practical problems of war, forms devoted at least one week of each term to war production, which amounted to 55 hours of production work by each boy.[84] Over the summers of 1915, 1916 and 1917, priority was given to workshop activity, the annual OTC camp was not held and instead boys and masters, 60 at a time, spent two weeks of their holidays fulfilling orders for the workshop.[85] During the war the production of its workshops was varied and included 13,376 torpedo components and

---

80 See Chapters 5 and 6.
81 Palmer, *The Life of F W Sanderson*, p. 165.
82 Ibid., p. 239.
83 Ibid., pp. 220-221.
84 Pendrill, *And We Were Young*, p. 256.
85 *The Oundle Munitions Gazette*, No. 1.

32,008 tools for the Woolwich Arsenal as well as bed screens for military hospitals.[86] The emphasis on engineering in the curriculum, the Headmaster's commercial acumen and the lower level of importance given to games were important factors in this impressive effort.

As has been argued in previous chapters it is unhelpful to see all public schools as being exactly the same. They varied and set out to be attractive to different groups of parents. Oundle's efforts were impressive for the reasons already set out. However, most schools wished to apply their resources towards supporting the war effort in the best way they could. Lloyd George, after being appointed Minister of Munitions in May 1915, set out to increase the number of organisations which could supply munitions and related components. Schools which offered technical training were able to provide this support to the munitions industry. Uppingham, whose approach was designed to bring the best out of every boy was slower to produce components, at the start of the war, but by the end of 1915 was stepping up its efforts. In October 1915 it switched its carpentry school to the production of splints.[87] The arrival of a new Headmaster, at the start of 1916, saw the purchase of a more powerful engine for the machine shop.[88] From the second half of 1916 all work undertaken in the metal shop was war-related with production including plunger bolts, and splints, bed tables and lockers for hospitals were manufactured in the woodwork shop.[89] During the war the school's production included 7,500 shell bases and over 2,600 dies and punches for .303 cartridge cases.[90] While not matching the efforts of Oundle, Uppingham's production figures demonstrate how a school's facilities could be effectively deployed to support the war effort. Christ's Hospital's Manual School taught practical skills which were especially useful for its many boys who came from less privileged backgrounds and left before the Sixth Form. From the summer of 1915, it supported the war effort by making essential components for the war effort. Like Uppingham it was able to provide substantial support and in the summer of 1915 20 boys (supported by instructors) worked seven and a half hour shifts, Monday to Friday, and a half day on Saturday, mainly producing clips and fittings. This was followed up in the Winter Term of 1915 with the production of parts for aircraft, the infantry and the artillery. Despite this substantial effort the school magazine expressed regret that the lack of volunteers meant more could not be done. Ironically, for a school not known for having a strong games ethos, despite the strong encouragement of the authorities, boys preferred to play games instead of volunteering at the Manual Shop.[91] Nonetheless, it was possible to maintain production for the rest of the war.[92] Unlike Oundle, the

---

86 Ibid., p. 223. Wednesday, August 4th, 1915, p. 1.
87 USA: Minutes of the Trustees 26 October 1915.
88 Halstead, *A School in Arms*, p. 101.
89 USA.
90 USM, April 1919, p. 94.
91 *The Blue*, Vol. XLIII., No. 3. December. 5, 1915, pp. 67-68.
92 CHA, The Home Front Exhibition.

school authorities appear to have suffered from a lack of commercial acumen with customers declining to pay for its services. Only after considerable efforts was it able to persuade its principal customer to make a payment in the summer of 1916 with the proceeds being used to purchase more equipment, strengthening both its educational facilities and capacity to fulfil orders.[93]

Those schools which were not able to support the munitions industry set out to provide practical support in other ways, as the examples of Winchester and Harrow demonstrate. Harrow used its workshop, in 1916, to produce metal bolts for the artillery and aircraft as well as splints and crutches for the local war hospital.[94] The lack of further reports about this activity in *The Harrovian* suggests that it was decided to apply its efforts for the remainder of the war to other priorities such as the training of potential officers and agricultural production, activities more appropriate to its curriculum. Rendall, at Winchester, saw the school as '*par excellence* to be the classical school.' In his view, because the demand for places meant it was able to select only 'intellectual' boys, unlike many other schools, he did not need to cater for boys for whom mechanical engineering would form a large part of their education. Therefore, there was no need to build an engineering workshop, although he did allow an expansion of the carpentry workshop's activities, presumably to produce relatively simple components.[95] Rendall's position can be understood; investing in an engineering workshop would have required substantial funds, with no guarantee this would be covered by revenue from the goods it produced. Unless the school made a strategic change to its educational approach there were too many risks in building a workshop. Apart from agricultural production, the school made other ad hoc contributions to the war effort. In October 1915, the school was diverted from its lessons for four days to process and index 40,000 National Register cards for men of military age.[96] All schools set out to apply their skills and abilities to support the war effort. While schools differed in the way they contributed to the home front what they had in common was that their support for the war effort was often mundane and practical. Practical support took precedence over those activities such as games which before the war were thought to be character building for boys. The war had a substantial effect on the schools both in terms of the demanding work to support the war effort and the increased level of austerity. It is little surprise that public schoolboys enthusiastically celebrated the end of the war.

---

93   CHA, Extracts from Council Minutes in 1915/16 about the Manual School and Munitions work.
94   *The Harrovian* Vol. XXIX., No. 5. April 1st 1916, pp. 21-22.
95   WCA, Report of the Head Master for the School Year ending August 1916, p. 4.
96   *The Wykehamist*, No. 546, November 1915, p. 454.

Marking Victory

Closer examination of these celebrations reveals that amongst the headmasters there were a variety of responses to the end of the war. Militarism did not underpin their response to the end of the war and there was little glorification of the war service of old boys. The way public schools celebrated the end of the war varied. Some were high spirited and extensive. At Uppingham, when news of the Armistice was received, school ended for the day and after a brief service of thanksgiving the school joined the town in the marketplace to celebrate and the day concluded with an impromptu concert.[97] Sherborne's celebrations were even more prolonged. On the Monday, when the Armistice took effect, school was cancelled until Wednesday morning. After a service of thanksgiving, the celebrations included letting off fireworks, a soccer match (Sherborne played rugby) between the boys and masters, and a dance.[98] The headmasters at Sherborne and Uppingham believed the cause the war was fought for was worthy and although neither was a militarist wanted to mark the end of the war in a significant way. Headmasters' views and approach dictated the way the war was marked. The Headmaster of Greshams, George Howson, who was a scientist, had established a broad curriculum (which was not classics based).[99] He opposed athleticism and although he was a member of the HMC committee he was often critical of other public schools. He granted a half day's holiday but the celebrations were more sober than those of the neighbouring town of Holt.[100] Howson had ambivalent feelings about the end of the war but wisely chose to allow celebrations, albeit they were subdued.

Other headmasters chose to ignore the nation's desire to celebrate the armistice with unfortunate results. Sanderson as Headmaster at Oundle had little insight into the national mood on 11 November 1918. *The Laxtonian* reported that three services were held between the Armistice and the end of term as acts of thanksgiving and memorial.[101] Unsurprisingly, the reports do not mention how badly Sanderson mishandled the situation A letter in the Oundle School Archives reveals that he declined to end school for the day and then attempted to put a stop to the town's celebrations in the evening. When he told the school the next morning that celebrations were not appropriate because the war was not over, it made the situation worse. It merely served to antagonise both boys and masters and led to a series of acts of disobedience which culminated in a demonstration involving many boys and some masters outside his house.[102] Sanderson's motivation for this action (which he apologised for the following

---

97 USM, No. 445. November 1918, pp. 422-424.
98 *The Shirburnian* Vol XXIX., No. 12. December 1918, pp. 362-363.
99 Tozer, *The Ideal of Manliness*, pp. 435-437.
100 Smart, *When Heroes Die*, p. 162.
101 Pendrill, *And We Were Young*, p. 314.
102 Oundle School Archives, Letter from Bramston House, Oundle (author unknown) 12 November 1918.

day) was the loss of his son in April 1918 which appears to have diminished his belief in the war.[103] Headmasters were the dominant figure at every public school but this episode reveals that they could not operate without the support of masters and boys. A similar incident took place at Berkhamsted where the Headmaster, Charles Greene, also refused to grant the day off. In the evening drunken troops broke into the school, with the assistance of a boy, whereupon many students took the opportunity to join the celebrations on the High Street. Greene's actions were driven by his strong feelings of anti-militarism and unfortunately these feelings flew in the face of the mood of much of the nation.[104] It was possible to have strong objections to militarism and still mark the end of the fighting. Mill Hill, with its strong streak of anti-militarism, thought it worthwhile to celebrate the end of the war but in a low-key manner.[105] These celebrations extended to its OTC, together with that of The Leys, forming the Honour Guard at the 'United Thanksgiving Service of the English Free Churches', attended by the King and Queen.

There was no common approach by schools about how the Armistice should be marked and there were also differences about commemoration after the war. How old boys who had died were to be commemorated was often the subject of vigorous debate. Many of the more senior old boys, who had not fought in the war, favoured a sacred memorial while those who had served favoured more practical memorials which improved the facilities at their *alma mater*. Sometimes these debates became heated but in general most schools had as part of their remembrance memorials which were both sacred and secular. Mill Hill's approach of building a Gate of Honour and a science block to commemorate those of its old boys who had died, reflected the approach of many schools.[106] The debate about appropriate memorials illustrated that those old boys who fought in the war saw nothing chivalrous about it and that there was no romance in war. Across the generations of public schoolboys there was no shared ethos.

Conclusion

An initial examination of public schools suggests that they enjoyed preferential treatment when compared with other schools, especially at the start of the war. Closer examination reveals that the apparent advantages were more to do with the location of public schools rather than them being afforded special privileges. In some cases, early in the war, the public schools used their influence with the War Office

---

103   Palmer, The Life of F W Sanderson, pp. 247-248.
104   Norman Sherry, *The Life of Graham Greene, Volume One 1904-1939* (London: Jonathan Cape, 1989), pp. 60-61.
105   *Mill Hill Magazine*, Vol. XLVI., No. 4. December 1918, pp. 72-73.
106   For a fuller discussion, see Timothy Halstead, 'Public Schools and Great War Memorials – Sacred and Secular', *Stand To!*, 120 (November 2020), pp. 63-65.

to halt the requisition of their facilities by the army. This was understandable as their OTC contingents provided training for potential officers at a time when the army was rapidly expanding and training resources were stretched. The ability of these contingents to provide training meant that their cadets who had the potential to be officers were allowed to remain until they were 18 and a half, whereas conscription of other men occurred when they reached 18. Public schools had to deal with the same problems as the rest of the civilian population. They suffered from food shortages and the effects of inflation as well as the effects on education which resulted from their staff leaving to fight in the war. Rather than being possessed by a romantic attitude towards war boys were sceptical of the more jingoistic speakers they heard and their response to war was phlegmatic. The demands of the war meant that games increasingly enjoyed a lower priority. Headmasters were keen to provide whatever pragmatic support they could for the war effort. The advent of a centrally directed war effort meant that from 1916 onwards, the contribution of public schools went beyond military training. Substantial changes were made to school life to support the war effort and manage the effects of food shortages. All boys found themselves spending substantial time cultivating potatoes and other vegetables for their own use as well as providing support for local farmers. During 1917-18 this support was extended to participation in Harvest Camps which became necessary after the conscription of agricultural workers. Boys who were 16 and older were well suited to this work as it involved unskilled manual labour. For many of the public schools the provision of manual labour remained their primary contribution. However, where schools had the appropriate facilities they produced components for the war effort. This work was mundane and far from romantic. It was physically demanding and combined with increasing austerity it is not surprising that boys and many schools greeted the end of the war with exuberant celebration, as did most of the civilian population. Exuberant celebrations at public schools were not a direct product of their ethos but reflected the prevailing national mood.

Conclusion

Public school ethos is a blunt instrument to explain their involvement in the Great War. The idea that this ethos made boys into romantic idealists with a set of values which made them keen to go to war is inadequate. It relies on the idea that the schools were essentially very similar in their approach, syllabi and values. All schools, it is claimed, took a similar approach to education; at the heart of this was the teaching of the classics and the playing of games. Such was the importance given to the playing of games that it became a cult. The result, it is argued, was that all pupils were imbued with a public school ethos; an ethos it is argued which was tantamount to an ideology. The promotion of teamwork and sacrifice led to a spirit of militarism and the belief it was right to die for your country (*Dulce et decorum est*). The approach which explained public school involvement in ideological terms developed in the 1960s and 1970's. Economic and social liberalism led to a decline in social deference towards the products of public schools and the questioning of the nature of their involvement in the Great War. There was also a deep awareness that Europe had suffered from the spread of Nazism and Communism. The Cold War was a part of everyday life and the memories of the Second World War were fresh. In seeking to explain the involvement of public school *alumni* in the Great War it is not surprising that an ideological explanation came to the fore.

Authors such as Peter Parker in *The Old Lie*, produced a great deal of evidence in support of the idea of public schoolboys being indoctrinated but ignored the evidence which plays down the idea the importance of public school ethos. The citing of public school fiction as a source of evidence that games were at the centre of the schools' lives does not bear closer examination. *Tom Brown's Schooldays*, which eulogised Thomas Arnold and Rugby has been misinterpreted. Arnold had no interest in games, apart from it being a useful way of keeping boys out of mischief. Neither did the book set out to promote a love of games as an essential and formative part of public school life. The idea it did arose from a misunderstanding of it by the founder of the Olympic movement. Although, there was plenty of literature which sought to romanticise the idea of public schoolboys being influenced by the teaching of the classics and the playing of games, there was a significant amount of public school fiction which took the opposite approach. P.G. Wodehouse in his *Mike* stories lampooned the games cult. Rudyard Kipling in *Stalky and Co* presented a group of schoolboys who had an ambivalent attitude to public school life, especially games and the classics, who were crafty and ingenious and set out to beat the system rather than be moulded by it. Similarly there is far less consistency in memoirs of public school life than has been claimed. Instead, they presented a variety of experiences of school life and included those of boys who despite having little inclination to play games had happy memories of their schools. It is dangerous to draw from memoirs and fiction an image of boys indoctrinated by the teaching of the classics and the playing of games.

Employing literature as a source is dependent on the idea that all schools took a similar approach. This misunderstanding partly arises from the Cavendish and Taunton Commissions reports, which set out, as part of their proposals for educational reforms, a hypothetical model of what represented good practice for the running of public schools. It included the idea of games as being part of the moral training of boys. It was a mistake by the Commissions to try to draw too many common features in public schools. The growth in industry and the professions meant that parents who sent their sons to these schools did not have a common set of educational requirements for their sons. No one school was able to cater for the entire range of different parental demands. It meant that different public schools had a different emphasis which met the needs of different groups of parents. The emphasis on the classics and games varied and not all public schools were Anglican and a significant number of schools were Catholic and non-conformist. The educational approach of these schools meant that the cult of games and a romanticised approach to war were less likely to take hold. The contribution of Catholic and non-conformist schools to the junior officer corps demonstrates that a model which explains the public school contribution to the junior officer corps in terms of ethos is insufficient.

The idea that classics and the exploits of military heroes recounted within them in some way brainwashed boys is at best simplistic and at worse wrong. In the period leading up to 1914, the of the classics significance started to wane. The public school movement engaged in a lively debate about how they should be taught. Classics were irrelevant for many boys. They did not have an aptitude for the classics and therefore lacked the means to be inspired by the tales of historically remote military heroes. Kipling's satire of the teaching of the classics, *Regulus* in *Stalky and Co,* reflects the experience of many. Parents expected to public schools to offer more than classics and in an increasingly competitive environment schools needed to offer an education which set them apart from competing establishments, to attract boys. Many schools introduced sixth form classes for subjects such as business and engineering as a response to the demand from parents for their sons to be given skills needed to work in family businesses. Although games remained important in public school life there were an increasing number of schools where the educational approach of the headmasters meant that the cult of games did not take hold. Analysing the contribution of these schools to the military effort there is no evidence that they made a lesser contribution to the junior officer corps. Those who excelled at games were less likely to have the type of education the army desired. The demand on the time of these boys meant it was often impossible to be proficient at games and to spare time to participate in the OTC. After the Boer War, the army became increasingly critical of the relevance of a public school education its requirements. Its efforts to redefine its educational requirements and improve professional standards increasingly led it to be in conflict with public school headmasters. The Army's educational reforms significantly reduced the status of the classics in its entrance exams and elevated the importance of the sciences and modern languages. This conflicted with the requirements of Oxbridge where the schools sent far more of their boys, than the army. Militarism and practical support for the army took second place to the educational priorities of the headmasters. The severe rift between the army and the headmasters only started to narrow after the establishment of the OTC in 1908. It meant that members of the OTC received training which concentrated on the technical skills required to be junior officers. These skills were of far more value to the army than a classical education, an ability to play games and a militaristic approach. Militarism was far less prevalent at public schools than has been suggested. Examining debates and articles in public school magazines shows schoolboys did not have an ideological belief in the British Empire and a militaristic desire to protect it . To them, the empire was a way a life which informed their understanding of the world but they were not uncritical of it.

The response of public schools to the outbreak of the war was patriotic, as was that of the whole country. Early accounts of the war although not militaristic underplayed its horrors. Later accounts, in school magazines, of the military activities of old boys did not attempt to hide the horrors of war. Headmasters were more concerned with providing practical support for the war than glorifying war to the boys under their care. The records of their meetings show men who were concerned getting clear guidance on the best way to do this and their exasperation, especially in the early stages of the war at the failure of the authorities to provide this. Rather than criticise from the side lines they were proactive in their offer of support. The records show them making proposals as to how guidance could be improved and their boys deployed more effectively both in the military effort and on the home front. Their predominant concern was National Efficiency and not imbuing boys with public school ethos.

When war broke out in August 1914, public schoolboys like all parts of the population responded to Kitchener's call for volunteers. There was a shared concern throughout the country about the threat to the empire. Public schoolboys were an obvious source of junior officers to lead the New Army and the War Office especially, sought those who had undertaken training with the OTC. The integrated nature of this training made it possible for them to make a more immediate contribution to preparing the New Army. The deployment of those with OTC training to provide training in the face of a chronic shortage of NCOs, even before their commission had been gazetted, demonstrates the importance attached to OTC training. The Junior OTC contingents did not entirely consist of those from public schools. Those schools outside the public school movement with OTC contingents also made significant contributions to the junior officer corps at the start of the war. The chaotic nature of the creation of the New Army meant that the War Office was unable to cope and forced to delegate junior officer recruitment to the COs of the new battalions. The COs given the urgent need to find junior officers did not insist on OTC experience, there were probably not enough men with this experience available. Instead, they set out to find men who they considered to have the right qualities to be leaders of men. They considered public schoolboys, without OTC experience, to have the right qualities to be leaders of men. Forced to rapidly recruit junior officers the battalion COs used their contacts to speed up the process. It meant that they also recommended men without public school backgrounds who were judged to have the right qualities. A public school background while helpful in gaining a commission was not essential, in the early stages of the war. Once it took back control of officer recruitment the War Office reinstated the approach which placed an emphasis on candidates having an OTC background with the right basic training, rather than the importance of public school ethos. It was an approach strongly supported by headmasters, who as already noted were keen to provide whatever practical support they could. The importance of a public school background declined throughout the war. As the army emphasised the importance of practical skills and returned to the pre-war integrated training approach of which the OTC was a part. Public schoolboys were no longer the sole source of officer cadets. To be accepted for officer training they had to meet clearly defined standards of efficiency. There was an increasing emphasis on clear guidance on training and active monitoring of it to ensure OTC contingents achieved a uniformly standard. The result was that those who excelled at games were no longer considered automatically to be the best candidates for commissions. With the emphasis on the right skills rather than ethos, in OTC contingents, those who were not good at games often demonstrated themselves to be better leaders than games players. Public school OTCs, with an established training infrastructure, remained an important source for officers. However, men in the ranks, who had shown leadership qualities on the front line were also a significant source of junior officers.

While in the chaotic expansion of the New Army at the start of the war a public school education was often used as a factor in the recruitment officers it does not adequately explain public school involvement. Status, class, curriculum and connections, as well as public school ethos, need to be taken into account in explaining the involvement of public schools in the Great War. The differences between the different public schools are too wide to be able to ascribe ethos as the dominant factor. The different educational approaches of each school are reflected in the way they contributed to the military effort. The air force, artillery and engineers needed men with educations in mathematics and science. It is no surprise that those schools whose curricula placed a strong emphasis on these subjects had a higher proportion of their old boys serving in. Apart from the curriculum the background of a school the background of a school would make them an obvious source for the skills the army needed. Epsom, which had been established by the medical profession to provide an education for the sons of doctors, and unsurprisingly had a long history of its old boys becoming doctors, was an obvious source of recruits for the RAMC. The school made a contribution to the medical services which far outweighed that of others. The army became an increasingly complex organisation which needed a variety of technical skills. The urgency of recruiting for these roles meant that patronage and social connections were an obvious way to speed up the process. These connections were not exercised in a way that meant the socially privileged had an advantage over the technically competent. The armed forces looked for recruits where it was confident it could find men with the right skills. The Old Blues of Christ's Hospital often came from less privileged backgrounds but provided a rich source of men who became paymasters in the navy. Several Old Blues were already paymasters at the start of the war and knew that the school's curriculum was likely to have produced men suitable for this role. What you knew and who you knew was equally important.

One of the reasons that public school involvement has been presented as unique is because their participation has been written about far more than other types of schools. This has led to the idea that there is something exceptional about public school involvement. The whole of the education sector supported the war effort and all schools suffered from it a variety of ways such as food shortages and blackout measures. Although public schools, especially at the start of the war, seemed to have been treated more favourably the reasons for this were usually far more nuanced than the social status of public schools. Public schools were usually located in places where the army had less need to requisition them. In some respects, public school boys did enjoy advantages but to enjoy them they had to meet specific standards of competence set by the War Office. Public schools were also eager not to set themselves apart by claiming privileges and the HMC agreed not to claim special privileges the law might entitle its members to. Public schools contributed to the whole of the war effort, and not the whole of the war effort. They played their part in the more closely managed war effort which developed from 1916. In addition to OTC training they expanded into supporting food production, both for themselves and the wider country. This was not done reluctantly. Public school headmasters had concentrated on OTC training at the request of the War Office. When called to provide further support the vast majority, willingly did so. They recognised that not only did their boys have the attributes to be junior officers but that the older ones had the attributes needed to partly replace conscripted agricultural labourers. The government placed a particular emphasis on supporting food production but all public schools sought to support the war effort in whatever way they could such as producing components for the war effort. To support this the playing of games was curtailed, to release time for boys to support food production and enable playing fields to be used for the production of food. Those activities which it is said contributed to public school ethos were cast aside. Schools were patriotic during the war, in common with of the rest of the population. This should not be confused with militarism. When the end of the war came exuberant celebrations at schools mirrored those amongst the rest of the population

Describing public school boys as the victims of Horace is an oversimplification of their involvement in the Great War. These men were prepared to take risks which they knew might lead to the loss of their lives. However, they also understood that to be reckless could lead to an unnecessary loss of life. They were not indoctrinated by public school ethos but did learn values and skills which made them good leaders of men. It was the skills boys learnt in the OTC which made them attractive to the army as candidates for commissions. There is no one size fits all approach to explaining public school involvement in the Great War. The army needed officers with a variety of different skills and expertise. The playing of games and the teaching of the classics were never likely to be enough to meet these requirements. The contribution of each public schools varied because they varied in their educational approach. Explaining public school involvement deserves a far wider explanation than one that reduces them to victims of Horace.

Bibliography

Archival Sources

The National Archives/TNA (Kew)
AIR/1/120/15/14/80: Officer Cadets for Officers Cadet Technical Corps
NATS 1/652: Employment of schoolboy labour: Public Schools report; Navy and Army Canteen Board
NATS/1/653: Harvest Camps Schoolboy Labour Reports of Cavendish Association
NATS 1/658: Commandant conference
WO 92/9034: Regulations for Officers Training Corp 1908 & Royal Warrant
WO 293/1: War Office Instructions, Aug.-Dec. 1914.
WO 293/2: War Office Instructions, Jan.-June. 1915.
WO 293/3: War Office Instructions, July.-Dec. 1915.
WO 293/4 Army Council Instructions, 1-1307, 1916
WO 293/5 Army Council Instructions, 1308-2449, 1916
WO 293/6 Army Council Instructions, 1-1032, 1917

Officer Service Files

WO 339/70723	Abel	John Duncan
WO 339/72970	Addington	Geoffrey William
WO 339/13666	Akroyd	Henry Cecil
ADM 337/56/166	Alexander	William Lindsay
WO 339/6854	Almack	Edward Poulton
WO 339/36496	Annan	James Gilroy
WO 339/52170	Archer	Ronald Hedley
WO 339/7602	Aytoun	Robert Merlin Graham
WO 339/95495	Badgery	Thomas Samuel Maxwell
WO 339/124614	Baker	Humphrey George Ambrose
WO 374/3955	Barker	Kenneth Edgar Mylne
WO 339/115814	Bascombe	Cecil Reginald
WO 339/58550	Beachcroft	Philip Maurice
WO 339/58484	Beatson	William Gordon
AIR 76/30/177	Beck	Edwyn Walter Tyrrell
WO 339/108894	Becker	Harry Thomas Alfred
WO 374/5560	Bell	Kenneth Pyman

WO 339/1270	Bindloss	Edward Hugh
WO 339/1391	Birley	Maurice
WO339/134148	Bowyer	Edward Barry
WO 339/27827	Brittain	Edward Harold
WO 339/60555	Browne	Burdett
WO 339/36949	Bunce	Hugh Pollock
WO 339/45176	Burlison	John Clement
WO 339/6987	Caldecott	John Leslie
WO 339/33904	Carey	Wilfred Hardacre
WO 339/19013	Carter-Wood	Joseph Allan
WO 339/42584	Chambers-Hunter	Charles Allardyce Jopp
WO 339/17833	Christopherson	Arnold Bayley
WO 339/137032	Clarke	John Holden Kempe
WO 339/21703	Colley	William Arthur
WO 339/5252	Collinge	Arthur
WO 339/32422	Constable	Oswald Clement
WO 339/133494	Cooper	Hugh
WO 374/22052	Edwards	Alfred Cecil Wall
WO 339/11428	Ellinger	Maurice Reginald
WO 339/60216	Hett	Alan Stanley
WO 339/24071	Ivatt	Henry George
WO 339/63675	Leir	Richard Thomas Marriott
WO 161/95/38	Johnson	William Dalrymple
WO 339/27667	Parr	Wilfred Wharton
WO 339/10422	Peachey	Hugh Graham
WO 339/8566	Pearson	Algernon George
ADM 196/62/386	Regnart	Cyrus Hunter
WO 339/16476	Thornely	Francis Bodenham
ADM 196/63/58	Trench	Bernard Frederic
WO 339/99018	Ward	Humphrey Plowden
WO 339/15795	Webb	Duncan Vere
WO 339/20320	White	William Lambert
WO 339/67763	Whitwell	Francis Albert
WO 33966398	Willey	Harold
WO 339/8764	Williams	George Gilbert Algernon
WO 374/75055	Williams	Ralph Vaughan
AIR 76/551/158	Williamson	James Sprout
WO 76/7/46	Wilson	John Menzies
WO 339/65351	Withy	Basil
AIR 76/559/9	Wood	Leslie Thomas Cyril
WO 339/2226	Wood	John Ironside
WO 339/44486	Wragg	Norman John
WO 339/80654	Wright	Desmond Arthur
WO 339/123636	Wynn	Roland Tempest Beresford
WO 339/55413	Young	Hugh

Bradford Grammar School
Roll of Honour, Sixth Mathematical

Brighton College
Council Minutes 1917 and 1918

Christ's Hospital
Reports on the Boys School 1903 to 1919

Commonwealth War Graves Commission
Casualty Database <http://www.cwgc.org/search-for-war-dead.aspx>

Epsom College Archives
Epsom College Midsummer 1914
Epsom College Register 1889-1914
Index of Old Epsomian Biographies between 1890 and 1914 Doctors: GPs, Consultants and the Most Eminent

Haileybury College
Arthur Fanshawe Hoare

Headmaster's Conferences
Reports of the Meetings of the Headmaster's Conference 1899-1919

Liddell Hart Centre for Military Archives
Burnaby, Lieutenant Colonel Hugo Beaumont Papers
Carr, Lieutenant General Laurence Papers
Lethbridge, John Papers
Liddell Hart, Capt Sir Basil Henry Papers
Caunter, Brig John Alan Lyde Papers

Lincolnshire Archives
Letters from Christopher Wakefield Selwyn

London Metropolitan Archives
Peachey Family

National Army Museum
2016-10-23, Colonel Maxwell Earle Papers
1990-09-7, Second Lieutenant Theodore Farquhar Twist Papers

Oundle
The Munitions Gazette, 1915
The Laxtonian 1908-1918

Somme Museum
Frank Thornley Collection

St Albans School
School Archives

The Imperial War Museum:
Ash, Lieutenant F H Papers
Briggs, Mrs L K Papers
Burton, Commander H C Papers
Cane, Major A S Papers
Eckenstein, Captain T C Papers
Ennor, Lieutenant F H Papers
Gray, Papers of Captain J E B Papers
Hale, Alfred Papers
Horridge, Captain G B Papers
Horridge, Captain J L Papers
Howitt, Brigadier F D Papers
Howitt, Captain H G Papers
Lee, Lieutenant Colonel A N Papers
Lewis, Major-General H V Papers
Openshaw, Group Captain E R Papers
13717, Gee, Charles Hilton Roderick (Oral History)
8766, Greenwell, Graham Hamilton (Oral History)
9474, Harbottle, George (Oral History)
10459, Holttum, Harold (Oral History)
9275, Heath, Charles Philip (Oral History)
7498, Horridge, George B (Oral History)
14985, Millard, Ernest (Oral History)
10699, Rymer-Jones, John Murray (Oral History).

Sherborne School Archives
Diaries of H R King
Headmaster's Report to the Governors 1907 – 1922

St Georges School Archives
School magazines 1914-1918

University of Cambridge Library
OP.2100.8.5, "B" Company No.2 Officer Cadet Battalion: Summary of lectures, private study and practical work for the 4 months' course, exclusive of drill, bayonet fighting and physical training.

Uppingham School
Harold Howitt Reminiscences
Charles Herbert Jones
R Sterndale-Bennett (1910-1921) Files
School magazines 1884-1930
Uppingham School Archives
Unknown OU: Games, Public School and Empire 1840-1900 A Study of Uppingham School to explore the effects of games on the British Empire unpublished BA dissertation (York)

Winchester College Archives
Reports of the Headmaster 1911-1922
Winchester College Calendar July 1907
Winchester College Calendar August 1914

Rolls of Honour

*1914-1919 The Book of Remembrance and War Record of Mill Hill School (*Reigate: Surrey Fine Art Press, n.d.)
Christ's Hospital Roll of Honour and Service Names of Governors, Members of Staff, and Old Blues serving in His Majesty's and Allied Forces in the World War 1914-1918 (Privately published, 1920)
Colfe's Grammar School Lewisham and The Great War 1914-1919 with Rolls of Honour and of Service (Privately published: 1920)
Downside and the War: 1914-1918 (Privately published, 1925)
Eastbourne College Roll of Honour (Privately published, n.d.)
Old Epsomians Known to have Served in the First World War (Privately published: 2017)
Final A List of Caruthusians who served in His Majesty's Forces and the Allied Armies August, 1914–November 1918 and in the Subsequent Russian Campaigns (Privately published, 1919)
The Great War 1914-1919: Old Georgians' Roll of Honour and Record of Service (Privately published, n.d.)
Handsworth Grammar School (Bridge Trust) Records of Service 1914-1918 (Privately published, n.d.)
Lancing College Roll of Service, Ninth Issue, July 1918 (Privately published: 1918)
Old Shirburnian Navy and Army List, 1914-1919 (Privately published: Sherborne, 1921)
Oakham, All Fighting Old Oakhamians <https://oakham-rutland.libguides.com/c.php?g=675068&p=4911855>
Oundle Memorials of the Great War MCMXIV-MCMXIX (Oundle: Privately published, 1920)
Shrewsbury School: Roll of Service 1914-1918 (Shrewsbury: Privately published, 1921)

Stonyhurst War Record A Memorial of the part taken by Stonyhurst Men in the Great War (Stonyhurst: Privately published, 1927)
Tonbridge School and the Great War of 1914-1918 A Record of the Services of Tonbridgeans in the Great War of 1914-1918 (Tonbridge: Privately published, 1923)
Third List of Old Uppinghamiams who served in H.M. Forces 1914-1919 (Oxford: 1919)
Wykehamist War Service Roll 1914-1919 (Winchester: Privately published, 1919)

School Rolls

Epsom College Register, 1889-1914 (Privately Published, n.d.)
Rugby School Register Volume IV From January 1892 to September 1921 (Rugby: George Over, 1929)
Shrewsbury School Register Vol. I. 1798-1908 (Shrewsbury: Wilding, 1928)
Shrewsbury School Register Vol. II. 1908-1958 (Shrewsbury: Wilding, 1964)
The Sherborne Register Fourth Edition (Sherborne: Privately published, 1950)
Uppingham School Roll 1824-1905 Third Issue (London: Privately published, 1906)
Uppingham School Roll 1853-1947 Seventh Issue (London: Privately published, 1948)
Winchester College A Register for the Years 1901 to 1946 (London: Edward Arnold, 1956)

School Magazines

Albanian
Berkhamsted
Brighton College Magazine
The City of London School Magazine
The Bradfordian: The Bradford Grammar School Magazine
The Carthusian
The Elizabethan
The Epsomian
Eton College Chronicle
The Harrovian
The Johnian
The Laxtonian,
The Leys Fortnightly
The Malburian,
The Meteor
The Mill Hill Magazine
The Pauline
The Shirburnian
The Stonyhurst Magazine
The Tonbridgian
The Wykehamist,

Published Sources

Official Army List, 1907-1918
Edmonds, Brigadier General Sir J. E., et al, *Official History of the Great War: Military Operations France and Belgium 1914-1918,* 14 Volumes (London: Macmillan and HMSO, 1922-1949)
The Cadet List being a List of All Cadet Units had received Official Recognition on 31st December 1915 (London: HMSO, 1916)
Schools Inquiry Commission, Report of the Commissioners, 1868
London Gazette, 1914-1918
War Office, *Field Service Regulations Part I Operations 1909 (Reprinted, with Amendments, 1912)* (London: HMSO, 1912)
War Office, *Infantry Training 1911* (London, HMSO, 1911)
War Office, *Officers Training Corps. Junior Division. Instructions for the Annual Camps. 1913* (London: HMSO, 1913)
War Office, *O.T.C. Examination for Certificates A and B, December 1908 to March 1912* (HMSO, 1912)

General
Adams R. J. Q and Poirier Philip. P., *The Conscription Controversy in Great Britain 1900-1918* (Basingstoke: MacMillan, 1987)
Amery, Leopold, Stennett. (ed.), *The Times History of the War in South Africa, 1899-1902, Vol. II* (London: Sampson, Low, Marston and Company, 1909)
Ashworth, T., *Trench Warfare, 1914–18: The Live and Let Live System* (London: MacMillan 1980)
Baker, Chris, *The Battle for Flanders: German Defeat on the Lys, 1918* (Barnsley: Pen and Sword, 2011)
Barnett, Corelli, *The Collapse of British Power* (Stroud: Alan Sutton, 1984)
Batten, Simon, *Futile Exercise? The British Army's Preparations for War 1902-1914* (Warwick: Helion, 2018)
Beach, Jim, *Haig's Intelligence: GHQ and the German Army, 1916-1918* (Cambridge: Cambridge University Press, 2015)
—— *Lord Gorell and the Army Educational Corps: 1918-1920 (*Cheltenham: Army Records Society, 2019)
Beckett, Ian, *Britain's Part-Time Soldiers The Amateur Military Tradition 1558-1945* (Barnsley: Pen and Sword Military, 2011)
—— (ed.), *The Army and the Curragh Incident (*Stroud: Army Records Society, 1986)
—— Simpson, K. (eds.), *A Nation in Arms: A Social Study of the British Army in the First World War* (Manchester: Manchester University Press, 1985).
—— Bowman, Timothy and Connelly, Mark, *The British Army and the First World War* (Cambridge: Cambridge University Press, 2017)
Stuart Bell, *Faith in Conflict: The Impact of the Great War on the Faith of the People of Britain (*Solihull: Helion, 2017)

Bidwell, Shelford and Graham, Dominick, *Fire-Power: The British Army Weapons and Theories of War 1904-1945* (Barnsley: Pen and Sword, 2004)

Bishop, T. J. H. in collaboration with Rupert Wilkinson, *Winchester and the Public School Elite* (London: Faber and Faber, 1967)

Blades, Barry, *Roll of Honour Schooling & the Great War 1914-1919* (Barnsley: Pen & Sword, 2015)

Blake, Robert (ed.), *The Private Papers of Douglas Haig 1914-1919* (London: Eyre and Spottiswoode, 1952)

Boff, Jonathan, *Haig's Enemy Crown Prince Ruprecht and Germany's War on the Western Front* (Oxford: Oxford University Press, 2018)

—— *Winning and Losing on the Western Front The British Third Army and the Defeat of Germany in 1918* (Cambridge: Cambridge University Press, 2012)

Bond, Brian, *From Liddell Hart to Joan Littlewood: Studies in British Military History* (Solihull: Helion, 2015)

—— and Cave, Nigel (eds.), *Haig a Reappraisal 70 Years On (*Barnsley: Leo Cooper, 1999)

——et al, *'Look To Your Front': Studies in the First World War* (Staplehurst: Spellmount, 1999)

Bowman, Timothy and Connelly, Mark, *The Edwardian Army: Recruiting, Training, and Deploying the British Army, 1902-1914* (Oxford: Oxford University Press, 2012)

Cannadine, David, *The Decline and Fall of the British Aristocracy* (London: Papermac, 1996)

Chandler, D. and Beckett, I. (eds), *The Oxford Illustrated History of the British Army* (Oxford: OUP, 1994)

Churchill, Alexandra, *Blood and Thunder The Boys of Eton College and the First World War* (Stroud: The History Press, 2014)

Edgerton, David, *The Rise and Fall of the British Nation: A Twentieth-century History* (London: Allen Lane, 2018)

Ensor, Sir Robert, *The Oxford History of England 1870-1914* (Oxford: Clarendon, 1936)

Ferguson, Niall, *The Pity of War* (London: Penguin, 1999)

—— *Empire: How Britain Made the Modern World* (London: Penguin, 2004)

Fox, Aimee, *Learning to Fight: Military Innovation and Change in the British Army, 1914-1918* (Cambridge: Cambridge University Press, 2018)

French, David, *British Economic and Strategic Planning 1905-1915* (London: George, Allen and Unwin, 1982)

French, David, *Military Identities: The Regimental System, the British Army, the British People c.1870-2000* (Oxford: Oxford University Press, 2005)

Galthorne-Hardy, Jonathan, *The Public School Phenomenon* (London: Hodder and Stoughton, 1977)

Gardner, Brian, *The Public Schools* (London: Hamish Hamilton, 1973)

Gregory, Adrian, *The Last Great War British Society and the First World War* (Cambridge: Cambridge University Press, 2008)

Grieves, Keith, *The Politics of Manpower, 1914-1918* (Manchester: Manchester University Press, 1988)
Haig-Brown, Captain Alan R, *The OTC and the Great War* (London: Country Life, 1915)
Haldane, Richard Burdon, *Education & Empire: Addresses on Certain Topics of the Day* (London: John Murray, 1902)
Harris, Jose, *The Penguin Social History of Britain. Private Lives, Public Spirit: Britain 1870-1914* (London: Penguin, 1994)
Harris, Paul, *The Men who Planned the War*: *A Study of the Staff of the British Army on the Western Front, 1914-1918* (Farnham: Ashgate, 2015)
Hodgkinson, Peter. E., *British Infantry Battalion Commanders in the First World War* (Farnham: Ashgate, 2015)
Honey, J. R. de S., *Tom Brown's Universe: The Development of the Victorian Public School* (London : Millington, 1977)
Hurst, Steve, *The Public Schools Battalion in The Great War* (Barnsley: Pen and Sword, 2007)
Jones, Spencer (ed.), *At All Costs: The British Army on the Western Front 1916* (Warwick, Helion, 2018)
Joll, James, *Europe Since 1870: An International History* London: Penguin, 1990)
Keegan, John, *The Face of Battle* (London: Pimlico, London, 1991)
Kennedy, Rosie, *The Children's War: Britain, 1914-1918* (Basingstoke: Palgrave Macmillan, 2014)
Koss, Stephen, *Nonconformity in Modern British Politics (*London: Batsford, 1975)
Lewis-Stempel, John, *Six Weeks: The Short and Gallant Life of the British Officer in the First World War* (London: Orion, 2011)
LoCicero, Michael, Mahoney, Ross and Mitchell, Stuart (eds.) *A Military Transformed? Adaption and Innovation in the British Military 1792-1945* (Solihull: Helion, 2014)
Mack, Edward. C., *Public Schools and British Opinion Since 1860*: *The Relationship Between Contemporary Ideas and the Evolution of an English Institution* (New York: Columbia University Press, 1941)
Madigan, Edward, *Faith Under Fire: Anglican Army Chaplains and the Great War* (Basingstoke: Palgrave MacMillan, 2011)
Mais, S. P. B., *A Public School in War Time* (London: John Murray, 1916)
Malcolm, Sir Neill, *The Science of War: A collection of essays and lectures 1892–1903 by the late Colonel G. F. R. Henderson CB* (London: Longmans, Green and Co., 1912)
Mangan, J. A., *Athleticism in the Victorian and Edwardian Public Schools* (Cambridge: Cambridge University Press, 1981)
Mein, Jonathan; Wares, Anne & Mann, Sue (eds.), *St Albans Life on the Home Front 1914-1918* (Hatfield: Hertfordshire Publications, 2016)
Middlebrook, Martin, *The First Day on the Somme* (London: Classic Penguin, 2001)
—— *The Kaiser's Battle* (London: Classic Penguin, 2000)
Mitchinson, K. W., *Defending Albion: Britain's Home Army 1908-1919* (Basingstoke: Palgrave Macmillan, 2005)

Moore-Bick, Christopher, *Playing the Game: The British Junior Infantry Officer on the Western Front 1914-1918* (Solihull: Helion, 2011)

Morgan-Owen, David. G., *The Fear of Invasion: Strategy, Politics and British War Planning* (Oxford: OUP, 2017)

Morris, A. J. A., *The Scaremongers: The Advocacy of War and Rearmament 1896-1914* (Abingdon: Routledge, 2014)

Newsome, David, *Godliness & Good Learning* (London: Cassell, 1961)

Ogilvie, V., The *English Public School* (London: B T Batsford, 1957)

Parker, David, *Hertfordshire Children in War and Peace, 1914-1939* (Hatfield, Hertfordshire Publications, 2007)

Parker, Peter, *The Old Lie: The Great War and the Public School Ethos* (London: Hambledon Continuum, 1987)

Pakenham, Thomas, *The Boer War* (London: Abacus, 1992)

Pennell, Catriona, *A Kingdom United: Popular Responses to the Outbreak of the First World War in Britain and Ireland* (Oxford: Oxford University Press, 2014)

Philpott, William, *Attrition: Fighting the First World War* (London: Little Brown, 2014)

—— *Bloody Victory: The Sacrifice on the Somme* (London: Abacus, 2010)

Playne, Caroline. E., *Society at War, 1914-1916* (London: Allen and Unwin, 1931)

Quigly, Isobel, *The Heirs of Tom Brown The English School Story* (London: Chatto & Windus, 2018)

Reader, W. L., *At Duty's Call* (Manchester: Manchester University Press, 1988)

Reynolds, David, *The Long Shadow* (London : Simon and Schuster, 2014)

Sainsbury, J. D., *Hertfordshire's Army Cadets* (Welwyn: Hart Books 2010)

Searle, G. R., *The Quest for National Efficiency: A Study in British Politics and Political Thought, 1899-1914* (Oxford: Blackwell, 1971)

Seldon, Anthony with Meakin, Jonathan, *The Cabinet Office 1916-2016: The Birth of Modern Government* (London: Biteback, 2016)

—— and Walsh, David, *Public Schools and The Great War The Generation Lost* (Barnsley: Pen and Sword Military, 2013)

Sheffield, G. D., *Leadership in the Trenches: Officer-Man Relations, Morale and Discipline in the British Army in the Era of the First World War* (Basingstoke: Palgrave Macmillan, 2000)

Sheffield, Gary, *Forgotten Victory: The First World War, Myths and Realities* (London: Review, 2002).

—— and Bourne, John, *Douglas Haig: War Diaries and Letters, 1914-1918* (London: Phoenix, 2006)

—— and Todman, D. (eds.), *Command and Control on the Western Front: The British Army's Experience 1914-18* (Staplehurst: Spellmount, 2004)

Sherry, Norman, *The Life of Graham Greene Volume One, 1904-1939* (London: Jonathan Cape, 1989)

Shrosbree, Colin, *Public Schools and Private Education: The Clarendon Commission, 1861-64, and the Public Schools Acts* (Manchester: Manchester University Press, 1988)

Simkins, Peter, *From Somme to Victory: The British Army's Experience on the Western Front 1916-1918* (Barnsley: Praetorian, 2014)
—— *Kitchener's Army; the Raising of the New Armies, 1914-1916* (Barnsley: Pen and Sword, 2009).
Simon, B. and Bradley, I. (eds.) *The Victorian Public School* (London: Gill and Macmillan, 1975)
Simpson, Andy, *Directing Operations: British Corps Command on the Western Front 1914-1918* (Stroud: Spellmount, 2006)
Spiers, E. M., *Haldane: An Army Reformer* (Edinburgh: Edinburgh University Press, 1980)
Springhall, J., *Youth, Empire and Society: British Youth Movements, 1883-1940* (London: Croom Helm, 1977)
Stephen, Martin, *The Price of Pity: Poetry, History and Myth in the Great War (*London: Leo Cooper, 1996)
Stevenson, David, *1914-18 The History of the First World War* (London: Penguin, 2005)
Todman, Dan, *The Great War Myth and Memory* (London: Hambledon and London, 2005)
Tozer, Malcolm, *Edward Thring's Theory: Practice and Legacy Physical Education in Britain since 1800* (Newcastle upon Tyne: Cambridge Scholars Publishing, 2019)
Tozer, Malcolm, *The Ideal of Manliness The Legacy of Thring's Uppingham* (Truro: Sunnyrest Books, 2015)
Travers, Tim, *How the War Was Won: Command and Technology in the British Army on the Western Front, 1917-1918* (London: Routledge, 1992)
Trevelyan, G. M., *A Shortened History of England* (London: Penguin, 1974)
Ugoloni, Laura, *Civvies Middle-Class Men on the English Home Front 1914-18* (Manchester: Manchester University Press, 2017)
Watson, Alexander, *Enduring the Great War Combat: Morale and Collapse in the German and British Armies* (Cambridge: Cambridge University Press, 2009)
Wearne, Sarah, *To Our Brothers: Memorials to a Lost Generation in British Schools* (Warwick: Helion, 2018)
Weiner, Martin. J., *English Culture and the Decline of the Industrial Spirit 1850-1980* (London: Penguin, 1987)
Williams, Captain Basil, *Raising and Training the New* Armies (London: Constable and Company, 1918)
Winnifrith, Tom and Barratt, Cyril (eds.) *Leisure in Art and Literature* (London: Macmillan, 1992).
Winter, Jay, *Sites of Memory Sites of Mourning* (Cambridge: Cambridge University Press, 1996)
Woodward, Sir Llewellyn, *The Age of Reform 1815-1870 Second Edition* (Oxford, Oxford University Press, 1962)
Wrigley, Chris (ed.), *A Companion to Early Twentieth Century Britain* (Oxford: Wiley-Blackwell, 2009)

Autobiographies, Memoirs & Personal Accounts

Blomfield, Captain C J, *Once an Artist Always an Artist* (London: Page & Company, 1921)

Brittain, Vera, *Chronicles of Youth 1913-1917* (London: Phoenix Press, 1981)

Bishop, Alan, and Bostridge, Mark (eds.) *Letters from a Lost Generation – First World War Letters of Vera Brittain and Four Friends: Roland Leighton, Edward Brittain, Victor Richardson, Geoffrey Thurlow* (London: Abacus, 1998)

Blunden, Edmund, *Undertones of War* (London: Penguin, 2010)

Cairnes, W. E., *An Absent-Minded War: Being some reflections on our reverses and the causes which have led to them* (London: John Milne, 1900)

Chapman, Guy, *A Passionate Prodigality: Fragments of an Autobiography* (London: Buchan & Enright, 1985)

David, Saul (ed.), *Mud and Bodies: The War Diaries and Letters of Captain N.A.C. Weir, 1914-1920* (London: Frontline Books, 2013)

Eyres, Harry, *Horace and Me: Life Lessons from an Ancient Poet* (London: Bloomsbury, 2014)

Furse, Ralph, *Aucuparius Recollections of a Recruiting Officer* (London, Oxford University Press, 1962)

Gibbs, Philip, *Realities of War* (London: Harper, 1920)

John P Graham, Forty *Years of Uppingham: Memories and Sketches* (London: Macmillan, 1932)

Graves, Robert, *Good-bye to All That* (London: Jonathan Cape, 1929)

Lewis, Cecil, *Sagittarius Rising* (London: Penguin, 1977)

Lindsay, Oliver (ed.), *A Guard's General: The Memoirs of Major General Allan Adair* (London: Hamish Hamilton, 1986)

Nevinson, C. R. W., *Paint and Prejudice* (New York: Harcourt, Brace and Company, 1938)

Robertson, Field-Marshal Sir William Bart., *From Private to Field-Marshal* (London: Constable, 1921)

Biographies

Bew, John, *Citizen Clem A biography of Atlee* (London: Riverrun, 2017)

Davies, Ross, *'A Student in Arms' Donald Hankey and Edwardian Society at War* (Farnham: Ashgate, 2013)

Fletcher, C. R. L., *Edmond Warre D.D., C.B. C.V.O. Sometime Headmaster and Provost of Eton College* (London: John Murray, 1922)

Haycock, David Boyd, *A Crisis of Brilliance* (London: Old Street Publishing, 2010)

Hibberd, Dominic, *Wilfred Owen* (London: Phoenix, 2003)

James, Lawrence, *Imperial Warrior: The Life and Times of Field-Marshal Viscount Allenby* (London: Weidenfield and Nicolson, 1993)

Jessel, Penelope,, *Owen of Uppingham* (London: A R Mowbray 1965)
Manning, Steven, *Evelyn Wood VC: Pillar of Empire* (Barnsley: Pen and Sword, 2007)
McCrum, Robert, *Wodehouse: A Life* (London: Penguin, 2005)
Parkin, George. R., *Edward Thring, Headmaster of Uppingham School: Life Diary and Letters* (London: Macmillan, 1900)
Prior, Robin and Wilson, Trevor, *Command on the Western Front: The Military Career of Sir Henry Rawlinson 1914–18* (Barnsley: Leo Cooper, 2004)
Sheffield, Gary, *The Chief: Douglas Haig and the British Army* (London: Aurum, 2011)
Terraine, John, *Douglas Haig: The Educated Soldier* (London: Phoenix, 2005)
Williams, Jeffery, *Byng of Vimy: General and Governor General* (London: Leo Cooper, 1992)

School Histories

Braithwaite, Roderick, *'Strikingly alive …' The History of the Mill Hill School Foundation 1807-2007* (Chichester: Phillimore, 2006)
Francis, Patrick, *Vivat Shirburnia Sherborne School and the Great War 1914-1918* (London: Impress, 2014)
Gourlay, A. B., *A History of Sherborne School* (Sherborne: Satwells, 1971)
Halstead, Timothy, *A School in Arms: Uppingham and the Great War* (Solihull: Helion, 2017)
Handford, Basil, *Lancing College History and Memoirs* (Chichester: Phillimore, 1986)
Leach, Colin, *A School at Shrewsbury: The Four Foundations* (London: James and James, 1990)
McClean, Daniel. J., *Rugbeians in the Great War* (Barnsley: Pen and Sword, 2019)
McDonnell, Michael F. J., *A History of St Paul's School* (London: Chapman and Hall, 1909)
Matthews, Bryan, *By God's Grace* (London: Whitehall Press, 1984)
Matthews, Bryan, *Eminent Uppinghamiams* (Cranbrook: Neville & Harding, 1987)
Merckyx, Elaine & Rigby, Neal, *Some Other and Wider Destiny: Wakefield Grammar School and the Great War* (Solihull: Helion, 2019)
Muir, T. E., *Stonyhurst 1593-1993* (London: James & James, 1992)
Winterbottom, Derek, *The Tide Flows On: A History of Rossall School* (Rossall: Rossall School, 2006)
Memorials of Rugbeians who Fell in the Great War Volume V (Privately published: Rugby, 1919)
Pendrill, Colin, *And We Were Young: Oundle School and the Great War* (Solihull: Helion 2017)
Pirt, Asher. C. J., *WSS Old Boys and the Great War 1914-1918* (Privately published: Watchet, 2013)
Richardson, Nigel, *Thring of Uppingham* (Buckingham: University of Buckingham Press, 2014)

Riley, Lieutenant Colonel J. P., *Schoolboys in Uniform A History of the Sherborne School Cadet Force 1888-1988* (Sherborne: Privately published, 1988)
Sabben-Clare, James, *Winchester College After 600 Years, 1382-1982* (Southampton: Paul Cave, 1981)
Scadding, Alan, *Epsom College A Celebration Benevolence and Excellence 150 Years of the Royal Medical Foundation of Epsom College* (Epsom: Privately published, 2005)
Smart, Sue, *When Heroes Die: A Forgotten Archive Reveals the Last Days of the School Friends Who Died for Britan* (Derby: Breedon Books, 2001)
Storrie, Paddy, *'Here I am; Send me': The War Dead of St George's School 1914-1918* (Harpenden: St Georges School, 2004)
Watson, Nigel, *Born Not For Ourselves: The Story of St Albans School* (St Albans: St Albans School, 2014)
Winterbottom, Derek, *Henry Nevinson and The Spirit of Clifton* (Bristol: Redcliffe, 1986)
Wilson, E. R. and Jackson, H. A. (eds.) *Winchester College A Register for the Years 1901 to 1946* (London: Edward Arnold, 1956)

Fiction & Poetry

Childers, Erskine, *The Riddle of the Sands* (London: Penguin, 2007)
Gardener, Brian (ed.) *Up the Line to Death: The War Poets 1914-1918* (London: Methuen, 1956)
Hornung, E. W., *Fathers of Men* (London: Smith Elder & Co, 1912)
—— *The Young Guard* (London: Constable, 1919)
Hughes, Thomas, *Tom Brown's Schooldays* (London: Virtue & Company, 1857)
Kipling, Rudyard, *The Complete Stalky & Co.* (Oxford: Oxford University Press, 1999)
Waugh, Alec, *The Loom of Youth* (London: Methuen, 1984)
Wodehouse, P G, *Mike: A Public School Story* (Rockville, Maryland: Tark Classic Fiction, 2008)

Periodicals

Ashmore, Major E B, 'The Officers Training Corps', *The Army Review,* pp. 247-243
Berghoff, Hartmut, 'Public Schools and the Decline of the British Economy', 1 (July – October 1911), *Past and Present* 129 (November 1990), pp. 148-167
Bond, B., 'Richard Haldane at the War Office, 1905-1912' *Army Quarterly* 86: 1(1963), pp. 33-43
Donaldson, Peter, 'The Commemoration of the South African War (1899-1902) in British Public Schools', *History & Memory,* 25: 2. (2013) pp. 32-65
Donaldson, Peter, '"We are having a very enjoyable game': Britain, sport and the South African War, 1899-1902', *War in History* 25: 1. (2018) pp. 4-25

Douglas, R., 'Voluntary Enlistment in the First World War and the Work of the Parliamentary Recruiting Committee', *Journal of Modern History*, 42: 4 (1970), pp. 564-585

Earle, Major M., 'The Army and the Public Schools', *The Army Review*, 1 (July – October 1911), pp. 254-260.

Fox, Aimee, 'The Secret of Efficiency? Social Relations and Patronage in the British Army in the Era of the First World War', *English Historical Review*, 135: 577 (December 2020), pp. 1525-1557

Fraser, Mary, 'Policing the Plough', *History Today*, 70: 5 (May 2020), pp. 42-49.

French, David, "Official History"? Sir James Edmonds and the Official History of the Great War, *RUSI: Royal United Services Institute for Defence Studies*, 131:1 (March 1986) pp 58-63

Fletcher, Anthony, 'Patriotism, the Great War and the Decline of Victorian Manliness', *History*, 99: 334, pp. 40-72

Grigg, John, 'Nobility and War: The Unselfish Commitment?', *Encounter* 74 (1990), pp. 21-27

Halstead, Timothy, 'Public Schools and Great War Memorials – Sacred and Secular', *Stand To!*, 120 (November 2020), pp. 63-65.

Halstead, Timothy, 'The First World and Public School Ethos: The Case of Uppingham School', *War and Society*, 34: 3 (August 2015), pp. 209-229

Halstead, Timothy, 'The Junior OTC: Playing at Soldiers or Nation in Arms?', *British Journal for Military History*, 3: 2 (February 2017), pp. 62-81

Humble, N. J., "'Leaving London": a study of two public schools and athleticism 1870-1914', *History of Education*, 17: 2(July 2006), pp. 149-162

Mangan, J. A., 'Muscular, Militaristic and Manly': The Middle-Class Hero as a Moral Messenger, *The International Journal of the History of Sport*, 27: 1-2, pp. 150-168

Miller, Alisa, Modern War and Aesthetic Mobilisation: Looking at Europe in 1914, *British Journal for Military History*, 2: 2 pp. 12-41

Nash, Paul, 'Training an Elite', *History of Education Quarterly*, 1:1 (March 1961) pp 14-21

Ottley, C. B., 'Militarism and Militarization in the Public Schools 1900-1972', *The British Journal of Sociology*, 29: 3 (September 1978) pp 321-339

Palmer, Richard. J., 'The influence of F.W.Sanderson on the development of science and engineering at Dulwich College, 1885-1892', *History of Education*, 6: 2 (1977) pp 121-130

Pattenden, Hugh, 'Old Perseans and the Great War: A Study in the Alumni of a Minor Public School', *History of Education*, 47: 5 (April 2018), pp 628-643

Pedersen, Joyce, Senders, 'The Victorian Public School', *History of Education Quarterly*, 19: 4 (Winter 1979) pp 467-475

Phillips, Christopher, 'Logistics and the BEF: The Development of Waterborne Transport on the Western Front, 1914-1916,' *British Journal for Military History*, 2: 2 pp. 42-58

Ripon, T. S. and Manuel, E. G., 'Report on the Essential Characteristics of Successful and Unsuccessful with Special Reference to Temperament', *The Lancet* (28 September 1918) pp. 411-415

Strachan, H., 'Essay and Reflection: On Total War and Modern War', *The International History Review*, 22: 2 (2000) pp 341-370

Teagarden, E. M., 'Lord Haldane and the Origins of the Officer Training Corps', *Journal of the Society for Army Historical Research*, 45: 182 (1967) pp. 91-96

Tozer, Malcolm, 'Cricket, school and empire: E W Hornung and his Young Guard', *The International Journal of the History of Sport*, 6: 2 (March 2007) pp. 156-171

Warre, Rev. Hon. Colonel E, 'On the Relation of Public Secondary Schools to the Organisation of National Defence', *Royal United Services Institution. Journal*, Vol 44: 273 (1900) pp. 1237-1268

Wilkinson, P., 'English Youth Movements, 1908-1930', *Journal of Contemporary History*, 4: 2 (1969) pp. 1-23

Worthington, Ian, 'Antecedent Education and Officer Recruitment: The Origins and Early Development of the Public School-Army Relationship', *Military Affairs*, 41: 4 (1977) pp. 183-190

Worthington, Ian, 'Militarization and Officer Recruiting: The Development of the Officers Training Corps', *Military Affairs*, 43: 2 (April 1979) pp. 90-96

Newspapers & Journals

Grantham Journal
Rutland and Stamford Mercury
The Independent
The Times 1900-1966
The Wipers Times

Dissertations & Theses

Allsobrook, David, 'An Investigation of Precedents for the Recommendations of the Schools Inquiry Commission 1864-1867 With an Analysis of Reasons for the Failure of the Endowed Schools Act, 1869' (PhD thesis, Leicester, 1979)

Badsey, Phylomena, 'The Political Thought of Vera Brittain' (PhD thesis, Kingston, 2005)

Badsey, Stephen, 'Fire and the Sword The British Army and The Arme Blanche Controversy 1871-1921' (PhD thesis, Cambridge 1981)

Berghe, Vanessa, 'Oliver Hill and the Enigma of British Modernism during the Inter-War' (M. Phil thesis, East London, 2013)

Duncan, Andrew, 'The Military Education of Junior Officers in the Edwardian Army' (PhD thesis, Birmingham, 2016)

Kang, Changboo, 'The British Infantry Officer on the Western Front in the First World War: With Special Reference to the Royal Warwickshire Regiment' (PhD thesis, Birmingham 2007)
Kennedy, Rosalind, Joan, Sarah, 'The Children's War: British Children's Experience of the Great War' (PhD thesis, Goldsmiths)
Methven, Paul, '"Children ardent for some desperate glory": Public Schools and First World War volunteering' (MPhil thesis, Cardiff, 2013)
Palmer, Richard John, 'The Life of F W Sanderson (1857-1922) with special reference to his work and influence at Oundle School (1892-1922)' (PhD thesis, Hull, 1981)
Roberts, I D, 'Jesuit collegiate education in England, 1794 1914' (MEd dissertation, Durham,1986)
Robbins, Simon, 'British Generalship in the First World War, 1914-1918' (PhD thesis, London 2001)
Sheffield, Gary, 'Officer-man Relations: Morale and Discipline in the British Army, 1902–22' (PhD thesis, London 1994)
Tozer, Malcolm, 'Manliness The Evolution of a Victorian Ideal' (PhD thesis, Leicester 1978)
—— 'Physical Education at Thring's Uppingham' (MEd dissertation, Leicester 1974)
Edward Whiffin, 'Public Schools, Politics and Associational Culture in England, 1899-1939' PhD thesis (University College London Institute of Education 2021)
Derek Whitfield, 'To what extent and why did the voluntary ethic characterise Winchester's response to war in 1914 and 1915?' (MA dissertation, Birmingham 2015)
Ian Worthington, 'Antecedent Education and Officer Recruitment: An Analysis of the Public School-Army Nexus, 1849-1908' (PhD thesis, Lancaster 1982)

Miscellaneous

Blackadder Goes Forth, TX 28, September 1989 to 2 November 1989
Carey, G. V., *The War List of the University of Cambridge 1914-1918* (Cambridge: Cambridge University Press, 1921)
Craig, E. S. and Gibson, W. M., *Oxford University Roll of Service* (Oxford: Clarendon Press, 1920)
Gillard, D. (2018) *Education in England: A History* <www.educationengland.org.uk/history>
Monty Python's Flying Circus, 'Upper Class Twit of the Year', TX 4 January 1970
O'Moore Creagh, General Sir G., *The V. C. and D. S. O. Distinguished Service Order 1886-1915: Distinguished Service Order. 6th September 1886 to the 31st December 1915* (London: Naval and Military Press, 2009)
—— *The V. C. and D. S. O. Book Distinguished Service Order 1916–1923* (London: Naval and Military Press, 2009)

Record of War Service 1919-1918 Officers Training Corps (Junior Division) Public School Officers and Other Members of the Staffs (London: privately published, 1919)

St George's School, School History <http://www.stgeorges.herts.sch.uk/About-Us/School-History>

Simkins, P., AGM April 14th 2012 – President's Address 'Everyman at War' Revisited, *The Western Front Association Bulletin 93 (2012)*

Spiers, Edward. M., *University Officers' Training Corps and the First World War* (Bedford: Council of Military Education Committees of the United Kingdom, 2014)

*Statistics of the Military Effort of the British Empire During the Great War (*London: HMSO, 1922)

The History of Epsom College <http://www.epsomcollege.org.uk/a-unique-history>

The Long, Long Trail <http://www.1914-1918.net/>

War Poets Association <http://www.warpoets.org/>

Index

Antecedent Education and Officer Recruitment, 54, 56–57, 62, 64, 68–70
Army, Regular, 52, 55, 64–65, 70–71, 77, 83, 89, 115, 139, 141–42, 157, 161
Army classes, 49, 57, 63, 65, 67, 95, 157–58
Army Educational Corps, 68, 199
Army Entrance Examination, 51, 55, 65–66, 105, 141–42
Army schools, 49, 55, 65, 67, 70, 137, 157, 181
Athleticism, 27–29, 31–32, 47, 52–53

Bloxham School, 149, 154, 160–61
Blunden, Edmund, 37–39, 82
Boarding schools, 45, 92, 95

Cadet Corps, 70–71, 96, 106, 108, 112, 150, 152, 154, 169
Cambridge, 32, 35, 101, 136, 142, 156, 160, 199–201, 203, 208–9
Cambridge University School of Instruction for Officers, 122
Chapman, Guy, xii, 39, 102, 204–5
City of London School insert 'Christ's Hospital, 34, 60, 61, 82, 88, 101, 118, 122, 147, 149, 152, 161, 162, 165, 168, 173, 182, 191
City of London School, 45, 198
Clarendon Commission, 44, 46, 202
Clarendon Schools, 47, 54, 64
Council of Military Education (CME), 54, 210

Director of Military Training (DMT), 101

Edwardian Army, 63, 68, 200, 208

Epsom College, 31, 50–52, 61, 64–65, 67, 93, 112, 119, 146, 149, 151–54, 156–58, 165, 169, 171, 173–74, 177, 206, 210
Eton, 25–28, 30–31, 38, 40, 54–55, 61, 68–71, 92–93, 115–17, 130–31, 147, 179, 181
Eton College Chronicle, 91, 114–15, 117–18, 130–31, 135, 141, 198

Field days, 76–77, 105–6, 116–17, 119, 137
Field Service Regulations (FSR), 74–75, 77, 105, 127, 129, 133

Games, organised, 26

Haig, Field Marshal Sir Douglas, 127, 162, 200, 202, 205
Haileybury School, 31, 35, 61, 69–71, 92, 147
Haldane, Lord Richard, 76, 83–84, 208
Handsworth Grammar School, 150, 152, 155, 197
Harrow, 29–30, 34, 54–55, 92, 110, 113, 116–17, 119, 138, 140–41, 144, 147, 181, 183
Harvest Camps, 178–80, 186
Headmasters Conference (HMC), 62–63, 65–67, 69–70, 72, 74, 89–90, 99–101, 103–4, 107–8, 110–12, 114, 124, 126, 138–39, 141, 156–57, 159, 163, 172–73, 178–79
High Church, 160–61
Housemaster, 40, 42, 174–75

Junior Division Officers Training, 86, 91–92, 108, 114, 117, 123, 129–30, 138–40, 142–43, 147–48

211

Kipling, Rudyard, 40–41, 43, 56, 206
Kitchener's Army, 84, 86, 89, 203

Lancing, 33, 52-53, 75-76, 92-93, 94, 118-119, 122, 128, 136, 138, 149, 160-161
Lancing College Magazine, 119, 121–22, 126, 129, 136, 138, 144
Latin, 28, 31–32, 41, 46, 62–63, 68, 171
Leaving Certificates, 62, 65

Marlborough College, 26–27, 34–35, 39, 87–88, 92, 113, 115, 131, 135, 140–42, 156, 160, 177
Military Education, 62–64, 157, 208
Mill Hill, 34, 42, 53, 60–61, 75, 82, 88, 93, 94, 105, 106, 112, 117, 118, 120, 136, 137, 140, 143, 144, 149, 152-153, 154, 155, 158-159, 170-171, 174, 185

Oakham School, 79, 116
Officer Cadet Battalions (OCBs) 101, 125, 128–35, 137, 139–41, 144–46, 148, 150–52, 163–64, 172
Officer training, 62, 68, 120, 123, 127, 142, 144, 146, 152, 163
Old Blues, 82, 161–62, 165, 191, 197
Officer Training Corps (OTC), 33, 55, 70–77, 83–84, 86, 88–90, 92, 94–97, 100–112, 116–31, 133–46, 149–52, 154–55, 169, 171–72, 174–75, 188–91
OTC camps, 179–80
OTC training, 33, 78, 114–15, 118, 129, 132–35, 138, 140, 168–69, 189, 191
Oundle, 49–50, 52, 64, 80, 92, 93, 95, 96, 100, 115, 116, 140, 143, 147, 149, 152-154, 156, 157, 158, 159, 165, 170, 174, 175, 176, 177, 181-182, 184
Oxford and Cambridge Schools Examination Board, 62

Pound Lane School, 169
Public School Battalion (PSB), 98–99

Qualifying Certificate, 62

Royal Army Medical Corps (RAMC), 146, 153, 157, 165, 190
Royal Garrison Artillery (RGA), 98, 155–56, 159

Roll of Honour, 150, 159, 168, 171, 195, 197
Rossall School, 55, 205

Sandhurst, 49, 57, 59, 61–62, 66–67, 69, 74, 99, 151, 157
Sassoon, Siegfried, 37–38
Second Anglo-Boer War, 54–55, 57–59, 61, 63, 65, 68, 71, 74, 77, 85–86, 95–96
Sherborne School, 47, 80, 161, 176
Shrewsbury, 45, 52, 60, 92, 93, 130, 149, 151, 154
Somme, Battle of the, 35, 38, 84, 88
South Africa, 56–57, 71–72, 199
St Albans School, 71, 79, 168, 206
Stalky & Co, 40–41, 187–88
Sterndale Bennett, Robert, 119, 121–23, 131–32, 134–36, 144–46
Stonyhurst College 53, 70–71, 93, 143, 149, 157, 160–61, 198, 205
Stonyhurst Magazine, 121, 142–43

Taunton Commission, 46, 92
Territorial Force (TF), 73, 86, 111, 120, 128, 146
Tom Brown's Schooldays, 29, 39–40, 42, 187
Tonbridge, 49, 52, 92, 93, 105, 106, 116, 121, 127, 135, 149, 157, 158, 160, 165

United Services College (USC), 40–41
University Officers' Training Corps, 210
Uppingham School, 25-26, 32–35, 47–48, 67, 70–71, 74–76, 81, 90–97, 105–6, 112–13, 115–16, 118–22, 132–35, 140–41, 143–44, 156–58, 172–74, 179–80, 182
Uppingham School Magazine, 34, 49, 119
Uppingham School OTC, 119, 121–23, 132, 135–36, 144

Wakefield Grammar School, 149, 152
War Office, 67–71, 73–74, 77, 87–91, 95–97, 99–100, 103–12, 114–19, 122–27, 129, 134–39, 141–42, 144–45, 163, 189–91
Westminster School, 117, 174
Winchester College, 45, 49, 51–52, 59–61, 64–65, 67, 74–76, 87–90, 100–101, 147, 149, 151–52, 168, 171–72, 175–76, 183
Woolwich, 59, 61–62, 64, 66, 74, 97, 99, 157–58
Wykehamist, The, 87, 133, 137, 168, 176, 183
Wykehamist, 133, 176

Wolverhampton Military Studies

www.helion.co.uk/wolverhamptonmilitarystudies

Editorial board

Professor Stephen Badsey
  Wolverhampton University
Professor Michael Bechthold
  Wilfred Laurier University
Professor John Buckley
  Wolverhampton University
Major General (Retired) John Drewienkiewicz
Ashley Ekins
  Australian War Memorial
Dr Howard Fuller
  Wolverhampton University
Dr Spencer Jones
  Wolverhampton University
Nigel de Lee
  Norwegian War Academy
Major General (Retired) Mungo Melvin
  President of the British Commission for Military History

Dr Michael Neiberg
  US Army War College
Dr Eamonn O'Kane
  Wolverhampton University
Professor Fransjohan Pretorius
  University of Pretoria
Dr Simon Robbins
  Imperial War Museum
Professor Gary Sheffield
  Wolverhampton University
Commander Steve Tatham PhD
  Royal Navy
  The Influence Advisory Panel
Professor Malcolm Wanklyn
  Wolverhampton University
Professor Andrew Wiest
  University of Southern Mississippi

Submissions

The publishers would be pleased to receive submissions for this series. Please contact us via email (info@helion.co.uk), or in writing to Helion & Company Limited, Unit 8 Amherst Business Centre, Budbrooke Road, Warwick, CV34 5WE, England.

Titles

1. *Stemming the Tide. Officers and Leadership in the British Expeditionary Force 1914* Edited by Spencer Jones (ISBN 978-1-909384-45-3)
2. *'Theirs Not To Reason Why': Horsing the British Army 1875–1925* Graham Winton (ISBN 978-1-909384-48-4)
3. *A Military Transformed? Adaptation and Innovation in the British Military, 1792–1945* Edited by Michael LoCicero, Ross Mahoney and Stuart Mitchell (ISBN 978-1-909384-46-0)
4. *Get Tough Stay Tough. Shaping the Canadian Corps, 1914–1918* Kenneth Radley (ISBN 978-1-909982-86-4)
5. *A Moonlight Massacre: The Night Operation on the Passchendaele Ridge, 2 December 1917. The Forgotten Last Act of the Third Battle of Ypres* Michael LoCicero (ISBN 978-1-909982-92-5)
6. *Shellshocked Prophets. Former Anglican Army Chaplains in Interwar Britain* Linda Parker (ISBN 978-1-909982-25-3)

7 *Flight Plan Africa: Portuguese Airpower in Counterinsurgency, 1961–1974* John P. Cann (ISBN 978-1-909982-06-2)

8 *Mud, Blood and Determination. The History of the 46th (North Midland) Division in the Great War* Simon Peaple (ISBN 978 1 910294 66 6)

9 *Commanding Far Eastern Skies. A Critical Analysis of the Royal Air Force Superiority Campaign in India, Burma and Malaya 1941–1945* Peter Preston-Hough (ISBN 978 1 910294 44 4)

10 *Courage Without Glory. The British Army on the Western Front 1915* Edited by Spencer Jones (ISBN 978 1 910777 18 3)

11 *The Airborne Forces Experimental Establishment: The Development of British Airborne Technology 1940–1950* Tim Jenkins (ISBN 978-1-910777-06-0)

12 *'Allies are a Tiresome Lot' – The British Army in Italy in the First World War* John Dillon (ISBN 978 1 910777 32 9)

13 *Monty's Functional Doctrine: Combined Arms Doctrine in British 21st Army Group in Northwest Europe, 1944–45* Charles Forrester (ISBN 978-1-910777-26-8)

14 *Early Modern Systems of Command: Queen Anne's Generals, Staff Officers and the Direction of Allied Warfare in the Low Countries and Germany, 1702–11* Stewart Stansfield (ISBN 978 1 910294 47 5)

15 *They Didn't Want To Die Virgins: Sex and Morale in the British Army on the Western Front 1914–1918* Bruce Cherry (ISBN 978-1-910777-70-1)

16 *From Tobruk to Tunis: The Impact of Terrain on British Operations and Doctrine in North Africa, 1940–1943* Neal Dando (ISBN 978-1-910294-00-0)

17 *Crossing No Man's Land: Experience and Learning with the Northumberland Fusiliers in the Great War* Tony Ball (ISBN 978-1-910777-73-2)

18 *"Everything worked like clockwork": The Mechanization of the British Cavalry between the Two World Wars* Roger E Salmon (ISBN 978-1-910777-96-1)

19 *Attack on the Somme: 1st Anzac Corps and the Battle of Poziéres Ridge, 1916* Meleah Hampton (ISBN 978-1-910777-65-7)

20 *Operation Market Garden: The Campaign for the Low Countries, Autumn 1944: Seventy Years On* Edited by John Buckley & Peter Preston Hough (ISBN 978 1 910777 15 2)

21 *Enduring the Whirlwind: The German Army and the Russo-German War 1941-1943* Gregory Liedtke (ISBN 978-1-910777-75-6)

22 *'Glum Heroes': Hardship, fear and death – Resilience and Coping in the British Army on the Western Front 1914–1918* Peter E. Hodgkinson (ISBN 978-1-910777-78-7)

23 *Much Embarrassed: Civil War Intelligence and the Gettysburg Campaign* George Donne (ISBN 978-1-910777-86-2)

24 *They Called It Shell Shock: Combat Stress in the First World War* Stefanie Linden (ISBN 978-1-911096-35-1)

25 *New Approaches to the Military History of the English Civil War. Proceedings of the First Helion & Company 'Century of the Soldier' Conference* Ismini Pells (editor) (ISBN 978-1-911096-44-3)

26 *Reconographers: Intelligence and Reconnaissance in British Tank Operations on the Western Front 1916-18* Colin Hardy (ISBN: 978-1-911096-28-3)

27 *Britain's Quest for Oil: The First World War and the Peace Conferences* Martin Gibson (ISBN: 978-1-911512-07-3)

28 *Unfailing Gallantry: 8th (Regular) Division in the Great War 1914–1919* Alun Thomas (ISBN: 978-1-910777-61-9)

29 *An Army of Brigadiers: British Brigade Commanders at the Battle of Arras 1917* Trevor Harvey (ISBN: 978-1-911512-00-4)

30 *At All Costs: The British Army on the Western Front 1916* Edited by Spencer Jones (ISBN 978-1-912174-88-1)

31 *The German Corpse Factory: A Study in First World War Propaganda* Stephen Badsey (ISBN 978-1-911628-27-9)